The Mythology of Kobe Bryant

"As a basketball guru, I find Dr. Adams's descriptive accounts of the late Kobe Bryant and what faith in God looks like in the relevant spheres of culture and sports to be an absolute masterpiece. Easily the best Kobe Bryant book ever written, . . . with great attention given to well thought out detail in the realms of Black culture, Scripture, theology, and history. Accurate, creative, and imaginative."

—**DERRICK HICKMAN**, head girls' basketball coach, University Heights Academy

"This book is unlike any other Kobe Bryant book on the market. The way Dr. Adams theologizes the life of Bryant within the culture of sports is fascinating, to say the very least. Most impressively, he defines the mythology of Kobe Bryant in a variety of ways—ways that speak to people from all walks of life. It's one thing to say that Kobe is the greatest basketball player ever. It's another thing altogether to argue cogently in the sphere of factuality."

—**JEREMY FRANKLIN**, founder, Life to Life Transitions, Lexington, South Carolina

"As an ex-basketball player, I am drawn to Dr. Adams's attention to detail with regard to the basketball sketch of the late Kobe Bryant and the culture of sports. As an ordained minister, I am very much inspired by his usage of Scripture as a way of talking about what it means to be the greatest at anything in life. As an administrator in the Christian County public school system, I understand the need for knowledge and truth. This new book is a basketball gem and a literary masterpiece."

—**MANCELL ELAM**, district diversity administrator, Christian County Public Schools

"I truly hope that Kobe's wife, Vanessa Bryant, and their beautiful children read this important book at some point in their meaningful lives. This book promises to be a tremendous blessing to them. The residents of Los Angeles, the states of California and Pennsylvania, along with Kobe Bryant fans in the United States and all over the world will fall in love with this book."

—**ELIZABETH SANDERS TOWNS**, content editor, EBeth Editorials

"This new book showcases Dr. Adams's unique ability to argue across cultures, disciplines, and genres. Dr. Adams has always been a historian of basketball. His argument that Kobe Bryant is the greatest basketball player ever is convincing and powerful. Most notably, his nontraditional use of the Bible, academic books, and online articles makes for an exciting engagement with what it means to live out our own lives to the fullest potential. An exciting, informative, and motivational read."

—**HENRY SNORTON III**, director, the Minority Economic Development Initiative

The Mythology of Kobe Bryant

Theology and the Culture of Sport

DARVIN ANTON ADAMS
Foreword by Lewis Brogdon

WIPF & STOCK · Eugene, Oregon

THE MYTHOLOGY OF KOBE BRYANT
Theology and the Culture of Sport

Copyright © 2022 Darvin A. Adams I. All rights reserved. Except for brief quotations in critical publications or reviews, no part of this book may be reproduced in any manner without prior written permission from the publisher. Write: Permissions, Wipf and Stock Publishers, 199 W. 8th Ave., Suite 3, Eugene, OR 97401.

Wipf & Stock
An Imprint of Wipf and Stock Publishers
199 W. 8th Ave., Suite 3
Eugene, OR 97401

www.wipfandstock.com

PAPERBACK ISBN: 978-1-6667-3564-2
HARDCOVER ISBN: 978-1-6667-9292-8
EBOOK ISBN: 978-1-6667-9293-5

10/18/22

This new book is dedicated to my wonderful children, Aiyana Marie Adams of Houston, Texas, Che'Nissia Dejuanae Thompson of Louisville, Kentucky and Darvin A. Adams II of Toledo, Ohio; and to my beautiful granddaughter Deavani D. Lewis of Louisville, Kentucky; and my canine son and daughter, Braxton Anton Gant and Truly Lee Gant of Manitou, Kentucky. My sincere prayer is that you all find something or someone on the earth that lovingly gives you spiritual inspiration and positive motivation to help you become the best version of yourselves. The sky is the limit to what you all can achieve in this life. With God all things are possible. My prayer is that you feel the power of the Holy Spirit in your inner selves and outer lives and be a contributing part of God's creative culture. Your daddy loves you all dearly and deeply. You all remain the absolute best part of my life.

Contents

Foreword by Lewis Brogdon | ix
Acknowledgments | xi
Introduction | xiii

1. The Greatest Ever: Basketball Details | 1
2. Family Man: The Magic Arms of a Tender Heart | 34
3. The (Un)Expected Death(s) | 53
4. Vanessa Bryant's Eulogy and God's Knowledge of Human Life | 66
5. It's Time to Dance: The Effect of Michael Jackson's Artistic Genius | 90
6. Twenty-four Claims and the Polarization of Otherworldly Greatness | 114
7. Kobe's Sixth Championship Ring: Inspiring the World and the Lakers | 134
8. The Culture of Sport and Saying Goodbye to the Inspiration of Zoom | 149

Bibliography | 189

Foreword

JESUS OFTEN TAUGHT IN parables. He did this because it not only provided a way to illustrate eternal principles in a way listeners could grasp, but it also taught people to see God and theological meaning in the mundane things around us. We tend to miss this. We look for God in places and spaces of worship, or institutions dedicated to the study of matters of the sacred. But God is omnipresent. God is everywhere, transcending and filling all things. Theologians often describe this as the "immensity of God." One of my former pastors, Dr. Derrick Miles, often called it "the bigness of God" in sermons and Bible studies. Miles is not only adding language from the Black religious tradition to Christian theology, but he is also employing African religious imagery for a cosmos believed to be sacred. Worshiping and thinking about an immense and big God means we must learn to look for God everywhere, a point repeated in Scripture. For example, one of the Psalms decrees, "The heavens declare the glory of God; the skies proclaim the work of his hands" (Ps 19:1), while Paul, a man I have studied for years, instructed the church at Rome that "the invisible things of [God] from the creation of the world are clearly seen, being understood by the things that are made, even his eternal power and Godhead" (Rom 1:20). These insightful declarations challenge us to pay attention to God beyond the sacred walls of our churches and halls of our theological schools.

One of the places outsides our walls and halls that is often neglected is culture. We rarely look for God and theological meaning in culture because we mistake prohibitions in the New Testament against "love of the world." In our quest not to be a "friend of the world," to use language from James 4, we create as much distance as we can from people in the world. Instead of guarding ourselves from "conformity to systems and ideologies of the world" (remember Rom 12:2), we close ourselves off from people, especially those who are different from us. This is unfortunate because we can hold these warnings in tension with the need to love and learn from people around us. It is as if we forget John 3:16, that God's love for the world—as in people—is what motivated his act of sending Jesus. People around us see God, talk about God, and struggle with questions of meaning in their own ways. Churches and Christian schools do not have the monopoly on the Creator. Instead of seeing this as an opportunity for dialogue and growth, too many churches ignore the vast fields of culture as sites of meaning, and they do so to our peril because the disconnect with culture is one of the driving forces behind the malaise and decline that is crippling our churches.

Paying attention to God's presence and works in the world means we must be students of culture. I have brought music, film, and literature into my classes, writing, and teaching for years because they are filled with profound questions and insights about God and matters of faith. Dr. Darvin Adams and I share a deep and abiding passion for culture, especially Black culture. I have known him for over fourteen years. He is a church leader with a compassionate heart and a deep commitment to social justice. He is also a budding theologian, who is respected in a historic African American denomination and the city of Hopkinsville, where he recently served on the city council. Darvin is the ideal person for a book like this. He models the same principles Jesus employed in parables. In this imaginative text, he invites us to see and think about God and theological meaning through the life of one of my favorite basketball players, Kobe Bryant. Kobe is a secular saint of sorts for Darvin and me. Whether you are a sports fan or not, you should know about Kobe and the significant impact he made on so many. This man's life is truly worthy of theological reflection. I applaud my best friend for this ambitious project and the insight it provides into the complex moment in which we all find ourselves. His deep love for Kobe's life and legacy, as one of the greatest to lace up basketball sneakers, will inspire you to look for, and see, God in new ways.

Dr. Lewis Brogdon
Director, The Institute for Black Church Studies
Associate Professor of Preaching and Black Church Studies
at the Baptist Seminary of Kentucky, Louisville

Acknowledgments

I HAVE BEEN CONSTRUCTING this new book piece by piece since I began writing my PhD dissertation in May 2016. It began as an article that I had originally wanted to send to *Slam Magazine* to be published. Because I did not have the time to publish much of anything during my nine-year PhD journey, I shared my initial thoughts with my best friend and New Testament theologian Dr. Lewis O. Brogdon Jr., and he was immediately interested. As former basketball players and ex-athletes, Dr. Brogdon and I would spend considerable time talking about the philosophical and theological connections between Christian theology and professional sports. More often than not, our conversations would end up focusing on the generational comparisons between the great Michael Jordan and Kobe Bryant. Depending on the day of the week, our respective workloads, and how far our sophisticated minds were willing to travel in our cultural depictions of each transcendent superstar, our conversations would always land somewhere between the effervescent labyrinth of Black religion in the United States and the Bible. And rightfully so. I, being a classically trained theologian with pastoral experience in the Black church, and Dr. Brogdon, being a classically trained New Testament scholar with pastoral experience in the Black church, our conversations on basketball and the culture of sport took us places beyond the physical church building and what we were hearing on ESPN. Our conversations on Jordan, Bryant, and the culture of sport were exciting, fulfilling, and invigorating.

Then the unthinkable happened on January 26, 2020, changing both the landscape of professional sports and the sacred conversations I was having with my best buddy. As the tragic result of a helicopter accident, Kobe Bryant transitioned into the glory of God, alongside his superstar daughter Gianna and seven other beautiful human beings. It was then that the Holy Spirit spoke to me in divine inspiration and gave me the vision to finish writing this important book. These brief reflections are my way of acknowledging what it took to complete this new text. In both sadness and thanksgiving I want to confess there are some dark images in this book in terms of the reader's ability to see the various nuances of life, death and purpose. In reading this new book, there are going to be some moments where the reader will be challenged in her or his own spiritual decision-making processes to believe that there is a Triune God—a Creator God the Father, a Lord and Savior Jesus Christ, and a Comforter in the Holy Spirit of God—all of whom are working together, active and present on earth and in heaven. Just like Kobe Bryant found his true purpose in life (inspiring others to achieve their own individual greatness), so too will this book draw you closer to the God of many good creations. My theology says that life and death are good things that come from the creative goodness of God. It should be noted that all Bible verses, Scriptures, descriptions, and exegetical work are referenced in the Zondervan NIV Study Bible.[1] The most important numbers in this new book are Gianna's jersey number, 2 (two), and Kobe's jersey numbers, 8 (eight) and 24 (twenty-four).

> Darvin Anton Adams I, BS, Masters of Divinity, PhD
> Theology & Ethics
> Garrett-Northwestern University in Evanston, Illinois
> Pastor, Lane Tabernacle CME Church in Hopkinsville, Kentucky
> Scholar-In-Residence, Second Episcopal District of the CME Church
> Adjunct Professor of Theology at the Simmons Bible College
> in Louisville, Kentucky
> Kentucky Licensed Funeral Director

---

1. Baker, *Zondervan NIV Study Bible*.

Introduction

For the first time in my forty-six years of living, I cried tears of deep mourning and joyful thanksgiving at the same time. I cried emotionally from both the pit of a deep, dark sadness and the church-happy wellspring of giving thanks and praise to God. I knew it was coming. I just could not stop it. I knew at some point during the 2020 NBA All-Star Weekend in Chicago that moment was going to grab me real tight and not let me go until I understood who was in control of all things visible and invisible. Stubbornly, I did not want to understand anything during that sacred moment. I did not want to hear from anybody or talk to anybody. I did not want to eat. I did not move from the dented spot on my mother's leather couch. The big-screen television screamed at me in immediate silence. Jennifer Hudson was about to sing Donnie Hathaway's popular song, "For All We Know," in honor of the late Kobe Bean Bryant. I just wanted to be in my present-day skin and be humbly still in hopes that God would allow us all the privilege of seeing what we will never see again in this earthly life—an image of Kobe. Maybe I was still in a deep dark pit of disbelief. Or maybe I was hoping this three-week nightmare would end and then life would go back to the way it was on January 25th. I thought I was sitting down to watch the NBA All-Star Game. I realized I was present for a far greater purpose. I was there to experience the mystical journey of the inevitable crying heart. And I was there in the presence of God to hear Jennifer Hudson sing. I knew it was coming. I just could not stop it. I was in mourning, and I was thankful for the what the Lord had done in the lives of Kobe and Gianna Bryant.

As Hudson sung the song of her lifetime, I saw images of Kobe on the giant screen in the middle of the United Center. I sat mesmerized in my puddle of grieving tears as the collage of pictures moved quickly. I did not view Kobe as a god or anything like that. I was not having a worship experience. But I was having a sacred moment. As a Black liberation theologian, I fight against all forms of idolatry—visible and invisible. The fight includes the worship of professional athletes. Just like all other athletes in the world, Kobe was a human being. But he was beloved in a way no athlete in history was beloved. And being loved meant I was called by God to be there to hear Hudson dive deep into the musical labyrinth of the historical moment. I don't know which image made me cry the most. The images of Kobe on the screen, the image of Jennifer Hudson reaching deep within to give voice to what we all were feeling and thinking, or the image of God welcoming Kobe and Gianna into heaven with open arms. I guess the combination of all three images trinitarianized me into deep theological reflection. I wondered if I was the only one in the world listening to Hudson do her best impression of Aretha Franklin, looking at Bryant on the big screen and thinking about the presence of God. The word "know" in Hathaway's lyrics prompted me to consider the knowledge of God in terms of slowly appropriating God's foreknowledge of and within the sacred moment.

As I willingly absorbed Hudson's spiritual melodies, I wondered about the meaning of knowing and what it meant to know and be known. Most of the people in the world who were mourning Kobe and Gianna's death did not know neither of them personally. They only knew of Kobe in terms of what they heard about him, read about him, and saw him doing. Knowing of someone or knowing about someone is not the same as knowing someone. I believe we can know someone and never meet them a day in our life. I also believe we can know someone personally and at the same time not know them at all. Of course, perspective is important. But the truth is we live in a society where everybody wants to be known. Most people want to be successful and popular. But few want to be of service by way of attempting to make a significant contribution to improving society. Everyone, however, wants to be known. What does it mean to know somebody? What does it mean to be known? For all we know about the people we see consistently, there very well could be a body of spiritual knowledge or a list of details we know nothing about. The point

I am trying to make is that I was not crying over the fact that someone I knew personally had died. There are a number of people I know personally who have died, and I had no response whatsoever. I did not have any emotions at all in terms of my connection to the deceased. I have both family members and friends who have passed away and I did not shed one single tear. I loved them all with the love of the Lord. However, I cried tears over the death of Kobe Bryant for one unchangeable reason: from a distance, Kobe consistently inspired me to be the best human being I could be. He inspired me to higher heights. He inspired me to reach for greater levels of achievement. He inspired me to be the best pastor, theologian, funeral director, and organizational leader I could be. Most notably, he inspired me to write. It can be said that Kobe's mythological universe represented and included the everyday reality of many people.

The greatest forms of inspiration are those that help you to overcome your doubts and fears. When you are inspired by something or someone, it helps you to get past that bad experience. It gives you the fuel that is needed to move forward with your life. Sometimes inspiration helps you forget about the things in life that have caused you the most pain. It helps you to understand the importance of not looking back to past mistakes. Listening to Jennifer Hudson and thinking about how Kobe had inspired me in my life, I remained teary-eyed as the All-Star Game approached. The truth is that Kobe Bryant was my modern-day hero. Outside the great Muhammad Ali[1] and Denzel Washington, all of my heroes died at an early age. Dr. Martin Luther King Jr., Minister Malcolm X, Roberto Clemente, and Bryant all passed away in their late thirties and early forties. I felt like I knew Ali, being that I had met him once in Louisville, only to find out that Ali's grandmother lived right around the corner from where I was born and raised on the east side of Hopkinsville, Kentucky. For all we know, I could have passed a younger Ali as he was

---

1. In his book, *Mamba Mentality: How I Play*, Kobe says he "learned a lot from studying and watching Muhammad Ali. One of the main takeaways was that you have to work hard in the dark to shine in the light. Meaning: It takes a lot of work to be successful, and people will celebrate that success, will celebrate that flash and hype. Behind that hype, though, is dedication, focus, and seriousness—all of which outsiders will never see. If you stop being dedicated to the craft, commercials and contracts will fade away. Muhammad (Ali) was also great at game planning. One of his strategies that I emulated was the rope-a-dope. A lot of people know that as a catchphrase, but I appreciate the psychology behind it, the idea that you can manipulate an opponent's strength and use it against them. That's really a brilliant concept, and one that I used often" (Bryant, *Mamba Mentality*, 59).

walking down the street I lived on. Ali inspired me in myriad ways. I knew he was the greatest fighter the world had ever seen. I was inspired by the way Ali used words to create poems. I was even more inspired by the fact that he courageously fought against many forms of injustice. To me, the way Ali fought against systemic injustices in the United States far outweighed the battles he fought in the boxing ring. But he blew me away when he told me he frequently visited Hopkinsville. In terms of athletes who both mastered and transcended their respective sport, I place Kobe Bryant right beside Wilt Chamberlain, Muhammad Ali, Marvelous Marvin Hagler, and Rafael Nadal.

Similar to Shaquille O'Neal not wanting to attend the Naismith Basketball Hall of Fame enshrinement of Kobe and others in the 2020 class, I was not looking forward to that year's All-Star weekend. I knew it was coming. I just could not stop it. I was wondering how the NBA was going to honor the game's greatest all-star in the city that Michael Jordan put on the American basketball map. At times it seemed like the league was torn between marketing the various images, cultures, and histories of the Windy City and honoring the basketball greatness of the self-proclaimed Black Mamba. In addition to the various images of Chicago's contribution to professional basketball, I thought the NBA did a credible job honoring Bryant and his daughter Gianna. It really did not matter how they showcased Kobe's legacy. My emotions were all over the place. I teared up every single time they either mentioned his name or showed pictures of Kobe and his daughter on the giant screen. I no longer needed Jennifer's Hudson's anointing to align me with the spirit of the moment. I was locked in as both a fan of NBA basketball and as one who was inspired by the tremendous work ethic of the late Kobe Bryant. As a historian of the game of basketball, I was just hoping the NBA would honor Kobe in a way befitting of his contribution to the game. In many ways, Kobe was the most unique basketball player the NBA had ever seen—on and off the basketball court.

The word "hero" contains a plethora of meanings. *Merriam-Webster's Dictionary* defines "hero" in four ways: 1) a mythological or legendary figure often of divine descent endowed with great strength or ability, 2) an illustrious warrior, 3) a person admired for achievements and noble qualities, and 4) one that shows great courage.[2] Like other formerly solely gender-specific terms, hero is often used to refer to both men and women,

---

2. *Merriam-Webster*, s.v. "hero." https://www.merriam-webster.com/dictionary/hero.

though heroine only refers to women. The original hero type of classical epics, on one hand, did such things for the sake of glory and honor. On the other hand are postclassical and modern heroes, who perform great deeds or selfless acts for the common good instead of the classical goals of wealth, pride, and fame. The antonym of a hero is a villain. Other terms associated with the concept of a hero, may include "good guy" or "white hat." When I say Kobe Bryant was my modern-day hero, I am saying he inspired me in a multitude of ways. I did not view Kobe Bryant as God, a god, or even a godlike figure. Only God is God. I heard a basketball commentator say that Kobe's generation of fans and players saw him as the god of basketball. He was not. Kobe was not the god of anything. I abhor the culture of idolatry in professional basketball. While I admired Bryant in a way I had never admired a professional basketball player, I never attempted to deify him. Kobe was different from the rest of the players. I read recently on-line where someone stated that Kobe was more human than he was hero. I would argue that Kobe was simultaneously human and hero. It is OK to be both. For me, the fact that Kobe was an authentic human being is what made him my hero. I was not expecting him to be perfect. I do not worship human beings. I do not worship professional athletes. They are just as flawed as anyone else in society. I admire their basketball talent, but that is about it. I have never needed someone's autograph or picture to solidify me as a human being. However, there were times in my life when I needed to be inspired. In the realm of professional sports, Kobe was my teacher of inspiration.

One of the things I loved most about Kobe was he embraced both roles. He embraced the role of hero, and he embraced the role of villain. Maybe both undergirded his biblical humanity. It did not bother Kobe that people considered him polarizing. He embraced the boos. He embraced the insults. He embraced the criticism. He embraced the doubts. He embraced the jealousy. He embraced the hate. He embraced the negative comments.

Here I must set the record straight. Kobe was considered a polarizing villain way before the Denver, Colorado situation. The only thing that was different after Kobe was accused of a crime was his critics now had something concrete on Kobe. They now felt like they had proof he really was less than perfect, because before then, the public was relatively unfamiliar with Kobe. We did not know Kobe. All we knew about Bryant was he was super-talented at basketball, he spent way more time working out in weight rooms and gyms than he did hob-nobbing with his teammates, and he got married at a young age. Not only was Kobe a mystery to many of us, but he was a convenient mystery. No one was checking to see if Kobe had any life flaws or addictive habits. All we knew was if he wasn't playing basketball games in a Los Angeles Lakers uniform, he was somewhere working out, trying to develop and improve his game. For those who admired Kobe, that was good enough. We were not concerned with his family life. We wanted to see him play professional basketball. We wanted to see the visible fruits of his basketball labor. We wanted to see Kobe perform.

I believe those visible fruits are what scared people into thinking Kobe was polarizing. The fact that the greatest talent the NBA had ever seen was the hardest-working player the game had ever seen meant an instant revolution within the culture of sport. By the word "revolution" I am saying Kobe forced the NBA to rethink their notions of greatness, even if it meant rubbing people the wrong way. Not only did he want to be the greatest basketball player ever, but Kobe also wanted us to witness him competing against what the world had originally labeled as the greatest. He wanted us to see his greatness on full display against those whom we thought were the greatest. In performing well against the greatest basketball players in the world, Kobe challenged the NBA with a type of invigorating force that had never been seen before. He challenged anyone and everyone to go put on their sneakers. He also challenged the world to think about what it meant to be great in life. In transcending the history of the Los Angeles Lakers uniform, Kobe also transcended the game of basketball.

Kobe did things on the basketball court that will never be done again. His basketball game and his words of thought inspired people to believe that if Kobe could be that great in what he did for a living, then we too could be that great in our own walks of life. Jennifer Hudson sure did sing that song before the All-Star Game. Not only did she bring me to tears, but she also kept me in tears throughout the course of the evening. I knew it was coming. I just could not stop it. Just like he did millions of people around the world, Kobe Bryant touched my life too. That is precisely why I am writing this book: to celebrate the life and legacy of a truly great human being, for others to see and feel what I see and feel.

The mythology of Kobe Bryant tells a plethora of wonderful stories about an amazing human being. It also represents, in my humble opinion, a factual account of what makes Kobe the greatest basketball player in the history of the NBA. The mythology of Kobe Bryant is defined as the ways and means in which Kobe's inspirational greatness transcended both the bias culture of sport and the ever-changing context of human existence as we know it. The mythological greatness of Kobe Bryant also gives creative space for a knowledgeable interpretation of what made Kobe, in the words of LeBron James, "immortal offensively because of his skill set and his worth ethic."[3] Whether it was founded in the unfathomable amount of work Kobe put in to develop and improve his basketball game from one year to the next, or the creation of the Mamba Mentality that helped him teach others how to grow into the best version of themselves, the symbiotic totality of Kobe's ability to inspire other people is worth celebrating.

For many different reasons, Kobe's life is worth celebrating. The life he lived serves as an example of the type of life we all should be living—mistakes included. One of the main themes of this book is that Kobe Bryant was a human being. Through statistical facts, descriptive narratives, and historical analyses, this book celebrates the life of Kobe Bryant and presents a clear argument as to why I believe Bryant is the greatest basketball player ever. Foundation-wise and word-wise, Kobe's *Mamba Mentality* is the central text for this book in that the words of Bryant are creatively brought to life to unpack the mythological contours of his overall greatness. The doctrine of Kobe's Mamba Mentality connects those who were inspired by him to the mythology of his detailed life.

Chapter 1 celebrates the life of Kobe Bryant by beginning the detailed argument of him being the greatest basketball player ever. By way of beginning the conversation of what the Bible says about what it means to be the greatest by serving others, I give theological reflections on the culture of sport and how Kobe fits into that particular model. Every chapter gives fresh details about certain parts of Bryant's life on and off the basketball court.

Chapter 2 celebrates the life of Kobe Bryant by lifting up Bryant's commitment to being a good husband, father, and all-around family man. In expanding the definition of family into the realms of human connections and sports organizations, I present Bryant as one who recognized the sacred value of family within and beyond blood relations. I also present Bryant as a real human being, one who was flawed and was loved by those who knew of his flaws. The comforting words of those who knew of Kobe's love for his wife and his four daughters showcase his abiding love for family—both blood family and spiritual family.

---

3. Zillgitt, "LeBron James Opens Up," para. 15.

Chapter 3 celebrates the life of Kobe Bryant by giving theological reflections on his unexpected death, while revealing what the Bible says about death in light of God's infinite knowledge and our lamenting a devastating loss. This chapter not only gives honorable recognition to the other seven human beings who died alongside Bryant and his daughter Gianna, but it also mentions the names of other athletes that have perished as the result of an accident.

Chapter 4 celebrates the life of Kobe Bryant by placing the lamentation spotlight on the integrity and strength of his lovely wife, Vanessa Bryant. In addition to breaking down Vanessa's outstanding eulogy of Kobe at the Staples Center, I will present a few tenets of Roman Catholic theology and how the Catholic Church interprets the infinite knowledge of God. This chapter also references the Bible in detailing God's knowing of what will happen in the lives of human beings.

Chapter 5 celebrates the life of Kobe Bryant by describing his experiential connections with the late Michael Jackson. Here I will attempt to unpack what the teenage Bryant gleaned from Jackson's tutelage in the spheres of one's personal work ethic, the learning of knowledge, basketball leadership, and the value of on-the-court performance. Jackson and Bryant had more in common than most people were aware of.

Chapter 6 celebrates the life of Kobe Bryant by diving deep into the mythological universe of Bryant's mindset. This chapter presents a factual case of how the mythology of Bryant both helped him and hurt him when it comes to being compared to other all-time-great NBA players. In presenting Bryant the basketball player as a warrior-hero type of athlete, I will illuminate the otherworldly greatness of Kobe's in-game brilliance and how he always found a way to improve himself while willing his team to victory.

Chapter 7 celebrates the life of Kobe Bryant by describing the ways he inspired people to be better versions of themselves. In growing into a basketball savant in the NBA and the most popular athlete in the world, Kobe achieved global championships in life that went beyond winning NBA Championships. Chapters 6–8 continue the conversation of Kobe being the greatest basketball player ever.

Chapter 8 celebrates the life of Kobe Bryant by describing his creative philosophy regarding shoes and what it means to be a source of inspiration to those who have yet to find their purpose in life. Very similar to the end of chapter 1, this chapter talks more about the powerful connection between Christian theology and the culture of sport. In discussing the ways that professional sports affects the culture of human beings, I utilize Scripture to give a thick description of Kobe's spirit and how God used him to make the world a better place. The Bible is a critical part of this new book, especially in chapters 1–5 and 8. It not only helps to comfort those who continue to struggle with the loss of their loved ones, but it also gives room for a certain type of theological reflection—one that helps the world understand what it means to be human.

1

The Greatest Ever
Basketball Details

A FEW DAYS AGO, I finally watched an episode of Kobe Bryant's show on ESPN entitled *Details*. This particular show demonstrates Kobe's visual genius in terms of his unique ability to break down NBA players' offensive patterns on the court. The way that Kobe uses the details of the game to present, in detail, how one can improve his or her offensive performance is fascinating to say the very least.. Kobe reminds me of a systematic theologian in that he recognizes the sport of basketball as a system of movements and patterns that are presented in the human mode of competition. He understands the subconscious even-flows of basketball and how the game itself is a product of something much greater than what is seen with the human eye. The words "journey" and "purpose" come to my exploratory mind in that Kobe studied the game of basketball in minute details. For Kobe, basketball represented a creative journey in life with God and a competitive sport of phenomenological purpose.

As I watched *Details*, I was amazed at how Kobe arrived at some of his observational conclusions. I was baffled by the mysterious fact that Kobe knew more about these NBA players than they knew about themselves. For Bryant, film study was all about detail. Kobe explains his philosophy: From a young age—a very young age—I devoured film and watched everything I could get my hands on. It was always fun to me. Some people, after all, enjoy looking at a watch; others are happier figuring out how the watch works. It was always fun to watch, study, and ask the most important question: Why?

In figuring out what worked and did not work, Kobe realized that the practice of watching film itself was a form of art and work. Watching film not only conditions the mind of the athlete, but it also helps to prepare his or her muscle reflexes. By way of understanding the details associated with watching film, especially in the sport of basketball, one is able to develop his or her instincts for moving around the court and making adjustments. Bryant was a master of details. He knew when things would happen before they happened. Kobe's championship teammate Pau Gasol says,

> One of the qualities that has made Kobe so successful, and always will, is his attention to detail. He always used to tell us: if you want to be a better player, you have to prepare, prepare, prepare and prepare some more. His dissection of the game was at another level. I'm a player who watches a lot of tape. I like to watch my opponents' latest game to see how they are playing at the point that I'm about to face them, but Kobe took it a step further than that.[1]

Kobe's undivided attention to the details of basketball not only prepared him for team success on the court, but it also inspired him to develop other parts of his game such as three-point shooting, offensive footwork, and finishing at the rim with his left hand.

For Kobe, film study is what brought out the details of the game. By way of watching game film, Kobe created strategic narratives and suggestions that helped certain players become more efficient on both ends of the basketball court. Because his own game was full of intricate details physically, mentally, and spiritually, I marveled at the way Kobe broke down every single aspect. I actually understood what he was saying. I got it. For Kobe, there were details within the details. A game within the game. A battle that was up-close and personal, and a battle that was distant and far reaching. In his feeble mind, Kobe was playing against the opponent right in front of him and competing against other generational Hall of Famers—all at the same time.

Kobe was both humble and vindictive in his pursuit of a unique basketball immortality. His competitive nature and his intellectual will to win and be the best are what drove him into the conversation of *being* the greatest ever to play the game of basketball. If there is any athlete in

---

1. Bryant, *Mamba Mentality*, 15.

the history of American sports that is worth writing about in the active spheres of theology and culture, it would be Kobe Bean Bryant. This book represents a journey of human experiences, in theological detail, of the sport of basketball as seen through the eyes of Kobe Bryant.

Let the journey begin.

The credible argument of Kobe Bean Bryant being the greatest basketball player ever begins and ends in the City of Angels: Los Angeles. Here I begin my reflections by stating that one of the most amazing things about Kobe Bryant being a career Laker was that he consistently embraced the pressure that came along with wearing the purple and gold. He understood the importance of winning championships while wearing the Laker uniform. Kobe was never fearful or intimidated by the Lakers' lore or the organization's championship pedigree. He performed at a very high level in front of the greatest group of basketball witnesses—those who have had their jerseys retired to the rafters of the Great Western Forum and now the Staples Center. A number of the greatest players in the history of the NBA have played for the Lakers. The Lakers could have their own NBA Hall of Fame. Kobe performed at a high level at the Great Western Forum and then the Staples Center, but he was also known as a road warrior when the Lakers traveled. He was just as impressive in the purple-and-black road jerseys with black tennis shoes as he was in the gold, white, and powder-blue home jerseys with white and gray tennis shoes.

Kobe always embraced the challenge of winning championships for the greatest sports organization in the world outside of baseball's New York Yankees. He had no fear at all about who was watching him play in Los Angeles. Whether it was the upper-echelon Hollywood crowd, the normal, everyday crowd, the downtown LA crowd, the common folk from middle-class backgrounds, the hard-core studs from Compton, Crenshaw, and other inner-city neighborhoods, or the Hispanic, Mexican, and Asian human beings who were season-ticket holders, Kobe always gave his fans the greatest basketball show on earth. He never failed to come through for those who came to witness his otherworldly basketball skills.

Make no mistake about it. The Staples Center is the house that Kobe built. While Jerry West, Elgin Baylor, Magic Johnson, and Kareem Abdul-Jabbar were the landlords of the Great Western Forum, Kobe was the undisputed king of the Staples Center. I understand that the Lakers' championship success in the Forum provided the financial currency needed to build the Staples Center. But any way you slice it, the Staples

Center in Los Angeles was Kobe's refuge. It was his gymnasium. His home away from home. In the annals of NBA history, I cannot think of any professional sports arena in America that is as intimately connected to one athlete as the Staples Center is to Kobe Bryant. When the Staples Center played host to some of the greatest concerts, award shows, or even other types of popular sporting events, Kobe Bryant was always recognized as the lord of the Staples Center. The greatest of the greats. He was always shouted out by other celebrities and superstars as the star of stars in Los Angeles, whether he was present or not. Everyone who visited the Staples Center knew they were visiting Kobe's house. Even though Kobe played his first three years in the Great Western Forum, his greatest years and greatest basketball moments took place in the Staples Center. Many of those historic moments inside Staples represent some of the greatest basketball moments in NBA history. Kobe scored more points in the Staples Center than any other NBA player has ever scored in one home building.

For me, it is a great thing for the city of Los Angeles to believe and know that Kobe was the greatest basketball player ever. The opinionated analysis of biased sports commentators will never change the mind of Los Angelenos, whether native or foreign. If there is one American city that basketball players would desire support from in terms of basketball superiority, it would be Los Angeles. Los Angeles is the capital of basketball in the United States. Not Boston. Not Chicago. Certainly not New York. While these basketball cities may have a respectable sports culture in place (especially Boston with the Celtics' 17 NBA Championships), none of them compare favorably to the city of Los Angeles. The combination of the Los Angeles streetball culture, the Rucker Basketball League, the UCLA Bruins (11 NCAA titles), and the Los Angeles Lakers (17 NBA Championships) makes Los Angeles the undisputed king of basketball cities. Quiet as kept, the Los Angeles Clippers are on the come up. They have transformed themselves into NBA title contenders. The Clippers are also a contributing part of the basketball culture in Los Angeles. Is there a better city in the world to be named and claimed as the greatest basketball player we've seen in history? I don't think so. The way the city of Los Angeles and the Lakers organization resonated with Kobe the person and connected to Kobe the basketball player was something the world had never witnessed before. No other city in the United States has ever identified with an athlete the way Los Angeles did with Kobe Bryant. They were a match made in heaven.

Spanning at least three different sports, there are numerous statues placed strategically outside the Staples Center. If the Lakers organization retired two of Kobe's jersey numbers, then there should be three statues of Kobe Bryant placed outside and inside the Staples Center in Los Angeles. The one inside should be of Kobe and Gianna watching a Lakers game while sitting in their courtside seats. Another statue should be the image of Kobe wearing his #8 home white Lakers jersey with his number one finger held high as he walked off the court after scoring 81 points against the Toronto Raptors. The last statue should be Kobe in his #24 road purple jersey shooting his patent fadeaway jump shot with defenders around him. These proposed statues would be indicative of what Kobe meant to the Lakers organization and the city of Los Angeles. While they are not always given the public opportunity or the national microphone like many of the media pundits, there are millions of people, players and coaches included, who believe Kobe Bryant is the greatest basketball ever, including people in basketball cities like in Phoenix, San Antonio, Atlanta, New York, Boston, Chicago, Dallas, and Miami. We simply do not get to hear and see these people saying as much on ESPN, FOX, NBC, or TNT. We have been programmed to think that if TV personalities do not say Kobe is the greatest, then he must not be the greatest. But my truth is that Kobe Bryant is the greatest ever to put a basketball in his hands.

Understandably, there is generational bias toward the great Michael Jordan because many Americans feel he represented their generation (the 1990s) of great sports athletes. TV commentators and basketball columnists believe that the more they say and write that Jordan is the greatest, the greater chance there will be of this being true. In other words, Air Jordan belonged to them. The truth is that not everyone agrees with the TV personalities and sports columnists. The sports commentators' arguments are faulty because they do not consider the whole body of work. They either pick and choose moments that help to solidify their argument, or they tend to stick with one predominant theory that they know will stick in the minds of their listeners. As one who knows basketball inside and out, TV commentators have never connected to my way of thinking the game. Just for the sake of keeping it simple, they mention such things as Jordan's 6-0 record in the NBA Finals, or what some commentators call "passing the eye test." My questions to them are: What the heck have you been looking at? Have you watched Kobe Bryant highlights on YouTube? If you have not, please take a look at "Kobe Bryant's Best Plays Against All 30 NBA Teams" and "The Tops 50 Plays of Kobe's

Bryant's Career." In arguing for Kobe's statistical greatness while playing for one team for twenty consecutive years, the affirmation of Bryant being the greatest player ever is founded in what he was able to achieve on the basketball court. I am not referring to the sale of tennis shoes or his appearances in commercials and movies. The nouns that come to mind in describing Bryant are "rarity," "ability," "talent," "work ethic," "creativity," and "inspiration."

Just for the sake of keeping things simple, I believe Kobe Bryant became the greatest basketball player ever when he won *multiple* championships (2009 and 2010) without Shaquille O'Neal in the same uniform. In particular, he became the G.O.A.T. when he won his fifth championship, leading the Lakers past their archrival, the Boston Celtics. When Kobe won those last two championships with a different set of Lakers teammates, he established himself as the alpha male whose exploits put him on equal footing with what Shaq accomplished during the Lakers' three-peat years. Whether we refer to the three-peat Lakers as the Shaq-and-Kobe Lakers or the Kobe-and-Shaq Lakers, we are still talking about the same Lakers. There is no pecking order in the names of the leading men. During the Lakers' three-peat from 2000 to 2002, there were several occasions where Kobe was the main guy or the leading superstar. He was the team's most offensively gifted player and its leader in assists, as well as its best perimeter player, clutch (fourth quarter) scorer, free-throw shooter, on-the-ball defender, ball-handler, and basketball mind on the team.

Philosophically speaking, the critique of Kobe's basketball greatness was more about him not being able to lead the Lakers to a championship without Shaq as a teammate. In the competitive mind of Kobe Bryant, this critique not only motivated him to prove he was always an alpha male (even in the company of another alpha male), but it also inspired his understanding of how unfair the original critique was. Kobe was aware of the fact that no other leading NBA superstar in championship history had to endure such biased contempt in being critiqued for not winning titles without their superstar sidekick. Even as the vaunted Lakers celebrated a trio of titles, Kobe was still frowned upon to some degree.

For the purpose of celebrating the life of Kobe Bryant in the presence of basketball historians, allow me to pick your brain in this line of factual questioning: Did Michael Jordan win multiple championships without Scottie Pippen? No. Did Magic Johnson win multiple championships without Kareem Abdul-Jabbar? No. Did Larry Bird win multiple championships without Kevin McHale? No. Did Kareem win multiple championships without Magic? No. Kareem did win one championship in Milwaukee with the great Oscar Robertson as his superstar sidekick, but the answer is no. Did LeBron James win multiple championships without Dwyane Wade? No. LeBron won one championship in Cleveland with Kyrie Irving as his superstar sidekick, but the answer is no. Did Shaquille O'Neal win multiple championships without Kobe Bryant? No. Shaq won one championship in Miami with Dwyane Wade as his superstar sidekick, but the answer is no. Let me give you all an important clue to what I am trying to say. The key word in this line of questioning is *multiple*. Here is the G.O.A.T. question of my factual argument. Did Kobe Bryant win multiple championships without Shaquille O'Neal? YES. Obviously, when it comes to winning NBA Championships, the great Celtics legend, Bill Russell, is the exception. He won a total of 11 NBA Championships. However, Kobe knew that the Shaq critique was unprecedented in the history of the NBA. He also knew that winning those last two championships without Shaq would take him to an unprecedented level of basketball immortality. Kobe ended the first decade of the new millennium the same way he started it—by winning multiple NBA Championships. Kobe destroyed the myth that he could not win an NBA Championship without Shaq.

During the Lakers three-peat from 2000 to 2002, Kobe was the Lakers' standout player in those super-intense Western Conference playoff series, which were actually more competitive and more exciting than the ho-hum NBA Finals against the Indiana Pacers, Philadelphia 76ers, and New Jersey Nets. Kobe Bryant showed up big time in the playoffs against the Portland Trail Blazers, Sacramento Kings, San Anotnio Spurs, and Phoenix Suns. If you disagree with my argument, ask Gregg Popovich, Rick Adelman, and George Karl about the greatness of Kobe Bryant in the NBA playoffs. For example, when we see Kobe shaking loose from an older Scottie Pippen and lobbing the infamous alley-oop to Shaq, it is assumed that this was the dominant course of action when it came to the Lakers winning over the course of three years. It was assumed that little brother Kobe passed the ball to big brother Shaq and Shaq did all the scoring in leading his team to victory. This is far from the truth. During that critical Game 7 against the Trail Blazers, Kobe was the reason why the Lakers survived. He led the Lakers with 25 points, 11 rebounds, 7 assists, and 4 blocks. Equally alongside of the Hall-of-Fame center, Shaquille O'Neal, Kobe Bryant was an ultradominant force on those Lakers championship teams. For the Shaq-Kobe (or Kobe-Shaq) Lakers, the NBA

Finals were a mere formality, the culmination of their dominance over the rest of the league.

With Kobe and Shaq, an argument could be made that the Lakers had the two most dominant players in the entire league. It should be noted that the NBA Finals MVP Award (which Shaq won three straight times) was not about how well or poorly Kobe performed during the Finals. Not only was Kobe the main reason the Lakers had gotten out of the Western Conference in the first place, but he also played well in those Finals. The awarding of the Finals MVP to Shaquille O'Neal was more about the relative ease with which he dominated the paint in all three series. Rik Smits (Lakers def. the Pacers 4 games to 2), Dikembe Mutombo (Lakers def. the 76ers 4 games to 1), and the combination of Todd MacCulloch (Lakers def. the Nets 4 games too) did not give Shaq much resistance down low. None of these centers were close to being considered an all-time great. Any real basketball mind knows this to be true.

But in leading his team to three straight NBA Championships, Kobe showed up and showed out when the Lakers needed him the most—those nail-biting, clutch moments. Where the younger Kobe's playoff greatness is concerned, you can always reference all of the Western Conference playoff series from 2000 to 2002: Game 7 of the 2000 Western Conference Finals, Game 7 of the 2002 Western Conference Finals, Game 4 of 2000 NBA Finals, Game 3 of the 2001 NBA Finals, Game 3 of the 2002 NBA Finals, and Game 2 of the 2004 NBA Finals versus the Pistons. Kobe's clutch performances in these massive games represented the true genesis of his postseason genius.

I will now argue Kobe Bryant's all-time basketball greatness in another comprehensive vernacular. In what the great Vanessa Bryant calls the "peak" of Kobe's basketball career,[2] he recently headlined what many basketball pundits are calling the greatest NBA Hall of Fame class ever (2020). Posthumously, Kobe is again the greatest star in the greatest class of basketball Hall of Famers ever. My questions to those who claim that Kobe did not pass the proverbial eye test during his playing days are: If Kobe Bryant was the hardest-working NBA player in history, the most skilled/talented NBA player ever, the greatest Laker ever, someone who only ever played for one team, the greatest player of his generation, the greatest player of the 2000s by a wide margin, a four-time All-Star-Game MVP, the greatest scorer in the history of high school basketball

---

2. "Vanessa Bryant Says."

in Philadelphia, the greatest and first guard ever to be drafted out of high school, the greatest scoring guard in the history of the NBA, at one time the greatest scorer in All-Star Game history, the greatest pure scorer in history (*scoring* 81 points in one game; 50 or more points in four consecutive games; 35 or more points in 14 consecutive games; 40 or more points in nine consecutive games; 62 points in three quarters, outscoring the entire Dallas Mavericks team; a then-record of 61 points in New York's Madison Square Garden; 60 points in his last career game; 50-plus points in one half three times; and 30 or more points in a quarter twice), then how can basketball analysts leave Kobe out of the mythical G.O.A.T. conversation?

If Kobe Bryant was the greatest pure scorer, tough-shot-maker, last-second clutch player, half-court isolation player, and mid-range shooter, and one of the greatest defensive players ever, how can we not say that he is the greatest play ever? If it is true what Phil Jackson says about Kobe going "beyond the veil"[3] as he became one the greatest scorers in both the NBA regular season and NBA Playoffs, that Kobe single-handedly put USA Basketball back on the world map, leading our national team to Olympic gold medals in both 2008 and 2012, how can we not say Bryant is the G.O.A.T.? If it is true that Kobe is the first player ever to have two different jersey numbers retired (8 and 24) by the same organization—the famed Los Angeles Lakers—the greatest draft pick in the greatest NBA draft ever (1996) and the greatest player in the greatest NBA Hall of Fame class ever (2020), then how can we not say in full faith, and with great pride, that Kobe Bryant is the greatest basketball player that has ever lived?

Here are a few more details. At the age of eighteen, Kobe Bryant was the youngest ever to win the Sprite Slam Dunk Contest. In leading all scorers with 31 points, Kobe should have been named MVP of the 1997 Schick Rookie Game. At the age of nineteen, Kobe was the youngest player ever to be voted to start in an NBA All-Star Game. By all accounts, Kobe played exceedingly well in his first All-Star game. He played so well against Jordan and his Eastern Conference compadres that the West All-Stars coach benched him for the majority of the second half. When he went to the bench for the final time, he was leading the West All-Stars in scoring with 18 points. You must remember that when Kobe was voted by the fans to start in this the 1998 NBA All-Star Game, he was not even

---

3. Young, "Phil Jackson on Kobe Bryant," para. 4.

starting for the Los Angeles Lakers. And if it were not for the 1999 NBA lockout, Kobe's career would have included his being voted by the fans to start in nineteen straight NBA All-Star Games, not eighteen. Kobe's basketball genius connected with the fans in such a way that he was even voted to start in the All-Star Games he was not physically able to play in. During the NBA All-Star season, Kobe was always the star of stars. He eventually became the All-Star Game's all-time leading scorer, passing his idol, Michael Jordan. I believe Bryant was humbled in his spirit whenever he passed Jordan statistically or did something that tied him with the great Jordan. It is not that he wanted to be Jordan or emulate Jordan. I do not think that was the case. It was universally known that Kobe was determined to be the best version of himself, but because Jordan was the standard of NBA greatness in the 1990s, Kobe used Jordan's accomplishments as motivation to pursue his own basketball greatness.

In addition to being named All-Star Game MVP a record four times, Kobe played well in several All-Star Games. As a testament to his basketball greatness, Kobe, unlike many of his contemporaries, was committed to playing hard in what many basketball pundits consider a glorified exhibition game. Kobe took the NBA All-Star Game seriously. I recall saying on national television that if these guys participated in the NBA All-Star Game with the purpose of trying to be cool and laid back, he would embarrass them in front of whole world. As a basketball historian, I am quite sure that those All-Star Games in which Kobe was playing opposite Michel Jordan (1998 in New York, 2002 in Philadelphia, and 2003 in Atlanta) were the ones that meant the most to him. Bryant's West team won two of those three games. Kobe also amassed a 5–3 record in regular season games versus Jordan-led teams.

Question: Who do you think Jordan came back to the NBA to play against when he was the owner of the Washington Wizards? Yes, Kobe Bean Bryant. While I do believe that Jordan needed to see for himself the high-flying acts of Kevin Garnett, Vince Carter, Tracy McGrady, and others, my gut tells me that Jordan's competitive juices led him back to the courts to compete against Bryant. Even though Jordan was way past his athletic prime, those four Lakers-Washington Wizards games, and those two All-Star games against Bryant, were epic sporting events to say the very least. As a scholar and theologian, I would be remiss if I did not say that the NBA did an excellent job of celebrating the life and legacy of Kobe Bryant throughout the 2020 All-Star Game weekend. Considering the difficulty of the grief-filled moment, I was very pleased that the NBA renamed the All-Star Game MVP Award the Kobe Bryant MVP Award. For numerous reasons, the posthumous honor bestowed upon Kobe Bryant was most fitting. I also agree with Brooklyn Nets' guard, Kyrie Irving, when he suggested that an image of Kobe Bryant should be the new NBA logo. I am sure Jerry West would be on board with this idea.

When Jordan came out of retirement for the second time to play for the Wizards, the NBA schedule confirmed that he and Kobe would get the opportunity to face one another at least three times. Our hope was that the mid-season All-Star Game would be the third meeting, along with the two Lakers-Wizards regular season games. Anyone with good basketball sense tuned in to the Jordan-Bryant dream matchup. They were both exciting and historic. It wasn't often we were able to get a glimpse of the two greatest players in NBA history, playing on the same court, at the same time, at the same position. While they did not always guard one another, just the mere fact that they were on the court together made for great theater. During Jordan's last season (a third go-round) things got a little testy between big brother Jordan and little brother Bryant. Because Bryant was not under contract with any shoe company, he would sport a pair of Jordan's basketball sneakers. According to former NBA player Gilbert Arenas, Jordan told Bryant (to his face) at the end of the Lakers-Wizards game that he could "wear the shoes but he could never fill them."[4] While I am sure that statement hurt Bryant's feelings, I am also sure that those words were not the words of a "big brother." They sounded like the words of someone who was concerned about the status of their own legacy, or someone who might have been concerned about the possibility of Bryant surpassing him in all-time greatness. Lest we contextually forget, Bryant was coming off of winning three straight championships with the Lakers (2000–2002), and he was the main reason why the West All-Stars team had defeated Jordan's East All-Stars two years in a row. In the 2002 All-Star Game in Philadelphia, Bryant's 31 points led the West to victory. Bryant was awarded his first All-Star Game MVP. The very next year (2003, in Atlanta), in what would be Jordan's last All-Star Game, Bryant did everything he could to spoil Jordan's farewell game. Even though the whole world was rooting for Jordan to go out an All-Star winner, Bryant personally made sure that did not happen.

Back to Jordan's shoe-filling statement to Bryant. Bryant's coach, Phil Jackson, confirmed Jordan's words to Bryant and stated that Bryant

---

4. Conway, "Gilbert Arenas," para. 4.

was deeply affected by the statement. According to many reports, Bryant stopped talking to his teammates for two straight weeks leading up to the Lakers-Wizards rematch in Los Angeles. The whole world knew this would be Jordan's last game in Los Angeles. They also knew the upcoming match-up would be the last chapter of Jordan-versus-Bryant. What the public did not know was that Jordan had made a challenging (and quietly hurtful) statement to Bryant. Obviously, that statement gave Bryant the fuel he needed to perform at an historical level. With Jordan on the court with him in a Wizards uniform, Bryant put on an offensive show for the ages. With Jordan staying completely away from Bryant and making sure his Wizards teammates guarded the Lakers' best perimeter player, Bryant went off for 42 points in the first half. He ended up with 55 points for the game. While shooting mostly three-point jump shots, Bryant effortlessly took over the Lakers offense. Hobbled with a sore knee, Bryant did not use a lot of energy in putting up those numbers. On that historic night, Bryant was efficient in his shooting, and he was determined to make his last game versus Jordan memorable. Basketball pundits declared this particular game the passing of the torch from Jordan to Bryant. What we had come to realize was that his 55-point night was just another day at the office for Bryant.

What Bryant did to the hapless Wizards, he did to the entire NBA. The beautiful thing about that night was that Jordan got to see in person what he had heard about and watched on TV—an historically great basketball player. Jordan later said something to the effect that it looked like Bryant was shooting the ball into a giant rim or an enlarged basketball goal. What it looked like to me is that Jordan made it a point to stay as far away from Bryant as possible as Bryant torched his Wizards with a masterful offensive display. I did not see Jordan spell Jerry Stackhouse, Richard Hamilton, or the other Wizards defenders by taking on the challenge of guarding the unguardable Kobe. Even as he wore a pair of Jordan's basketball shoes in his final game against Michael Jordan, Kobe Bryant was in the process of filling his own shoes. He was building his own basketball legacy.

Considered by many to be a basketball savant or professional basketball's version of Albert Einstein, Kobe Bean Bryant worked his way into a conversation that only has room for two people. Those two people are Michael Jordan and Kobe Bryant. The crux of this particular conversation revolves around the ongoing debate of who is basketball's greatest player. As much as people want to place LeBron James in the G.O.A.T.

conversation, those comparisons are force-fed. If you know anything about forcing things into places where they do not fit, you are aware of the fact that the force itself does great damage to both the edges of the peg and the inside of the hole. Put simply, it does not fit. Attempting to compare James to Jordan without any mention of how James stacks up against Bryant is an insult to the game of basketball. Even Jordan himself says that only Bryant deserves the comparison.[5] Kobe was such a polarizing figure. His two-way prowess is significant enough to convict his greatest critics. Society makes it a point to consistently disrespect Bryant when it comes to the conversation of who is the greatest basketball player ever. Whether we want to accept it or not, Kobe Bryant is now the fourth-leading scorer in NBA history (and was once the third, passing Jordan in 2015). Bryant was the first player in NBA history with over 30,000 points and 6,000 assists. He is one of three players in NBA history with at least five NBA Championships and 30,000 points (Abdul-Jabbar and Jordan being the other two). Bryant is one of two guards in the history of the NBA who has cracked the 30,000-point plateau (Jordan being the other). I am not sure if we will ever see an NBA guard score 30,000 points again.

While he has always been a sweetheart of a guy, LeBron James is 4–6 in the NBA Finals. He has lost multiple NBA Finals in both Cleveland and Miami while being swept in both uniforms. And he could very easily be 3–7 if it were not for sharpshooter Ray Allen. Certainly, divine intervention intervened on behalf of the 2013 Miami Heat. Lest we forget, the Miami Heat had four future Hall of Famers on that 2013 title team. They were lucky to survive Game 6 of the 2013 NBA Finals. One would suggest that, given the plethora of talent assembled on that team, the Heat were supposed to win the NBA title in every year of their "Big Three" existence. The Heat were 2–2 in the NBA Finals during their four-year run with James, Dwyane Wade, and Chris Bosh leading the way. Even though James won two titles in Miami, I believe his matriculation away from Cleveland did more harm to his basketball legacy than good. Representing the Eastern Conference in the NBA Finals was not a challenge for the Heat. Actually, it was rather easy.

On the other side of the basketball hemisphere, Kobe Bryant was a very respectable 5–2 in the NBA Finals. Representing the Western Conference in the NBA Finals was always a difficult task in the post-Jordan era. In terms of competition, the Western Conference has been superior

---

5. Freeman, "Michael Jordan Thinks," para. 4.

to the Eastern Conference since 1998. Thus, my list of players in the conversational pecking order when theorizing about the greatest basketball player ever is: Jordan, Bryant, Chamberlain, and everybody else. Given the subject matter, theorizing about the hypothetical is the absolute best any of us can do. Nobody knows the truth about who the G.O.A.T. really is. The best we can do is give an intelligent opinion or speak from a factual perspective about who we feel is the best basketball player of all time. My intellectual understanding is that every single facet of this particular conversation—the greatest NBA player of all time—is arguably fluid.

For many people, the affirming of Kobe Bryant as the greatest basketball player in NBA history is basketball blasphemy. Whether we are at the barber shop, the gymnasium, the park, a restaurant, the grocery store a church, or even in front of a big-screen TV watching football, if Kobe Bryant's name is mentioned in the same breath as Michael Jordan, Kobe automatically becomes the villain. In referencing the smallest details of Jordan's many accomplishments, Kobe instantaneously becomes less than perfect. Kobe the human being quickly becomes a rapist, a man of arrogance, a ball-hog, a snitch, an adulterer, a spoiled brat, a problem child, an aloof, selfish ballplayer, a systemic nightmare, and a breaker of organizations. I have heard people refer to Bryant as everything other than what he really is—arguably the greatest *basketball player* in the history of the game.

As a scholar, I am always willing to research the numbers and argue epistemological greatness. Championship player, coach, and executive Pat Riley (Lakers, New York Knicks, and Miami Heat) once said that Kobe was "he rates right there . . . with Jordan"[6] in terms of ranking the living hierarchy of basketball greatness in the world. NBA Commissioners David Stern and Adam Silver have made similar statements. Riley made this comment in the context of LeBron James, Dwyane Wade, and Carmelo Anthony needing to improve their games for the purpose of being mentioned in the same breath as Jordan and Bryant. This statement was made before Kobe began winning championships again with a new sidekick. Championships four and five changed the G.O.A.T. conversation.

If one is allowed to argue that Kobe Bryant is the greatest Laker of all time (and he is for sure), then the Jordan comparisons must go to a deeper presuppositional level, analytically and factually speaking. First, the placing of Bryant above the likes of all-time Lakers greats Kareem

---

6. Dr. KaMilan, "Pat Riley about Kobe and MJ," 0:15–0:17.

Abdul-Jabbar, Magic Johnson, Shaquille O'Neal, Jerry West, Wilt Chamberlain, and Elgin Baylor is a huge honor. Any of these Hall of Famers would have easily been the greatest player of any other NBA franchise. Because society has allowed the media's obsession with Michael Jordan to be etched into its collective psyche—even crossing generations—affirming Jordan as the one and only G.O.A.T., the NBA media landscape has become a hotbed for developing basketball zombies by shutting the basketball world off from arguing whether or not someone other than Jordan might be the game's greatest player.

Second, my argument for Bryant being the G.O.A.T is an argument based on facts and not personal feelings, shoe sales, off-the-court revenue, and corporate sponsorships. The opening question is *not* "What does Kobe Bryant do better than Michael Jordan?," the real question is, "What can Kobe Bryant *not* do on the basketball court?" Kobe defends the other team's best perimeter player with the heart of a gladiator, dribbles the basketball with an *And 1* skill set, rebounds with a ruthless vengeance, and scores as if he knows he is the greatest shot-maker in the history of the game—almost as if he invented scoring.

I believe Kobe when he said the 2012 U.S. Olympic Basketball Team could defeat the 1992 Dream Team.[7] I am more than sure that Jordan, Magic, & Co. would have had a very difficult time defending the likes of Bryant, James, Kevin Durant, Anthony, and Kevin Love (if on the court at the same time) and their respective versatility as rooted in their combined abilities to spread the floor, penetrate, and make the three-pointer. Not to mention the fact that Kobe stated on more than one occasion that he would personally take on the challenge of guarding Jordan in that mythical pick-up game. Bryant's hypothetical wish includes the fact that he would have wanted Jordan to guard him on the other end of the court. Unlike many of Jordan's peers, generational and intergenerational, Kobe did not fear Jordan in the least bit. Even though Jordan vehemently disagreed with Bryant in regards to Bryant's Olympic Team defeating Jordan's Dream Team, Bryant remained cordial with his idol Jordan by stating, "So what, he (Jordan) knows that I am bad mother[expletive]. I'm not really tripping."[8]

How many Lakers records does Kobe hold anyway? Nine: most games played, most minutes played, most field goals made, most three-point field goals made, most free-throws made, most steals, most career

---

7. Turbow, "Kobe's Hoop Dreaming."
8. BSO Staff, "Kobe Bryant's Response," para. 4.

points (more than 8,000 points ahead of second-place Jerry West and 9,000 points ahead of Kareem Abdul-Jabbar), most playoff points, and highest usage percentage. How many NBA records does he hold or share? Fifteen: He holds nine records by himself and shares six others.

Kobe is the youngest player ever to start in an NBA All-Star Game, and he is the youngest ever to win the NBA Slam Dunk Contest. He scored the most points in a single game of the modern NBA era (81), and he has scored more points and made more free-throws than any guard in NBA history. He is also the oldest player ever to score 60 points in a single game. Kobe also holds the record for most points ever scored in one's final career game (60). He still holds the record for most consecutive three-point shots made in one half (nine), and he holds the record for scoring the highest percentage of his team's points in one game (66.4 percent) when he scored 81 points in 2006. Kobe also holds the record for the most scored by an opponent in the famed Madison Square Garden (61).

Kobe is tied for the most NBA All-Star Game MVP awards (four, with Bob Pettit) and he is also one of four players in NBA history to amass nine All-Defensive First Team honors (with Michael Jordan, Kevin Garnett, and Gary Payton). Kobe is tied for most consecutive games (four) of scoring at least 50 points (with Wilt Chamberlain), and he is tied for most consecutive games of scoring at least 40 points (nine, with Wilt Chamberlain and Michael Jordan). Kobe is also tied for most consecutive games (thirteen) of scoring at least 35 points (with Wilt Chamberlain). He is the only player in NBA history to score 30 points in a single quarter on two different occasions.

I recently read an article stating that Kobe, Jordan, and Hakeem Olajuwon were the only players in NBA history "to have fifteen 30 or more point games in a single playoff run."[9] That 2009 season marked Kobe's first championship without Shaquille O'Neal as one of his teammates. What many do not know is that Kobe led the NBA in total scoring four times in his career. Three times he led in field goals made, and twice he led in points per game, free throws, and field goal attempts. At one time Kobe held the record for the most three-point field goals made in one game (twelve). Setting all of these records while playing twenty years with one organization, is unheard of in today's culture of sport and professional team sports.

---

9. Jha, "Only Michael Jordan, Kobe Bryant, and Hakeem," para. 1.

Kobe broke John Stockton's record for the most years of basketball service with one team. Stockton, the NBA's all-time assist leader, played nineteen seasons for the Utah Jazz, alongside Karl Malone; but they were not able to win one single NBA title. Dirk Nowitzki played twenty-one consecutive seasons for the Dallas Mavericks, breaking Kobe's record. For the record, Kobe never took a break from the game he loved. Kobe did not call a press conference every time he felt uninspired to play basketball the following season. Kobe did not pursue another sport because he was disinterested and disenchanted with the current stable of basketball players and their inability to challenge his throne. Kobe did not cease competing when he felt the fear of failure and losing creeping up in his bones.

Year after year, Kobe worked out his body and mind in various gymnasiums, training rooms, and weight rooms with hopes of becoming a better ballplayer. The funny thing is that after Kobe was unanimously chosen by several media outlets as the best NBA player of the 2000s, he was in the process of winning his fifth championship with a new set of Lakers teammates. In other words, he was still the best player in the NBA. As if being lauded as the greatest player of the 2000s was his call to begin thinking about retirement, Bryant yawned yet again at his critics and put together one of his finest seasons ever in 2013, his seventeenth year in the NBA.

The fact that Kobe was awarded only one MVP is absolutely ridiculous. Kobe was snubbed multiple times in the NBA Regular Season MVP voting. He should have won four or five NBA MVP Awards. In addition to his 2008 MVP campaign, Kobe should have won the NBA MVP Award during the years he averaged 35.4 and 31.6 points per game (2005 and 2006, respectively), as well as the 2002–03 season. It is amazing to me how so many people have jumped on Stephen Curry's bandwagon in hopes of him being named the MVP of the 2020–21 season. This is because he ended up the league's leading scorer and he helped his team qualify for the postseason play-in tournament. Why is it that when Kobe led the league in scoring, the powers that be created reasons not to name him the MVP of the regular season when he led the NBA in scoring, but instead they found a way to name Steve Nash the MVP? Go figure.

Some fifteen-plus years later, many basketball pundits are now willing to publicly advocate for Curry over the likes of Nikola Jokic of the Denver Nuggets, Joel Embiid of the Philadelphia 76ers, Giannis Antetokounmpo of the Milwaukee Bucks, Chris Paul of the Phoenix Suns, and Donovan Mitchell of the Utah Jazz. How could Bryant's scoring numbers during those two years, which were higher than Curry's (31.5) be less worthy of an MVP Award when Bryant the player was light years better than Steve Nash? Why is it that Curry's leading the NBA in scoring is MVP-worthy and Kobe's years of leading the NBA in scoring are not?

Even though the Lakers were not title contenders, Kobe Bryant was the undisputed best basketball player in the world. Michael Jordan and LeBron James would have never lost the regular-season MVP Award to Steve Nash. Neither would Stephen Curry. The TV analysts would have made sure of that. During the 2009–10 regular season, Kobe hit six game-winning shots and went on to lead the Lakers past the Celtics for his fifth NBA Championship. He should have won the MVP that year as well. Because Kobe is not the most politically correct or most beloved player in the NBA (the word that comes to mind is polarizing), he was oftentimes robbed of being named MVP of the NBA's regular season. But yet, according to Shaq, Kobe became the absolute best player in the NBA during the Lakers' first championship run in 2000. While it does not seem like the MVP snubbings affected Bryant's performance on the basketball court, it can be affirmed that Kobe was the best player in the entire world throughout the entirety of the 2000s.

But at the same time, Bryant's lone MVP does not define his basketball greatness. With such retired greats as Bob Pettit, Russell, Wilt, Kareem, Moses Malone, Magic, Bird, Jordan, and Karl Malone winning multiple NBA MVPs, one would think that Kobe's basketball talent would have merited him more MVPs. But again, the regular-season MVP did not define Kobe's transcendent game. Anybody with good basketball sense knows that *the number of NBA titles won* is the only category that truly matters when it comes to affirming one's basketball greatness. In 2010, fourteen years after he was drafted out of high school, Kobe was still playing at an elite level and with insane athleticism. His skill set enabled him to still be able to dunk the basketball jumping off of one foot, two feet, and the wrong foot as well.

Above the likes of Wilt, Russell, Kareem, Oscar Robinson, Magic, Bird, and many other dominant ballplayers from different eras, society has placed Jordan at the pinnacle of professional basketball without actually seeing him play against other generations' greatest players in person and in their respective primes. While Jordan was not the first to go 6–0 in the NBA Finals (Bill Russell), he became the chosen name that we were sure about in terms of him being what Pat Riley would call the "best of the best of the best."[10] Sadly, people were declaring Jordan as the greatest basketball player ever after he won his first three championships from 1991–93. Go figure.

I believe that Kobe Bryant is the historical bridge between Jordan and LeBron James. When I say "historical bridge," I am referring to the fact that Kobe competed against both Michael and LeBron in regular season games and All-Star games. Jordan and James never played against each other. Because Bryant competed hard and shot the ball well against Jordan and James, I am inclined to think he got the best of both superstars in both regular season games and All-Star games. This is precisely why the world needed to see Bryant and James battle in the 2009 NBA Finals. This clash of basketball superpowers was to be the next best thing to Jordan-versus-Bryant in an NBA Final. In his infinite knowledge of NBA history, Bryant knew the supreme importance of competing against Jordan and James in real time. Bryant was sure he was superior to both Jordan and James. The fact that Bryant did not take a backseat to either superstar allows me to present my argument in a different way.

If the NBA Finals is the sole criteria for placing Jordan above every other NBA great in history, then let us analyze who Jordan competed against in those six NBA Finals. When the Bulls defeated an over-the-hill Lakers squad from the 1980s, Jordan torched the 6'3" Byron Scott for over 30 points a game. There was no competition at the two-guard position. Magic was way too slow to guard the athletic Jordan. When the Bulls defeated the Trail Blazers in 6 games, an athletic Clyde Drexler provided Jordan with his toughest individual competition in the NBA Finals. Many basketball observers thought that Drexler had a similar athleticism and skill set as Jordan. The truth is he did not. All Drexler could do was glide his way to an open-court dunk. When the Bulls defeated Charles Barkley's Phoenix Suns, Jordan had his way with such players as 6'0" point guard Kevin Johnson, slow-footed sharpshooter Dan Majerle (6'6") and relative unknown Richard Dumas (6'7"). None were known for their defensive prowess, but yet they found themselves guarding MJ on the game's biggest stage. When the Bulls eliminated the Seattle SuperSonics in the 1996 Finals, 6'3" Gary Payton and 6'3" Hersey Hawkins drew the assignment of guarding Jordan. David Wingate and Vincent Askew took vacation pictures with Jordan too. Are we done yawning yet? When the Bulls beat the old-school Utah Jazz for their fifth and sixth

---

10. Dr. KaMilan, "Pat Riley about Kobe and MJ," 0:19–0:20.

championships, Jordan absolutely abused both the limping, 6'3" starting shooting guard Jeff Hornacek and the athletically challenged, 6'7" Byron Russell on many late-game plays. Shandon Anderson also spent some time on Jordan. None of these three Jazz defenders had a prayer of guarding Jordan.

In the words of the legendary Dr. J., Jordan "caught it (the NBA) at the right time. . . . [the modern NBA] should be more competitive, but the actuality is it's probaby more diluted."[11] I believe Jordan took full advantage of the opportunity to dominate those less-athletic opponents. The late Bill Russell echoed Erving's sentiments, noting that the competition during Jordan's era simply wasn't as good.[12] In the words of NBA Hall of Famer Grant Hill, "Kobe hit more 'tough' shots than Jordan and Jordan got more 'star treatment' in his view, [but] Jordan was more efficient in mid-range."[13] My interpretation of Hill's words is that Jordan got what he wanted on the offensive end. Kobe, on the other hand, had to be more creative when it came to scoring. This is the same Grant Hill who later stated that Kobe Bryant was "the best player he played against."[14]

Let me be clear. I am not saying Jordan is not a great NBA champion, or even an all-time great, because he truly is. I am only suggesting that the competition at shooting guard and small forward during Jordan's tenure in the NBA was nowhere near his own athletic and psychological prowess. Also, how good were those five teams the Bulls defeated for their six titles? Were any of those teams better than the best Lakers team ('87), the best 76ers team ('83), the best Celtics team ('86), the best Pistons team ('89, and the best Rockets team ('86) from the 1980s? Heck, none of those teams the Bulls defeated in the NBA Finals (Lakers, Trail Blazers, Suns, SuperSonics, and Jazz) were better than the 2008 Celtics led by Coach Doc Rivers, Kevin Garnett, Paul Pierce, Ray Allen, and Rajan Rondo, or even the 2014 San Antonio Spurs. Did any of those runner-up teams defend as well as Garnett & Co., or score as well as David Robinson, Tim Duncan, Manu Ginobli, Tony Parker, & Co.? Other than Magic's Lakers, what other team had even won an NBA title prior to meeting Jordan's Bulls in the NBA Finals? None of them. Other than a handful of the Lakers and former Celtic guard Danny Ainge with the

---

11. ESPNSportFirstTake, "First Take," 4:51–4:52, 5:24–5:29.
12. Klas, "Bill Russell Thinks."
13. Hansford, "Lakers News: Grant Hill Says," para. 3.
14. Gharib, "Lakers Video," para. 6.

Trail Blazers and Suns, did any of those runner-up teams have an NBA champion on their roster? No. Of course Jordan and the Bulls had their way with those five teams from the depleted Western Conference.

Prior to the Jordan era, the NBA was a league that was dominated by players 6'9" and taller. Inclusive of an athletically declining Dr. J. (6'7") and the athletically challenged Magic (6'9") and Bird (6'9"), front-line players were the most dominant players in the NBA. This trend continued throughout the latter half of the 1980s and throughout most of the 1990s. When Jordan entered the NBA in 1984, the league was not a guard-dominated league. The NBA was a forward-and-center-dominated league. Not only did Jordan usher in the super NBA athlete or dominant two-guard era, but he was also the prototype. Think about it. Jordan's greatest rivals in the 1980s and 1990s were the likes of the late Dennis Johnson, Craig Ehlo, Joe Dumars, John Starks, Reggie Miller to a lesser degree, a young Ron Harper, a lost Nick Anderson, and Drexler. Jordan never faced the super NBA athlete that he himself had already transformed into. One could argue that Jordan was challenged by athletic small forwards like Xavier McDaniel, Dominique Wilkins, and Dennis Rodman during Detroit's "Bad Boy" days, but he was never threatened by an athletic shooting guard who was courageous and talented enough to challenge Jordan's throne... at least until Kobe Bryant came on the scene, albeit in a later generation.

Most NBA players were scared to challenge Jordan because they felt athletically and mentally defeated before the ball was even tipped. The psychology of Jordan overwhelmed his fellow competitors at both the two-guard and small forward positions. Athletically speaking and skill-wise, Jordan's greatest basketball challenge came in the form of his own teammate, Scottie Pippen. More often than not, Pippen guarded the opposing team's best perimeter player while Jordan conserved his energy for dominant efforts on the offensive end of the court. When Jordan came back to the Bulls after his first retirement (1995), Pippen had developed into arguably the best player in the NBA. Jordan did not have a true rival, nor did he have a single NBA peer who was nearly as athletically gifted as he was. Kobe Bryant, on the other hand, had a plethora of athletic shooting guards and small forwards that he not only had to deal with effort-wise on a nightly basis, but he also had to transcend them skill-wise too. A gifted defender, Bryant made it a point to guard the other team's best perimeter player even it meant guarding the opposing team's point guard. Not only has Bryant outlasted every single player from what many consider to be the greatest NBA draft ever (1996), but he has also defeated the numerous generations of NBA super athletes that came before and after him. In this particular line of thought, Bryant's NBA career has been both historical and transcendent.

Like Jordan, Bryant had no true rival. Maybe Jordan and Bryant were each other's true rival from each of their generational spaces. But there were a number of athletically gifted shooting guards and small forwards he competed against. Among them: Vince Carter, Ray Allen, Tracy McGrady, Kerry Kittles, Paul Pierce, Jerry Stackhouse, Grant Hill, Penny Hardaway, Brandon Roy, Jason Richardson, Antoine Walker, Allan Houston, Ron Mercer, Derrick Anderson, Shane Battier, Ron Artest, Tayshawn Prince, Eddie Jones, Rip Hamilton, Bruce Bowen, Doug Christie, Reggie Miller (in the latter years of his career), Steve Smith, Manu Ginobli, Latrell Sprewell, Ricky Davis, Gerald Green, Jalen Rose, Joe Johnson, Glenn Robinson, Shawn Marion, Monte Ellis, Josh Howard, Matt Barnes, Aaron Afflalo, Andre Iguodola, Peja Stojakovic, Ruben Patterson, Bonzi Wells, Paul George, Dahntay Jones, Danny Granger, Scottie Pippen in his later years, Dwyane Wade, Carmelo Anthony, even LeBron James and Kevin Durant could be thrown into this group of athletes due to their superior athleticism. Not all of the players I mentioned are worthy of all-time accolades or even Hall of Fame consideration. However, that is not my point. My point is that, on the whole, Kobe successfully competed against a greater level of NBA athlete, and as a result of the increased athletic competition Bryant outshot, outhustled, outdefended, outscored, outworked, outwilled, outclassed, outplayed, out-won, and outlasted all of them. I do not need many experts to agree with me on this. This argument is more than legitimate. Again, Jordan came back to the NBA for those two years (2001–02 and 2002–03) as owner of the Wizards for a reason. He wanted to see what he had missed out on by not competing against those new-age NBA athletes, many of whom could jump way above the rim and touch the top of the square just like he once could.

Upon learning that he was named to the NBA 75th Anniversary Team, Isiah Thomas made a statement to the effect that he was the only NBA great who had won multiple NBA Championships without a Top 50 teammate playing alongside him. Someone out there in the basketball universe please inform Mr. Thomas that Kobe Bryant won multiple NBA titles without a single Top 50 player or Hall of Famer playing on his team (2008–09 and 2009–10). Those back-to-back Detroit Pistons title teams had three Hall of Famers (Thomas, Dumars, and Rodman), an All-Star forward in Mark Aguirre, and a plethora of talented players up and down the roster. Bryant's championship teams were way less talented than Thomas's title teams. However, what Bryant and Thomas have in common is that they led their respective organizations to consecutive NBA Championships without other all-time greats on their team.

In terms of affirming the unmatched NBA legacy of Kobe Bryant, I need the world to know that as much as I love Pau Gasol, I am not fully convinced of his NBA Hall of Fame status. If he is an NBA Hall of Famer, it would only be that way because he played with Kobe Bryant, and they won multiple championships together. Gasol was one of the least-talented star sidekicks I have ever seen in the history of the game. Unlike many Lakers legends who played major roles in helping their teams win NBA Championships, I see no reason to hang Pau's jersey in the rafters of the Staples Center. Please do not mention the word statue in my presence. Pau Gasol was not on the level with Abdul-Jabbar, McHale, Pippen, Cousy, Jones or any of the supporting cast of the "Bad Boy" era Detroit Pistons. Nor was he better than Tim Duncan's championship support system of David Robinson, Tony Parker, Manu Ginoboli, and Kawhi Leonard. In my humble opinion, Kobe was the only first-ballot NBA Hall of Famer on those Lakers back-to-back title teams in 2009 and 2010. Here the interpretation is that Kobe did something unprecedentedly historical.

I am not saying that Kobe won those championships by himself, but it sure seems that way. Less-talented players have been voted into the NBA Hall of Fame. Subsequently, there is a distinct difference between being voted into the NBA Hall of Fame and being an all-time great basketball player. So who knows? Sadly, I saw too many NBA power forwards and centers use and abuse the seven-foot Gasol in the paint. Kevin Garnett, Kendrick Perkins and Glenn "Big Baby" Davis dominated the physically weak Gasol in the 2008 NBA Finals. It was painful to watch the Celtics' front line push Gasol around like he was invisible. They treated Gasol with no respect whatsoever, handing Bryant his second defeat in the NBA Finals. Nevertheless, Bryant's five titles with two different groups of Lakers qualifies him to be a part of the mythical G.O.A.T. conversation.

Recently, I have heard Jordan and Shaq refer to Kobe Bryant as their little brother. Whether the reasoning for developmental mentorship in the NBA was difference in age or difference in life experience, Jordan and O'Neal consistently refer to Bryant as the little brother or the younger brother. While I am sure that the "little brother" title has nothing to do with talent or ability, the context in which the label was used seems to express eternal doubt about one's ability to ascend to another plane or a higher level. The term was used as if to indicate Kobe would always be considered the little brother, or less than, or not as good as, the big brother. Even though I have heard Shaq refer to Kobe as both the greatest Laker ever and the greatest NBA player ever (and he sounded sincere), my questions are: Who said the little brother could not eclipse the big brother? Who wrote into constitutional law that the student could not eclipse the teacher? Who said that just because someone looks up to another person, they would never be better than them or they would never go beyond them in their shared field of study? As I think about it in raw terms, the little brother identification seems more like a cultural death sentence that insinuates that the little brother will never ascend to the level of the big brother.

Coming from the big brother, the title of "little brother" sounds more like the placing of limits or chains on one's ability to flourish. Obviously, Kobe looked up to Jordan and O'Neal because he needed guidance and information from them both. As Shaq referred to Kobe as his little brother on numerous occasions, both superstars knew that Kobe was not anybody's little brother or second option. What Kobe lacked in experience, he made up in raw talent, hard work, and prophetic courage. Kobe, the existential bridge between Michael Jordan and LeBron James, did not take a back seat to anybody. Just as he challenged both players on the basketball court, thinking that he was better than both of them, Kobe challenged everybody he came in contact with. No one was exempt from Kobe's offer of competition. On my read and examination of Bryant's competitive nature, it seemed like Kobe was obsessed with surpassing everyone he viewed as a threat to his dominance, especially at shooting guard and small forward positions.

I recall many NBA players saying Jordan got what he wanted in terms of not having to work hard to get to his spots closer to the rim. This was part of the reason why Jordan had a higher field goal percentage. Kobe, one the other hand, had to be creative in the totality of his offensive splendor. Unlike Jordan, Kobe was more comfortable on the offensive end in that creative space. He was a better perimeter shooter than Jordan. As a shooting guard, Kobe took more shots from the perimeter than Jordan. Both were comfortable taking the ball to the hoop and finishing at the rim and around the rim. It baffles me to hear basketball pundits say that Kobe did not have the athletic dominance that Jordan did. What games were they watching? Kobe's basketball athleticism was similar to that of Jordan. What am I saying? Not only was Kobe robbed of the respect he deserved as an electrifying dunker, but the truth is that Kobe dunked on people in the same way Jordan did. Everyone knows that Vince Carter and Dr. J. are the greatest in-game dunkers in the history of the NBA. But in terms of comparing the in-game athleticism of Jordan and Bryant, I would say that they were on the same level. There were some in-game dunks that Jordan did that Kobe could not do. And there were some in-game dunks that Kobe did that Jordan could not do. My point is that Jordan and Bryant had similar athleticism that allowed them to dominate the game above and below the rim.

For the dunker, dunking the basketball on someone was just as much an act of offensive punishment as it was an act of theatrical creativity. For Bryant, dunking the basketball changed the molecules of the arena. One can argue that the slam dunk changes the momentum of the game. It can either inspire your team to come back from a large deficit, or it can put a huge stamp on the dominance your team has already exhibited. Either way, the slam dunk sends a powerful message.

As Kobe grew older, he still found ways to dunk the basketball on people during the course of the game. He picked his spots and chose his moments wisely. But make no mistake about it, Kobe dunked on a large number of NBA players, and he did so in many different ways. Because his hands were not big enough to instantly palm the basketball, Kobe had to be creative. Some of the greatest in-game dunks in NBA history came from Kobe. Bryant dunked on guards, forwards, and centers. A number of Bryant's most spectacular dunks came in those half-court, isolation situations where Bryant would slip the screen with his dribble and jump over his opponent to dunk on them.

As much as people want to say that Kobe emulated Jordan in everything he did and said, what the basketball pundits fail to admit is that they were noticeably different in the way they played the game. Jordan says that Kobe would beat him one on one because Kobe stole all his moves. Not only did Jordan fail to admit there is a strong evolutionary nature to the game of basketball, but he also failed to realize that winning one-on-one basketball games is not about your opponent knowing your moves; it is more about one's ability to stop your opponent from scoring. Jordan once conceded that a younger Kobe Bryant would beat him one on one now. However: "In my prime . . . no contest. . . . Let's just say, that I'd have a better chance of stopping him than him stopping me."[15]

Either way, I believe Kobe would not only win the mythical one-on-one game with Jordan, but he would do it in such a dominant way that it would force Jordan to rethink some things in terms of what it meant to compete against someone who could do the same things he could, and even more. I believe Kobe would have out-talented the great Jordan to no end in a one-on-one battle. Jordan never experienced that level of competition in his prime years of playing the two-guard position, because the closest anyone came to matching his on-the-court abilities was one of his teammates, Scottie Pippen.

According to former NBA player Jalen Rose, Jordan was the original and Kobe was the remix.[16] In this vein of thought, I do not think Rose was placing either player over the other. The important thing to know about remixes is they serve a dual purpose. First, remixes share a similar quality to the original in that they understand the fundamental principles of the existential origin. Second, remixes offers a more creative look or cultural perspective—one that is seemingly different from the original. The greatest remixes are the ones that both demonstrate a fundamental understanding of the original *and* create a different form of activity/performance that could never be emulated. Just as Jordan emulated Dr. J, David Thompson, Elgin Baylor, Walter Davis, Connie Hawkins, and Jerry West, he himself was very emulatable. However, as Magic Johnson so eloquently put it on numerous celebratory occasions, we (the NBA) will never see the likes of Kobe Bryant again. In the case of Jordan-versus-Kobe, I believe the remix was better than the original. In other words, Kobe eclipsed and surpassed Jordan in a number of on-the-court basketball categories.

Jordan tried his best to emulate Julius Erving, David Thompson, and anyone else who had been successful at jumping high and palming the basketball. Jordan was not the first of his kind. He stole moves from the players who came before him. What separated Jordan from the aforementioned group of players was that he had an above-average jump shot and he was smart as all get out. In a respectful mentioning of the earlier generation players that Jordan patterned his game after, the question now becomes: How were Kobe and Jordan different? Kobe was a better

---

15. "Michael Jordan vs. Kobe Bryant," para. 2.
16. Talwalkar, "Jalen Rose," para. 5.

shooting guard. With emphasis upon the two-guard position, Kobe was a better pure shooter. Phil Jackson said the only difference between Jordan and Bryant was the size of their hands. Jackson also believed Jordan was more developed as a leader. In summary, Jackson stated that both Jordan and Bryant were championship players. I am sure Kobe Bryant was one of best in-game dunkers in the history of the NBA. Kobe dunked on his NBA colleagues jumping off of two feet, one feet, the wrong foot, at the end of an alley-oop, slipping a pick-and-roll during a half-court offensive set, going baseline and taking off one side of the rim and coming around to the other side. Kobe was just as athletic as Jordan, if not more.

THEOLOGY AND THE CULTURE OF SPORT: WHAT DOES THE BIBLE SAY ABOUT BEING THE GREATEST?

With the Jordan/Kobe comparison in full view, the question is: How does theology properly reflect on matters of sports and competition? As an ex-basketball player and one who is concerned with the holistic condition of African American people in particular, and poor people in general, I define theology as a holistic discourse within the study of God in religious faith, Christian practice, human experience, and spirituality, that gives cultural reasoning for the liberating truth of God to come to light in any context. In essence, I believe in order for one to identify the critical norms and sources of one's theology, he or she must be operating from a working definition of theology that gives meaning to one's critical approach to biblical hermeneutics, theological praxis, and research analysis. As a trained theologian, I have always been curious about the spiritual purpose of sports. I have also pondered the existential connection between the playing of a particular sport and the presence of the transcendent God.

I agree with theologian Lincoln Harvey and others who claim that "The nonproductive nature of sport is one of the reasons why it is so hard to find a reason of sport."[17] Watching a professional basketball game in person, or even on television, it is understood from the beginning that there is no communal purpose for the game itself. Being the best team or the best player on the basketball court serves no developmental purpose in terms of helping to improve society or provide a service to those in

---

17. "Christian Perspective On Sport," para. 15.

need of resources. Because basketball is considered a team sport, it is hard to see purpose in winning a game or a series of games. Other than for the fans' bragging rights or the celebratory events that comes along with organizational success, it is difficult to see the true purpose of sports in general, and basketball in particular.

But the truth is that sports does, in fact, have meaning. They (sports) are ordered toward goals and targets, and these goals and targets give the activity its purpose. Basketball players do not shoot because it makes their food taste better; their purpose for trying to score is not founded in attaining academic degrees or winning Nobel Prizes. The basketball player only shoots because scoring a bucket for the accumulation of team points is the true purpose of the game. In the game of basketball, scoring the most points and winning the game is the point of playing. And the purpose lies within the game, not outside it. Most would agree that the sport of basketball, just like all team sports, is an unnecessary but meaningful sport. In a way that was different from those who came before him, Kobe Bryant showed us why the game of basketball is a meaningful sport. While the culture of sports is fused with claims of absolute truth, opinions, and generational bias (very similar to religion), there are some exceptions to the rule. Every athlete is not the same. What this means is that athletes participate in sports for different reasons. This leads us to the fact that every sport is different in nature. There are similarities and differences across the board. What makes sports meaningful to the world and different in the eyes of the fan is the individual athlete. How the individual athlete affects and inspires the world is what makes sports a beautiful part of society.

Another important reason why sports has meaning is because sports are competitive in nature and within the mindset of the athlete. Athletes love competing because they are competitors. They compete for the purpose of winning, being able say they are better than their opponents. Even if it is just for one game, the goal of the competitor is to win that one game and claim they are the best. Here the interpretation is that competition has often been one of the most difficult aspects of a Christian understanding of sport. Can one love their neighbor while trying to block their shot, foul them with the intent to do bodily harm, or insult them for the purpose of gaining a psychological edge? The etymology of the word "competition" is helpful, for the Latin *com-petito* literally means "to strive together," rendering sport a "mutually acceptable quest for excellence."[18] Michael W. Goheen and Craig G. Bartholomew rightly argue that it is cooperation, not rivalry, that is at the heart of competition: "In sports, teams or individuals agree cooperatively to oppose one another within the stated goals, rules, and obstacles of the game."[19] Cooperation, while helping to maintain levels of sportsmanship and unity, is no longer the goal of sports. Competition has become the sole purpose for one's participation in play. Whether we are talking about professional sports or elementary school league sports, the prevailing notion of play is that each team or each individual wants to win the game.

NBA Hall-of-Farmer Isiah Thomas once said that "the secret to basketball is that it's not about basketball."[20] He was pointing to the fact that the greatest sports teams succeed when the athletes put their egos and differences aside for the greater good of the team, working collectively toward the same end. When we see a team doing this well, in any sport, it paints a compelling picture of community and the church and, even more, the greater community of the Triune God, allowing us to see his beauty and character in a whole new light. But even in sacrificing for the greater good, which is found in team success, therein lies the importance of competing. If an individual sacrifices his or her personal goals for the overarching team goal, the team itself has to compete at a high level in order to win the game. Whether the driving force of winning is found in the active embodiment of cooperation or competition, sports is still less important than God. In sum, God's image-bearers are called to develop God's creation for the good of others *and* to delight in God's creation because of its intrinsic good. Within this context of playfully developing and delighting in God's creation we can say that sports are part of God's intention and design for creation.

Please allow me to reintroduce to you an athlete by the name of Kobe Bean Bryant. While my competitive argument for Kobe Bryant being the greatest basketball player ever is not a theological one, there is a systematic way in which I can present Bryant as a great human being and a child of God. My initial question is: What does the Bible say about being the greatest? What does it mean theologically to be the greatest in any field of study or a sport? Without moving into the realm of idolatry or

---

18. Carson, *Themelios*, 396.
19. Treat, "More than a Game," para. 19.
20. Camilo, "Bill Simmons and the 'Secret of Basketball,'" para. 2.

worshiping people because they are exceptional athletes, the question is: What is the litmus test for ranking certain people amongst other people? No one in any sport is greater than God the Father, Jesus the Son, and the Holy Spirit. No athlete is on the level of the Triune God. What that means is a athletic greatness is a lower-level kind of greatness based on opinion and research. Being great at anything in life does not mean we deserve to be worshiped. According to the Bible, being the greatest or being called the greatest is the opposite of self-exaltation. Matthew 18:1–5 says:

> At that time the disciples came to Jesus and asked, "Who, then, is the greatest in the kingdom of heaven?" He called a little child to him and placed the child among them. And he said: "Truly I tell you, unless you change and become like little children, you will never enter the kingdom of heaven. Therefore, whoever takes the lowly position of this child is the greatest in the kingdom of heaven. And whoever welcomes one such child in my name welcomes me.

According to the biblical text, the greatest in the kingdom of heaven is the one who changes their ways of human arrogance and becomes like little children. The lowly position of a child is one of innocence and humility. For Jesus, the greatest in the kingdom of heaven is the one humbles himself, denying who they believe themselves to be in the world. This teaching includes adults as well. Those adults who become like little children by way of humbling themselves are the greatest in the kingdom of heaven. Luke 22:24–30 says:

> Also a dispute arose among them as to which of them was considered to be greatest. Jesus said to them, "The kings of the Gentiles lord it over them; and those who exercise authority call themselves Benefactors. But you are not like that. Instead, the greatest among you should be like the youngest, and the one who rules like the one who serves. For who is greater, the one who is at the table or the one who serves? Is it not the one who is at the table? But I am among you as one who serves. You are those who have stood by me in my trials. And I confer on you a kingdom, just as my Father conferred one on me, so that you may eat and drink at my table in my kingdom and sit on thrones, judging the twelve tribes of Israel.

Here Jesus quoted from the Pentateuch when arguing with the Sadducees, since those books had special authority for them. The reference (Deut 5:5–10) is to Levitical law, which was given to protect the widow and guarantee the continuance of the family line. Notice that Jesus refers to this line of questioning in terms of the dispute as to who is the greatest in the kingdom. This sounds like NBA pundits disputing who is the greatest basketball player ever. The text suggests that the greatest should be like the youngest and the one who rules is the one who serves. According to Jesus, the greatest is not the one at the table. The one who serves is greater than the one at the table. Humble servants who are committed to serving others are the greatest in the kingdom of God.

Mark 9:34–35 reads this way: "But they kept silent, for on the way they had argued with one another about who was the greatest. And he sat down and called the Twelve. And he said to them, 'If anyone would be first, he must be last of all and servant of all.'" Due to the fact that the disciples kept quiet, there seemed to some level of embarrassment. Questions of rank and status (Who is the greatest?) were normal, as they played an important role in the life of Jewish groups at this time, but they had no place in Jesus' value system. Mark refers to the question of who is the greatest in the kingdom as an argument. Again, it sounds like people in inner-city barbershops arguing about who is the greatest basketball player ever. Mark, the first-century theologian, responded to the twelve disciples' inquiry. Mark teaches that the greatest in the kingdom is the one who is committed to serving all people regardless of their own reputation and status in society. Whether one is first, last, or somewhere in between, he or she must prioritize serving others as the most important part of their lives.

Matthew 23:11–12 explains: "The greatest among you will be your servant. For whoever exalts himself will be humbled, and whoever humbles himself will be exalted." Matthew is known for using messianic language in affirming Jesus Christ as the Messiah of the world. According to Matthew, Jesus is God clothed in human flesh. In the same vein, Matthew believes the greatest people in the world are humble servants. Humility is both a lowly disposition amongst your peers and the opposite of exaltation. Humility is also the spiritual fate of those who attempt to exalt themselves over others. God's exaltation or God's promotion is the result of our self-humbling. In the eyes of God, there is an abundance of greatness in serving others with the spirit of humility. Referencing James 4:6, 1 Peter 5:5 says: "Young men, in the same way be submissive to those who are older. All of you, clothe yourselves with humility toward one another, because 'God opposes the proud but gives grace to the humble.'" Peter talks about what it means to be submissive. The theme that runs throughout 2:13—3:6 is those who are older, or those who hold the office of elder. Peter may have had in mind the foot-washing scene that is reported in John 13, in which he figured prominently. Although he was at first rebellious, he writes now with understanding (see John 13:7).

Matthew 22:36–40 records: "'Teacher, which is the greatest commandment in the Law?' Jesus replied: '"Love the Lord your God with all your heart and with all your soul and with all your mind." This is the first and greatest commandment. And the second is like it: "Love your neighbor as yourself." All the Law and the Prophets hang on these two commandments.'" The exegesis of verse 37 is critical: *with all your heart . . . soul . . . mind*. With your whole being. The Hebrew of Deuteronomy 6:5 has "heart . . . soul . . . strength," but some manuscripts of the Septuagint (the pre-Christian Greek translation of the Old Testament) add "mind." Jesus combined all four terms (heart, soul, mind, and strength) in Mark 12:30. Here Matthew teaches that following the commandments of love embodies the greatness in and of God. Loving God, loving your neighbor, and loving yourself are all characteristics of what it means to be great. Love is not only the greatest commandment, but the action of love is the by-product of serving others and remaining humble in doing the work of the Lord.

How about James 4:7? It says, "Submit yourselves, then, to God. Resist the devil, and he will flee from you." For the New Testament writer, James, resisting the devil was an essential part of submitting oneself to God. In Ephesians 6:10–20, the apostle Paul summarizes what it means to take your stand against the devil's schemes. With the understanding that our struggle is not against flesh and blood, Paul's scope has a cosmic flavor. From the very beginning, Paul has drawn considerable attention to the unseen world, and now he describes the spiritual battle that takes place against evil in the heavenly realms (Eph 6:12). First Peter 5:8–9 says: "Be self-controlled and alert. Your enemy the devil prowls around like a roaring lion looking for someone to devour. Resist him, standing firm in the faith, because you know your brothers throughout the world are undergoing the same kind of suffering." Resisting the devil is a substantive part of demonstrating self-control. According to James, greatness in God implies one's decisioned commitment to submit themselves to the will of God and to resist the work and presence of the devil. James teaches that if we resist the devil, Satan will leave our presence. He will flee from us. Here there is an obvious connection between the greatness of God and one's decision to submit to God.

While not probable, it is very possible for people to submit their lives to God by way of committing themselves to their athletic craft or professional calling. Whether they know it or not, many professional basketball players are doing the work of God just by playing the game they love. They are both sources of spiritual inspiration and cultural icons of monumental influence. While not all of them aspire to, or are capable of, all-time greatness, many of them are drawing people closer to God. Ministerially, this drawing happens when people come to a greater realization of their individual purpose. To me, this is where greatness begins and ends. Being the greatest in the kingdom of God means being committed to serving others with humility, loving God and your neighbor, and staying away from anything that exalts us above other people. According to the Bible, greatness is the embodiment of godliness as founded in submitting ourselves to God and resisting the devil.

What does all this biblical teaching on who is the greatest and greatness in God have to do with how we decide who is the greatest basketball player ever? The first thing the Bible teaches us is that the debate itself should never become an argument or a dispute. The second thing is that we should establish some guidelines or at least debate our opinion with facts and credible statements from credible people. In addition to one's accomplishments on the basketball court, such characteristics as godliness, inspiration, service, humility, and love for the sport of basketball are important. These aforementioned attributes also contribute to creating a positive culture of sport in any given society.

2

Family Man
The Magic Arms of a Tender Heart

By all accounts, Kobe Bryant was a family man in every sense of the word. The Bryant family provided the world with an abundance of pictures. Whether you were a Kobe fan or not, you saw endless images of the Bryant family at his basketball games. It seemed like Vanessa and the girls attended all of Kobe's games. The home games at the Staples Center for sure. In every celebratory moment Kobe was involved in (and the non-celebratory ones too), his wife and daughters were there with him. Not as admirers, cheerleaders, and fans, but they were supportive and present as members of his immediate family. Kobe's family were present with him in documentaries, during interviews, press conferences, tributes, book signings, and business deals. Looking at his family pictures, you could see Kobe loved his family dearly. He loved his wife Vanessa, and he loved his four daughters. The more their family grew in number, the happier Kobe became. Kobe and Vanessa were the backbones of their wonderful family. Their daughters were the bones that held it all together. Beautiful in their own rights, Natalia, Gianna (sometimes referred to as GiGi), Capri, and Bianka are spitting images of their mother and father. Even from a distance, we could tell that Kobe was proud of his family because they represented an extension of him. Kobe's family was his life.

In terms of describing Kobe Bryant as a family man, it is difficult to separate his basketball life from his family life. Regarding most everything Kobe did in his NBA career, his family was present to support him and celebrate those moments with him. As many times as we witnessed Kobe kissing the love of his life, Vanessa, after the game was over, or even in the tunnel when he first came in contact with his wife, we also witnessed him kissing his daughters with the same loving affection. Whether he kissed his wife and his daughters last or vice versa, one could tell that Kobe's immediate family was a super-important part of his life. In order for the world to understand what family meant to Kobe, we must ask his wife Vanessa. If anyone could testify to Kobe's family-first attitude, it would be her. Vanessa's eulogy of her husband at the Staples Center gave us some insight into Kobe's commitment to being a good husband and father. Vanessa confesses that, "He was my sweet husband and the beautiful father of our children. He was mine. He was my everything,"[1] she said. She added,

> Kobe and I have been together since I was 17 and a half years old. I was his first girlfriend, his first love, his wife, his best friend, his confidant, and his protector. He was the most amazing husband . . . more than I could ever express or put into words. He was the early bird, and I was the night owl. I was fire, he was ice and vice versa at times. We balanced each other out. He would do anything for me. I have no idea how I deserved a man that loved and wanted me more than Kobe.[2]

Vanessa described her husband as a devoted father who was often identified as "the MVP of girl dads-or MVD."[3] According to Vanessa, "Kobe had a tender heart."[4] She spoke of her husband's heart because Kobe somehow knew where she was at all times. Specifically, when Vanessa was late to his games. Kobe would worry about Vanessa if she was not in her customary seat at the start of each game. If Vanessa was not present, Kobe would ask security where she was at the first timeout of the first quarter. Vanessa was amazed at the fact that Kobe, the professional, could play the game of basketball at such a high level and still be concerned by making sure that his family made it to the game safely. For Vanessa, this was just another example of how family came first to Kobe. It is no secret that Kobe loved his wife. He loved being married to Vanessa. Vanessa publicly expounded on their love: "Kobe wanted us

---

1. Moreira, "Vanessa Bryant Recalls," para. 2.
2. Andrew, "Read Vanessa Bryant's Speech," para. 19.
3. Moreira, "Vanessa Bryant Recalls," para. 13.
4. Andrew, "Read Vanessa Bryant's Speech," para. 24.

to renew our vows. He wanted Natalia to take over his company, and he wanted to travel the world together. We had always talked about how we'd be the fun grandparents to our daughter's children. He would have been the coolest grandpa."[5]

In addition to being a devoted husband, Kobe took fatherhood seriously. For Kobe, being a great father included picking his kids up from school. In the words of Vanessa: "When Kobe was still playing, I used to show up early to be the first in line to pick up Natalia and Gianna from school, and I told him he couldn't drop the ball once he took over. He was late one time, and we most definitely let him know that I was never late. So he showed up one hour and 20 minutes early after that."[6] When Kobe retired from the NBA in 2016, he proudly became his kids' personal transporter to and from school. By way of parental presence, Kobe would wait for his daughters to get out of school. It was important for Kobe to be there at his daughters' school when the learning day ended. He knew his daughters would be just as happy to see him as he would be to see them.

Vanessa describes Kobe's fathering skills as incredibly hands-on. Here she gives supporting details in regards to Kobe's passion for being a dad and a father to his four daughters:

> He never left the toilet seat up. He always told the girls how beautiful and smart they are. He taught them how to be brave and how to keep pushing forward when things get tough. And when Kobe retired from the NBA, he took over dropping off and picking up our girls from school, since I was at home pregnant with Bianka and just recently home nursing Capri. (As a parent) He always knew there was room for improvement and wanted to do better. He happily did carpool and enjoyed spending time in the car with our girls. He was a doting father, a father that was hands-on and present. He helped me bathe Bianka and Capri almost every night. He would sing them silly songs in the shower and continue making them laugh and smile as he lathered them in lotion and got them ready for bed. He had magic arms and could put Capri to sleep in only a few minutes. He said he had it down to a science: eight times up and down our hallway. He loved taking Bianka to Fashion Island and watching her play in the Koi pond area and loved taking her to the pond. He loved being Gianna's coach. He told me he wished he would have convinced Natalia to play basketball so they could have spent even

---

5. Andrew, "Read Vanessa Bryant's Speech," para. 20.
6. Andrew, "Read Vanessa Bryant's Speech," para. 22.

more time together. But he also wanted her to pursue her own passion. He watched Natalia play in a volleyball tournament on her birthday, on January 19th, and he noticed how she's a very intelligent player. He was convinced she would have made a great point guard, with her vision of the court.[7]

It is known that Kobe's daughters and Vanessa were his entire world. It is also known that within the realm of family, Kobe was an inspirational teacher of life lessons. While a guest on *Jimmy Kimmel Live!* in October 2018, Kobe said, "I love having girls. They are so incredible to me." On coaching Gianna he said, "The best thing that happens when we go out, fans will come up to me and she'll be standing next to me and they'll be like, 'Hey, you gotta have a boy! You and V gotta have a boy to have somebody to carry on the tradition and the legacy.' She's (Gianna) like, 'Hey, I got this! You don't need a boy for that.'"[8] Teaching Gianna the game of basketball brought great joy and exceeding bliss to Kobe's heart. Ever the proud father, Bryant often took to social media to show off his girls' hoops skills. Coaching his girls' teams was one of Bryant's proudest roles in his post-NBA life. "A valuable lesson that I can teach them is what it means to pursue excellence and the commitment level that comes with that,"[9] he told *People* of being a coach in a 2017 interview. "They're having a blast. They've gotten extremely, extremely good over the course of the last year, and are continuing to work and get better, man. It's been fun."[10] After retiring from the NBA, Bryant stayed near the basketball court through his role as coach for his daughters.

Known as "Mambacita," in reference to her father's nickname, GiGi had already garnered national attention for her impressive fade-away shot. For Bryant to teach his daughter the fundamentals of the game he loved so much and to witness her development as a gifted and talented basketball player, these were heavenly moments for him and Gianna. The same way that Kobe was committed to developing his own craft of playing basketball, he was just as committed (if not more) to being there with Gianna on her journey to basketball greatness. Teaching Gianna the game of basketball showcased Kobe's ability to be a father. Even coaching Gianna and teaching her the basic nuances of basketball,

---

7. "Read Vanessa Bryant's Words," paras. 8–10, 12, 13.
8. Mack, "Kobe Bryant Told Jimmy Kimmel," para. 5–6.
9. VanHoose, "Kobe Bryant Was," para. 12.
10. VanHoose, "Kobe Bryant Was," para. 12.

Kobe's commitment to family extended beyond his own legendary career. For Kobe, the essence of family was revealed in the beauty of coaching Gianna. He enjoyed growing Gianna and other basketball players from the ground up. Here Kobe was supremely involved in his daughter's journey of developing athletic prowess. Kobe's interaction with Gianna was just one way he expressed his all-out love for family. Bryant loved having all girls, telling *People*: "It's pretty cool for me 'cause it's Daddy's little princesses."[11] In his post-NBA life, Bryant continued to sit courtside in the Staples Center, often joined by GiGi. Being surrounded by women, Bryant was an advocate for women basketball stars, once telling *CNN* that "I think there are a couple of players who could play in the NBA right now honestly."[12]

When I speak of the greatness of Kobe Bryant the family man, I am affirming that he is fondly remembered by those who knew him personally as one who always took family seriously. As I did my research, I found that many big names took to social media to remember Bryant as the quintessential family man. "As I scrolled through Kobe's feed, and Alex and I talk memories and moments we remember about him . . . this is the truth that rings out the loudest . . . family is what matters most,"[13] Jennifer Lopez wrote on Instagram.

> Abdul-Jabbar called Bryant an amazing role model for so many around the world. "I just remember a great family and a brilliant athlete. He was so [supportive toward] his little girls. That's the person that I miss," Abdul-Jabbar said, according to *USA Today*.
> He recalls the bond he had with the Bryant family and a specific moment when he played peek-a-boo with a young Gianna.[14]

Former New York Yankees great and MLB Hall of Famer Derek Jeter remembers Bryant as family man who "Just Loved Being a Dad."[15] In his reflections on Bryant, Jeter emphasized that Kobe was a family man, first and foremost: "All I ever needed to know about Kobe Bryant was this: that throughout our friendship, the most meaningful conversations

---

11. Kimble, "Kobe Bryant Says," para. 5.
12. Trenamum, "Kobe Bryant Backs Women," para. 3.
13. Fillingham, "Jennifer Lopez and Alex Rodriguez," para. 5.
14. Etienne, "Kareem Abdul-Jabbar Remembers Kobe," paras. 5–7.
15. VanHoose, "Derek Jeter Remembers Kobe Bryant."

we had—they were always about family."¹⁶ Jeter added: "When I think of Kobe, I really just end up thinking about those special few personal conversations that we were lucky enough to share together, each time one of us had a new baby daughter."¹⁷ Shaquille O'Neal wrote on Twitter "Kobe was so much more than an athlete, he was a family man. That was what we had most in common. I would hug his children like they were my own and he would embrace my kids like they were his. His baby girl GiGi was born on the same day as my youngest daughter Me'Arah."¹⁸

In addition to his immediate family, there were Kobe's parents, Joe and Pamela Bryant, and his beautiful sisters, Sharia Bryant Washington and Shaya Bryant. Even though Kobe and his parents were not always on the same page, they are the ones who made Kobe a family man in the first place. Kobe said his parents were his backbone. I am quite sure Mr. and Mrs. Joe Bryant provided a good life for their son. By all accounts, Kobe loved his sisters, and they loved him too. Kobe's home life with his parents and sisters in such cities as Houston, San Diego, parts of Italy, and Philadelphia shaped his thoughts on what it meant to be a part of a loving family. Put another way, Kobe's upbringing as Joe and Pamela's only son played an important role in his development as both a basketball player and a family man. The experiences associated with having a tumultuous relationship with his mom and dad did not take away from the love that Bryant and his parents had for one another. The truth is there is no such thing as a perfect family. All families have some form of dysfunction and imperfection. Kobe Bryant's family was no exception.

The main point of this particular reflection is that Mr. and Mrs. Joe Bryant were great parents to Kobe. His parents and his sisters instilled in him the importance of family and having faith in God. Bryant's parents will always be his parents. Despite their respective differences, they all continued to love each other and embrace one another as family. Kobe continued to share a close relationship with his sisters and their children. Thankfully, things with Kobe and his parents appeared to be on the mend in the months after Kobe's retirement in 2016. Family friend and former coach, Wayne Slappy, told *The Daily Mail* that Bryant and his father were recently seen hugging at an event. "I just remember being with him up at his camp in Santa Barbara, and seeing him hug his dad. You know

---

16. VanHoose, "Derek Jeter Remembers Kobe Bryant," para. 3.
17. VanHoose, "Derek Jeter Remembers Kobe Bryant," para. 4.
18. Skilbeck, "Shaquille O'Neal Reflects," para. 3.

how they loved each other from how they looked at each other, how they smiled."[19] Kobe loved his mother, father, sisters, nieces, and nephew deeply. In raising Kobe the right way, his parents taught him the eternal value of love and faith. I am sure Kobe's family did not love him the way they did because he prospered financially from a professional sport. They loved him because he was their son, grandson, brother, and uncle.

I have lived in predominantly Black neighborhoods throughout the course of my life. As an ordained pastor of almost twenty years and licensed funeral director for fifteen years at the time of this writing, I have dealt with my fair share of Black family dysfunction. My family has served the Black community in Hopkinsville, Kentucky for over ninety-five years. I have seen and experienced dysfunction in the Black family unit in the church, in the community, in organizations, in politics, in sports, in everyday relationships, and in the all-important realm of finances. I do not know of any Black family that has not had issues and disagreements over money, especially where the choosing of a life's mate is concerned. Where money is concerned, holy matrimony and personal jealousy sometimes go hand in hand. I do not know of one Black family that has not experienced longstanding silence amongst family members. I do not know of any Black family that has not had money issues and were not in need of financial support to make ends meet. Every family I know has gone through difficult moments with each other within the family unit for one reason or another. The Bryant family is no different from any other Black family in the United States. They were blessed to have two professional basketball players in the immediate family (Mr. Joe Bryant and Kobe Bryant), but this did not mean the Bryant family was exempt from having issues and problems.

The same dysfunction that Kobe experienced at home with his wife is the same dysfunction he experienced at home as a child with his parents and sisters. While the level of dysfunction varies from family to family, the amazing truth is that all of our families have some active form of dysfunction in it. This is what it means to be a normal family. To experience some moments of dysfunction and then allow God to heal the situation for the purpose of helping the family to find its way back into the grace of God's love. The love of family as a part of God's unconditional love for humanity will never die. It will always be present as long as we know our people. The only reason the dysfunction within Kobe's family

---

19. Boswell, "'Can You Imagine?,'" para. 17.

became public is because it was Kobe's family, plain and simple. There was no need for anybody outside the Bryant family to continue discussing what was going on in their family. Their personal problems were their business, and the family unit should have been given the respectful space' to deal with these problems accordingly. That includes the situation in Denver and whatever problems Kobe and his parents had. Their celebrity status only made things worse, but there was a certain amount of normality within the family dysfunction.

When I think of the word "family," the thoughts that come to mind are ones of familiarity, identification, and connection. Still affirming Kobe Bryant as a family man, I believe the true strengths of any family are found in their innate ability to be familiar with one another, identify with one another, and connect with one another despite the presence of dysfunction. As with all situations in the Christian life, Jesus is the standard. There are two instances in the Bible that reveal Jesus' thoughts about family. The first instance is when Jesus' parents thought he was lost at a public event. They began looking for the young Jesus only to find him in a cave conversing with religious leaders about the knowledge and presence of God. When Jesus' parents found him in the cave, Jesus responded to their lack of familiarity by asking them, "'Why were you searching for me?' he asked. 'Didn't you know I had to be in my in my Father's house?'" (Luke 2:49). When the young Jesus says, "in my Father's house", he is pointing to his personal duty to his Father in heaven. Jesus contrasted his "my Father" with Mary's "Your father" (Luke 2:48). At twelve years of age, Jesus was aware of his unique relationship to and with God. But he was also obedient to his earthly parents (Luke 2:51). In this particular line of questioning, Jesus assumed his earthly parents would know what he was doing with his life. In not being completely familiar with the identity of their son, we see signs of a disconnection between Jesus and his parents. In the mind of the young Jesus, his parents should have known what Jesus was doing away from them.

Another instance where Jesus gave his thoughts on family was when he was approached by those near him and informed the now-adult Jesus that his family was present. Matthew 12:47–50 says, "Someone told him, 'Your mother and brothers are standing outside, wanting to speak to you.' He replied to him, 'Who is my mother, and who are my brothers?' Pointing to his disciples, he said, 'Here are my mother and my brothers. For whoever does the will of my Father in heaven is my brother and sister and mother.'" Mark 3:35 uses the same words: "'Whoever does the will of my Father in heaven is my brother and sister and mother.'" The teaching point is membership in God's spiritual family is more important than membership in our human families. Along the same lines, Luke 8:21 puts Jesus' reply this way: "'My mother and brothers are those who hear God's word and put it into practice.'" Jesus' reply was not meant to reject his natural family; it was meant to emphasize the highest regard for those who believed in him. In other words, Jesus was saying his family members were those who did the will of God. Jesus wasnnot disrespecting his mother and brothers, but he wanted to publicly identify those whom he considered to be his family. In explaining why he considered his disciples as his true family Jesus was referring to the spiritual connection he shared with his disciples in their service to God and humanity. The point I am making here is that family means different things to different people. Whether we look at our own family situation or we reference what the Bible says about the family of Jesus, the notions of familiarity, identification, and connection help us understand the dynamics of existing within a family unit. It is not easy being a member of a family unit. Love for one another and faith in God helps us to endure.

Moses writes in Exodus 20:12: "Honor your father and your mother, so that you may live long in the land the LORD your God is giving you." Honoring those in authority is essential for both spiritual balance and social stability. From the outside looking in, it seemed like Kobe honored his parents the best way he knew how to. Even though their differences and disputes over money and Kobe's choice of life mate (Vanessa) were well documented, I am sure Kobe did his best to honor his father and mother. He loved his parents deeply. In addition to the high-profile group of people who inspired Kobe along the way during his Hall-of-Fame basketball career, his father and mother taught him how to be successful in life. They taught Kobe what it means to believe in God and stay true to the identity of one's family. While I am not sure what type of particular advantage Mr. Joe Bryant gave to Kobe, basketball-wise, the fact that Kobe followed in his father's footsteps by playing professional basketball is proof that he honored his father and mother. Kobe honored his father and mother because they raised him with cultural excellence and unconditional love.

Mr. and Mrs. Joe Bryant were great parents to Kobe and his two sisters; and they continue to be outstanding grandparents to all seven of their grandchildren. Following the biblical text, I am sure Kobe highly prized his parents, cared for them, showed respect for them, and obeyed them as best he could. God gives two biological parents. Joe and Pamela Bryant were loving gifts from God in the life of their chosen son, Kobe Bean Bryant. I believe God is pleased with both the way Kobe's parents raised him and the way he fathered his four beautiful daughters.

What Kobe described as a disgusting little trick became one of the many lessons he learned from his dad. I recall seeing Bryant soaked in a purple Lakers road jersey. The Lakers were playing against their crosstown rival, the Los Angeles Clippers. Bryant was being guarded by defensive specialist Matt Barnes. Kobe was dribbling the ball beyond the top of the key, and he had his jersey in his mouth. He was doing as his dad told him to do. Kobe was sucking the sweat out of his own jersey. With the jersey in his mouth, he put on a dazzling display of offensive moves. Kobe dribbled one way to his right and then changed directions, going back to his left. With Barnes off-balance and leaning the opposite way, Kobe rose up for one of his patent mid-range jump shots. What made the offensive move and jump shot so cold-blooded was that his jersey was in his mouth the whole time. He was simultaneously sucking the sweat out of his jersey and putting Barnes on ice skates. Watching that basketball move, I said to my best friend: "Lord Jesus. Look at what family will do to you. Kobe is such a family man. Did you know that Kobe's middle name, Bean, was his father's nickname when he was playing professionally in the United States and overseas?"

Now, thinking about the taste of the various flavors of jelly beans, one of the questions that pops into my mind is: What does it mean to be a family man and an all-time great basketball player for twenty years at the same time? To label Kobe Bryant a family man is a great compliment. It is what any father worth his grain in salt would love to hear someone say about him. It is all a man could ever hope for—that someone would say he was a family man. But what exactly are we saying here? Are we saying Bryant was perfect in his husbandly duties? Of course not. Are we saying Bryant was a perfect father to his four daughters? Of course not. He could not have been. He was a professional basketball player who spent large amounts of time working out away from home, practicing away from home, and traveling to other cities play games. A major reason why Bryant was not the perfect husband and father is because his lack of presence at home with his family would not allow him to be. But just because he was not the perfect husband and father to Vanessa and his daughters, that does not mean Kobe was not a family man. He was.

For those critics of Bryant who are waiting for me to fly you to Eagle, Colorado, the plane ticket is on the way. But for now I want to talk about what it means to be a professional athlete and a family man "in absentia." To a large degree, the best thing a professional athlete does for his or her family is they take care of them financially. Paying bills and attaining material things are easy accomplishments for those families whose husband or father is a professional athlete. Because professional athletes make millions of dollars in salary, they are more than able to provide for their respective families. But does providing money for his or her family automatically make a professional athlete a family man or family woman?

While Kobe spent a considerable amount of time away from his family playing basketball, he found ways to show affection to them and love them from a distance. But that is not the same as being at home and being in the same space, within hugging and reaching distance of their loved ones. My argument for Kobe being a family man, or a man who showed great love to his family, is not one of perfection; rather it is an argument that centers on the fact that Kobe Bryant was a human being. He was not a god or a superhero. He was a great athlete and a well-known celebrity. But Kobe was not perfect by any stretch of the imagination. What he was, what he is, and what he will always be is a human being. All athletes are human beings. None of them are God. We may treat them as such, but athletes are no different from your next-door neighbor. They are everyday, common people just like you and I. Being a human being is the everyday embodiment of being imperfect. Kobe Bryant, like the rest of us, was created in the image of God. The fact that he was an imperfect person has no bearing on his family man status. The fact that he made mistakes does not make him less of a family man, and his intrinsic humanity does not make him more of a family man. Bryant's humanity is what makes him a family man. His imperfections are what makes him human.

The Bible says that all have sinned and fallen short of the glory of God and the high mark of God's calling (Rom 3:23). To be the embodiment of God's glory is what God intended for human beings. The glory that human beings had before the fall (Gen 1:26–28; Ps 8:4–8; Eph 4:24; Col 3:10) believers will once again have through Christ (Heb 2:5–9). Kobe Bryant is a part of the "all." So are you. We all are. Kobe Bryant, the all-time-great NBA player, is no different from any other player who has spent considerable amounts of time away from their families. The only difference is he got caught up publicly in the web of his own private activities. In other words, Kobe got caught. Plain and simple.

Kobe's celebrity status made him a prime target for someone who was looking for a financial upgrade in their life. What Kobe did was no different from what any NBA player has done, is doing, and will continue to do, as long as their celebrity status and significant time away from their family allows them to. The only thing that unfortunate situation in Denver showed us about Kobe Bryant was that he was a human being. As he stated himself, he committed adultery. At the end of the day, Bryant was no more of a rapist than most NBA players are faithful husbands/boyfriends to those they call their significant other. Professional athletes are part of the human race.

Whoever says that Kobe's legacy in life is complicated is absolutely correct. I say that because all of our legacies within the living of this earthly life are complicated. Complicated means less than perfect or flawed. According to the greatest theologian in history, Saint Augustine of Hippo, the world is fallen because it majors in complication.[20] In examining the complicated narrative of Kobe Bryant, we must all examine the complicated narratives of our own lives. We all have complicated things in our lives that render us fully human and less than perfect. Because Kobe was accused of sexual assault, that does not mean that he did not take marriage and family seriously. That does not mean that he did not love his wife and daughters. That does not mean that he does not love the Lord with all his heart, soul, and mind. What it means is that Kobe's humanity prompted him to make a simple mistake. Kobe was not a criminal by any stretch of the imagination. He was a normal human being who got caught up in some ungodly foolishness. Just like the rest of the human world, Kobe learned from mistakes and responded beautifully to the darkness of human adversity.

In the midst of learning from his mistakes, Kobe continued to be the best husband and father he could be. I would argue that Kobe became an even better husband and father following his situation in Colorado. Bryant became a greater family man when it seemed like his actions had destroyed himself and his family. Judgmental hypocrites in society may have given up on Bryant, but his family did not give up on him. The Los Angeles Lakers did not give up on him. The city of Los Angeles did not give up on him. Kobe's teammates did not give up him. While his opponents may have said something about Bryant in the privacy of their own conversations, I am sure they did not give up on Bryant. Most

---

20. Drakos, "3 Ways."

importantly, Kobe did not give up on himself. By way of inspiring the world to greater greatness, Bryant continued to believe in himself. I am quite sure the love of God played a role in Bryant's ability to move on with his life. God had a greater purpose and plan for Bryant the husband and Bryant the father of four daughters.

For Bryant, being an exceptional father meant raising exceptional daughters. It meant raising a beautiful quadrilateral of women. It meant being the best girl dad he could possibly be. Bryant was an advocate of the WNBA, women's college basketball, and any other outreach that involved girls' activities and their participation in sports. His oldest daughter, Natalia, was near and dear to Bryant. Being the oldest child and being at home with Bryant the longest, Natalia got to spend the most time with her daddy. Natalia is a standout volleyball player whom Bryant believed would also make an outstanding point guard. Bryant lauded and praised Natalia's court vision as an athlete who loved competing. Kobe loved Gianna in the same way he loved all of his daughters—dearly and deeply. I am sure Gianna's interest in basketball and following in her daddy's footsteps brought the two even closer. While most of his father-daughter pictures were of him and Gianna, I am willing to bet Natalia was just as close to her to her dad, if not closer. With everything he had, Bryant believed in girls' basketball, girls' soccer, women's college basketball, the WNBA, and the WFIBA. Bryant also advocated for equal pay for women.

Not only did Bryant love and celebrate his immediate family with his wife, daughters, and parents, but he also had extended families he leaned and depended on. The Los Angeles Lakers organization, Lakers owner Jerry Buss, and the NBA logo—Jerry West—all considered Kobe as their son. Jerry's daughter, Jennie Buss, stated on more than occasion that Kobe was like family to the Buss family. Kobe also had his Lakers teammates and the greater NBA family, many of whom considered Kobe a brother. According to Bryant, the Lakers were a family.

For Bryant, the love of family meant two things: passion and sharing. Passion in life ensures the long-term survival of the family unit. And sharing within the family makes the environment extremely conducive to continued excellence and greater greatness.

Kobe considered two-time NBA Championship teammate Pau Gasol a member of his family, and according to Gasol, the family feeling was mutual. This is another example of how Kobe's family worked within and beyond his bloodline. His father connected Kobe to the great Abdul-Jabbar, not even knowing he would one day play professional basketball for the Los Angeles Lakers. Kareem embraced Kobe as a son and a brother in Lakers fraternity. Their bond is eternal. The same holds for Magic Johnson. Kobe met Magic during his first year in Los Angeles. If any of the retired Lakers embraced Kobe as a brother, it would be Magic. Magic loved Kobe to the core. He treated Kobe like a member of his own family. Magic took Kobe under his wing and supported him in every step of his NBA journey. In my humble opinion, Magic Johnson should have been appointed by Kobe's wife, Vanessa, to introduce Kobe into the Naismith Basketball Hall of Fame in 2021. To keep this huge honor in the Lakers family, Magic would have been the logical choice. He, of all the Lakers greats, was the most familiar with how Kobe impacted the city of Los Angeles and knew the intimate details of what Kobe did for the Lakers organization and the NBA.

Lakers legend, Los Angeles native, and three-time NBA champion with the Lakers, Byron Scott was like family to Bryant as well. I suspect Kobe was more emotionally tied to Scott than he was any of the Lakers greats. Their bond was both strong and different in terms of their unique sharing of information and affection. Both Bryant and Scott played the two-guard position. Both won multiple NBA Championships playing for the Lakers. Both possessed a deep passion for the game of basketball. As a theologian of the Spirit, I am sure it was not by accident that Byron Scott was Kobe's last head coach in the NBA. The many lessons Scott taught Bryant were both invaluable and nurturing. If anyone is familiar with Kobe's journey toward becoming the greatest basketball player in the history of the game, it would be Coach Scott. Just like with Kareem and Magic, Bryant considered Scott as family.

Kobe considered Lamar Odom to be family as well. He had such an affectionate admiration for Odom that he saw Lamar as the glue of the back-to-back championship teams in 2008–09 and 2009–10. In some ways, Odom was Kobe's little brother. Odom leaned on Kobe for advice and companionship. Their relationship was both familial and friendly. Where Odom is concerned, his connection to Bryant worked well because it led to them having a good friendship, and they won 2 NBA titles together. Bryant explains his love for Odom in three ways: 1) he was a community guy; 2) he was big-hearted; and 3) he was super-talented.

With the concept of family in mind, Kobe says that "Jerry West and I had a father-son type of relationship."[21] After all, Jerry West, the then-

---

21. Bryant, *Mamba Mentality*, 56.

General Manager of the Los Angeles Lakers, was the one who pulled the executive trigger on trading Vlade Divac for the seventeen-year-old Bryant. It was termed by many as the "Draft-day trade." It can be argued that West was the one who discovered Kobe Bryant. Even though Bryant was drafted by the Charlotte Hornets, West's vision of Bryant wearing the purple and gold led him to acquire the "Showboat" teenager from Lower Merion High School in Philadelphia. If the truth be told, Bryant and West had a lot in common. Both were high-scoring shooting guards. Both relied on the fundamentals of the game. Both enjoyed putting pressure on the defense by shooting efficiently off the dribble. Both were considered intellectual geniuses of the game of basketball. After watching the teenage Kobe's first workout with the Lakers, West was convinced he had just witnessed the greatest NBA draft workout ever. Bryant worked out against the 6'7" Lakers great and defensive specialist Michael Cooper. West saw enough promise in Kobe's game to make an executive decision.

I could not find where Phil Jackson referred to Kobe Bryant as a son or nephew. Nor could I find where Kobe referred to Jackson as a father-figure or uncle. However, I think I found some evidence of something much deeper between the two than the language of family. When it came to the Bryant-Jackson dichotomy, I found that their relationship with one another was of the utmost importance. Jackson began coaching Bryant when the latter was at the tender age of 20. Bryant's game was on the upswing. He was somewhere between flourishing and medium-well. Kobe aspired to be the greatest basketball player. He had hopes and dreams of replacing Jackson's former player, Michael Jordan, as the best to ever do it. Jackson had hopes of bringing a talented team together for the purpose of winning an NBA title. Even as Jackson guided the Lakers to three straight championships from 2000–02, his relationship with Kobe was just beginning. Due in large part to Jackson's nurturing (and Kobe's natural development as an all-world athlete), Bryant's second tenure with Jackson was more personal for the both of them.

With the highest level of respect (and family love too), Kobe viewed Phil as someone who taught concepts within basketball, but more so the macro concept of basketball. He was able to teach—without lecturing—the importance of being a team and how to get from Point A to Point B to Point Championship. He was also able to get guys to understand energy, flow, and meditation.[22]

22. Bryant, *Mamba Mentality*, 63.

Just as Jackson was Kobe's basketball coach, life mentor, and philosophical teacher, Kobe the father found a way to honor Jackson's teachings by coaching his gifted daughter Gianna. Just as Jackson had taught Bryant the intricacies of the triangle offense (and there were some tough patches between Jackson and Bryant over Kobe's lack of executional patience), Kobe taught his daughter and her teammates the same triangle offense. The fact that Kobe, the proud son/student, called his former coach Jackson to inform him of the good news, shows that their connection transcended that of just a player-coach relationship. For Kobe, Phil Jackson was family.

Lakers teammates Shaquille O'Neal, Derek Fisher, Brian Shaw, and Luke Walton were all relatively close to Bryant, as they were the foundational pieces of those five championships in the 2000s. To some degree and in some experiential ways, they could also be considered family to Bryant. What I have realized is that if Kobe used the language of family to describe his connection or relationship to a certain person, then he must have considered them family. While the idea of family is defined by one's blood relatedness, the ethos of family as a form of connectedness takes on many forms. Thus, Kobe the family man took on many shapes and forms. Bryant was a product of many environments and audiences. Kobe cherished his Lower Merion Academy family in Philadelphia. I am sure many of his schoolmates, classmates, teachers, and coaches had an endearing connection to Bryant. He also cherished his Team USA family with whom he won two Olympic gold medals (2008, 2012). Kobe's Italian roots highlights his European family. By the way that Kobe was treated in such places as China, Japan, Spain, England, and South America, it is safe to say he had extended families across the globe. In Los Angeles and other American cities, Kobe was loved like family by Mexicans, Asians, Dominican Republicans, Puerto Ricans, and Jamaicans. Kobe's ability to speak multiple languages fluently presupposes his familial ties to people, places, and cultures within the United States and beyond American borders.

Affectionately, Kobe considered the Staples Center crowd his family. He scored more points in the Staples Center than any NBA player had ever scored in any home arena. Certainly, the city of Los Angeles was an extended part of Kobe's family. According to those who have spent considerable time in Southern California, words cannot and do not describe what Kobe meant to the various cultures of Los Angeles. Bryant was a family man in that he cherished all forms of family. He cherished being connected to different groups of human beings for different reasons.

Whether it was the blood ties of close family or the kindred spirit of distant family, Kobe understood the importance of both. In Bryant becoming his daughter's coach, I am reminded that playing professional basketball was not the only thing Kobe and his dad had in common. Just as Mr. Joe became a successful coach, I believe Kobe would have eventually followed in his father's footsteps and became a coach as well.

In his own words:

> When I was growing up in Italy, I grew up in isolation. It was not an environment suited to me. I was the only black kid. I didn't speak the language. I'd be in one city, but then we'd move to a different city, and I'd have to do everything again. I'd make friends, but I'd never be part of the group, because the other kids were already growing together. So this is how I grew, and these are the weaknesses that I have.[23]

He adds:

> I hate it because it doesn't teach our players how to play the right way, how to think the game, how to play in combinations of threes. I think everything is a reward system. I think coaches who are teaching the game are getting rewarded in one fashion or another. It's just a showcase. I think it's absolutely horrible for the game. I think they are doing a disservice to our young basketball players right now. That's something that definitely needs to be fixed and it's going to definitely be one of the things that I focus on.[24]

The previous statements speak directly to what it meant for Bryant to be raised outside of the United States. Because his father played professional basketball overseas, Bryant was exposed to a different way of life. He was also exposed to a different type of basketball. Even though he critiques his upbringing of growing up in Italy, Kobe is thankful for learning the fundamentals of European basketball. He understood the importance of learning these fundamentals within the realization that he could not have learned the basics of the game playing in the American AAU circuit. In addition to learning the fundamentals of European basketball, Kobe realized the conceptual/developmental advantage associated with learning other languages (outside of English and engaging a culture that was, for the most part, unfamiliar to Black Americans). Even as Kobe

---

23. The PostGame Staff, "Kobe Bryant," para. 7.
24. Conway, "Kobe Bryant Comments on AAU," paras. 3, 8.

confesses his human weaknesses, he also understands the strengths of being a Black kid that was raised outside of the United States. For Bryant, the reality of family took on many different meanings.

In his article, "Kobe Bryant: Reflections on Fatherhood, Passion and Immortality," John C. Richards confesses that, "As a father, my heart hurt that Bryant could no longer continue to nourish and develop his growing relationship with his daughter."[25] The way Bryant fathered his future basketball star Gianna was an inspiration to many. The same could be said for the way he fathered all four of his daughters. The world stood in awe of how Bryant was fathering Gianna as a parent and developing her as a basketball coach. Their bond was authentic and organic. It did not take a rocket scientist to figure out that Kobe and Gianna were connected on various levels. In attempting to change the narrative on Black fatherhood, Richards adds that, "While I did not care for Kobe Bryant as a player, I admired him in retirement as a father. His active involvement in his daughters' lives and his presence after missing special moments because of a rigorous NBA schedule was refreshing."[26] For Richards, the refreshing part of Bryant's ability to be a great parent to his children was his attention to detail. Bryant paid attention to the needs of his children. Whether it be in the form of fatherly advice, a protective presence at home, or just plain old-fashioned love, Kobe inspired other men to be better fathers to their children. Lining up what we saw in media images and pictures of him with his daughters, Kobe was a committed father behind closed doors. Richards concludes that,

> Our country is rife with mischaracterizations about black fatherhood. Kobe had joined the litany of NBA black father ambassadors to help shape and change the false narrative of fatherlessness in black and brown communities. We lost the opportunity for Bryant's story as a father to play out. But we are also reminded of ordinary, everyday, working Black fathers who put the same effort and love into their children's lives.[27]

By way of his love for family, Kobe acknowledges his wife and daughters in his groundbreaking text, *The Mamba Mentality*: "My story, my career, my dedication would not exist without my wife, Vanessa. Thank you for your partnership, patience, and equally competitive spirit.

25. Richards, "Kobe Bryant," para. 2.
26. Richards, "Kobe Bryant," para. 4.
27. Richards, "Kobe Bryant," para. 7.

You are my ultimate teammate. Natalia, Gianna, and Bianka, I hope you find the inspiration in this book to go build your own Mentality. Each of you, above all else, is my pride and joy."[28] In the words of Vanessa Bryant, Kobe "worked his ass off for 20 years. Gave it his all.... All he wanted was to spend time with our girls and me and make up for lost time.... He wanted to be there for every single moment... in our girls' lives."[29]

---

28. Bryant, *Mamba Mentality*, 10.
29. Loumena, "Vanessa Bryant Shares Instagram Post," paras. 1, 3.

3

The (Un)Expected Death(s)

ON SUNDAY, JANUARY 26, 2020, I preached my weekly sermon to the Lane Tabernacle Christian Methodist Episcopal Church congregation in Hopkinsville, Kentucky. I could tell something was not quite right with my spirit. Every now and again, I feel the presence of spiritual heaviness, sensing that something or someone somewhere is somehow not in a good spiritual order. In the preaching of my sermon, I felt a deep sense of mourning and grieving. But I did not know the origin or the source of the discomfort. All I knew was that something was wrong. I came home and dried myself off with a towel and sat down on the couch in my family's living room. As I normally do, I began watching a movie while thinking about what I wanted to eat as a snack before the family gathered to eat our Sunday dinner. My cellphone rang loudly. It was my oldest daughter, Aiyana, who lives in Houston. Aiyana was loud and hysterical on the phone. She asked me had I heard the news? I had no idea what she was referring to. She then revealed to me that *TMZ* had put it out that Kobe Bryant had died in a helicopter accident in California. Obviously, I was taken aback by the news, but I did not panic. My initial thought was that the news of Bryant's demise was made up for the sake of publicity or gossip. I told Aiyana I would check with ESPN to see what was going on. Months earlier I recall having dreamed one night that Kobe Bryant had died in some type of accident. I woke up quickly and stayed up as long as I could so that when I fell back to sleep, my subconscious would not take me back to those depressing and hurtful images. On Sunday, January 26, I turned on ESPN. I told my daughter I would check for breaking news at the bottom of the TV screen. I was so darn nervous, and I was hoping that news of Bryant's death was false. After fifteen or twenty minutes of watching ESPN, the bottom portion of the TV screen then read, "Breaking News: NBA legend Kobe Bryant was killed in a helicopter accident earlier this morning in Calabasas, California."[1] I called my daughter back to confirm what she had originally told me. Kobe died.

By then, Aiyana was crying to the point of where I knew she was shedding real tears. As huge fans of Kobe Bryant's competitive fire, we both needed David's words that weeping may remain for a night but rejoicing comes in the morning (Ps 30:5). We admired and respected Bryant for different reasons. My initial response upon seeing the breaking news on ESPN was one of numbness. Similar to a human being who is approaching death by way of gasping for their last breath, I tried my best to mentally hold on to the possibility that if there was, in fact, an accident involving Kobe, then maybe he could have survived it. My critical thinking at that moment led me to believe that if anybody could have survived a helicopter accident, it would have been the Black Mamba. To make matters worse, ESPN confirmed what would end up being three life-changing realities for me: 1. Kobe's 13-year old daughter, Gianna, was traveling there with her dad. 2. Seven other people were also present in the helicopter with Bryant and his daughter. 3. There were no survivors.

Just thinking about that moment pushes me back into a tearful disposition. The truth is I could not believe something like that had just happened. Not now. Not to that particular group of people. Not during this sacred moment in time. Not on a Sunday morning which is universally declared the Lord's day. Once I was able to process everything, I immediately began mourning and grieving. I tried my best to hide my tears from my parents. I would tear up really bad and then wipe the tears from my eyes while my family was not looking at me. And then I would repeat the process. I was not in a good space. I struggled to get myself together. I then prayed to God that he would send the Holy Spirit down to comfort those who had been affected by the tragic accident. I prayed for the Bryant family in particular and the world in general.

As a fourth-generation funeral director in my family's business, Adams & Sons Mortuary, and an ordained pastor in the CME Church,

---

1. *ESPN*, January 26, 2020.

The (Un)Expected Death(s)

I know a little something about death. I have seen death. I have smelled the scent of death. I know what death looks like. I have felt the temporary sting of death, over and over. I understand the dynamics of death in terms of what it means to miss someone who has gone on to Glory. My understanding is that it is natural for people to miss those loved ones who have died. In other words, it is hard to say goodbye to people we know personally. I did not know Kobe Bean Bryant personally—I never met the man—but for some strange reason I knew him. I was familiar with him. I was able to tell people some things about him. Most important, Kobe was a source of great inspiration to me and for the world. And because he inspired me in a plethora of endearing ways, I did not have to know him personally. When I learned the truth of his death, I was completely devastated. I was hurt and sad. Since Kobe's demise, I have mourned his death on several occasions. I grieved Kobe's death like I had known him for most of my life. Like most, I will miss seeing Kobe on television playing basketball games, giving interviews and motivational speeches. I will also miss reading about Kobe Bryant and the greater greatness he was shooting for in his post NBA days. Instead of questioning God by way of pondering Kobe's eternal residency (I have a good idea where Kobe and Gianna are now residing), the theologian in me prompted thoughts about what the Bible says about death and dying. Believe it or not, the Bible has a lot to say about death and the afterlife. As Christians, we are to be confident about what God's word says about death and how our earthly/bodily death relates to the blessed assurance of living eternally with God in heaven. I say all of that to say this: I did not expect Kobe Bryant to die in the fashion that he did. No one expected Kobe to perish at the age of forty-one. Even though death is expected in terms of our earthly life one day coming to an end, I did not expect Kobe to transition away from us so soon.

Hebrews 9:27 says, "Just as man is destined to die once, and after that to face judgment." Romans 6:5 says "If we have been united with him like this in his death, we will certainly also be united with him in a resurrection." Because Jesus conquered death, sin and evil through his resurrection, he paved the way for us to be united with him in a resurrection similar to his. Second Corinthians 5:6–8 records that, "Therefore we are always confident and know that as long as we are at home in the body we are away from the Lord. For we live by faith, not by sight. We are confident, I say, and would prefer to be away from the body and at home with the Lord." Paul teaches that while we are still living here in our earthly dwelling, this does not mean we are deprived of the Lord's spiritual presence with us in our daily lives. God is with us in our earthly existence (v. 6). *By faith, not by sight.* Second Corinthians 4:18 says we are to "fix not our eyes on what is seen, but on what is unseen. For what is seen is temporary, but what is unseen it eternal." Here Paul teaches that the experiences and circumstances of this present life are visible to the Christian; but these are merely temporary and fleeting. To fix our eyes on them would cause us to "lose heart" (2 Cor 4:1, 16). By contrast, the unseen realities, which are no less real for being invisible (Heb 11:1, 7, 26–27), are eternal and imperishable. Accordingly, we look up and away from the impermanent appearances of this present-world scene (Phil 3:20; Heb 12:2).

First Corinthians 15:51–57 says,

> Listen, I tell you a mystery: We will not all sleep, but we will all be changed—in a flash, in the twinkling of an eye, at the last trumpet. For the trumpet will sound, the dead will be raised imperishable, and we will be changed. For the perishable must clothe itself with the imperishable, and the mortal with immortality. When the perishable has been clothed with the imperishable, and the mortal with immortality, then the saying that is written will come true: "Death has been swallowed up in victory. Where, O death, is your victory? Where, O death, is your sting?" The sting of death is sin, and the power of sin is the law. But thanks be to God! He gives us the victory through our Lord Jesus Christ.

When Paul mentions the mystery in verse 51, he is referring to the things about the resurrection body that were not understood but are now revealed (Rom 11:25). *We will not all sleep.* Some believers will not experience death and the grave (1 Thess 4:15). In verse 52, Paul writes the words *in a flash* to teach the fact that the change to an imperishable body will occur instantly at the great trumpet call that announces the consummation or redemption (Matt 24:31; 1 Thess 4:16–17). In verse 56, where Paul says, "The sting of death is sin," he is implying that it was sin that brought humanity under death's power (Rom 5:12–21). The reason why the power of sin is the law is because the law of God gives sin its power, for the law of God reveals our sin and condemns us because of our sin (Rom 7:7–12). Lastly, when Paul writes, "He gives us the victory through our Lord Jesus," he is teaching that Jesus Christ gave us the victory over the condemnation for sin that the law brought (v. 56) "and over death and the grave" (vv. 54–55) "through the death and resurrection of Jesus Christ" (Rom 4:25).

The two takeaways from these four primary scriptures (Heb 9:27; Rom 6:5; 2 Cor 5:6–8; 2 Cor 5:51–57) are, first, that death is not the end of anything. Scripture teaches that while our present physical bodies will decompose, our souls will live forever, either in God's presence or eternally separated from him. And second, because Jesus overcame death, so will we. Jesus demonstrated this unchanging truth of his overcoming death when he was resurrected. This means that, though our physical bodies will cease to function, our souls will immediately enter into God's presence. Later, when Christ returns, our souls will be reunited with our physical, then glorified bodies, which will be raised from the dead. Put another way, death is not the end for Kobe and Gianna Bryant. And because Jesus overcame death, Kobe and Gianna Bryant will also overcome death. This does not mean our understanding of death has crystallized into something great and wonderful. What it means is that even in death, God is better than good. God's goodness carries a purpose and a plan for those existing on both sides of life. Our overcoming death is an act of God and not of our own doing.

I hear a lot of people in the Christian church ask: Why do people die? My answer is simple. People die because they were created by God to live and then to die. People are born into this world for the purpose of living and then one day dying. Athletes die. Celebrities die. Rich people die. Poor people die. Black people die. White people die. Mexican people die. Asian people die. Americans die. Non-Americans die. Middle-Easterners die. We all die (Heb 9:27). Death is always expected. The perplexing part about dying is that we do not have the specific knowledge of when, where, and how we will die. Ironically, this is similar to the biblical fact that we do not have the specific knowledge about Christ's return and the end of the world, we do not know when we will die. The one thing we do know is that one day we will all perish. Some scholars and religious leaders refer to death as a calling from God. We sometimes read on the program of the deceased that he or she was called to his or her eternal rest. The mystery of death does not revolve around the question of if but about when. Sadly, Kobe Bryant was not the first professional athlete to die in an accident, and he probably will not be the last. Bryant's death hurts to the core because he was accompanied by his daughter, Gianna. Both Kobe and Gianna left behind a multitude of family members who will continue to love them dearly and cherish their precious memories.

Within the conversation of death and the afterlife, there is still much to be desired knowledge-wise.

Three more takeaways from what the Bible says about death and the afterlife are that, first, we do not have to fear death. God never wants us, his beloved creations, to live in fear, uncertainty, or confusion. In Christ, he offers us a certain, glorious, and joy-filled destination, a future free of pain, sorrow, and sickness. This invitation is open to all who trust not in themselves or their good works but instead in Jesus and the price he paid. Second, spiritual death is separation from God. To our way of thinking, death means the end of something and the complete cessation of life. In Scripture, however, death primarily means separation—separation of a human's spirit from his or her body and from human beings from God. And finally, heaven will be better than anything we can imagine. Heaven will be better than all the earthly pleasures combined across the span of time. Regarding this, the Bible says, "No eye has seen, no ear has heard, no mind has conceived—what God has prepared for those who love Him" (1 Cor 2:9). These blessings are probably not limited to either present or future blessings; both are involved in God freely giving us his secret wisdom that comes from the Spirit of God. Physical death is inevitable this side of heaven, but this was never God's intent for his beloved creation. Nor is it where he wishes for us to remain. In Christ, he offers us life—to experience, through relationship with him, all the good and lovely and amazing blessings He has planned for us. He wants to surround us in his love, from now into eternity, and in so doing, to cast out all fear.

I know these biblical reflections on death and the afterlife will not bring Kobe, his fabulous daughter Gianna, and the seven other beautiful people wh operished with them back to earth and back into their family's presence. But it does offer some important perspectives, if not spiritual solace, concerning their unexpected deaths, especially where the notion of fear is concerned. While we are sure of the fact that Kobe and GiGi's physical bodies perished in a helicopter accident, we can also have faith in the fact that Kobe did not fear his inevitable moment of dying. I know Kobe's long-time friend and competitor, Tracy McGrady, stated that "Kobe wanted to die young,"[2] but that is not to say that Kobe had a fear of death. A tearful McGrady used the word *crazy* in his reflections on Kobe's mentality. Wanting to die an early death may have seemed crazy to McGrady, but to Bryant it may have signaled the fact that Kobe had

---

2. Lauletta, "Tracy McGrady Says," para. 5.

gotten over his fear of death at a young age. Maybe Kobe's thoughts about death were his way of normalizing what he believed about life in general. The reason I believe that Kobe did not fear death is because fear was not a part of his makeup. While I did not know him personally, it did not seem like Kobe feared much of anything in his earthly life. As a believer, I am sure that Kobe did not fear for his daughter as he held her tightly in his arms until he could not hold her anymore.

Within his own relationship with God, I believe Kobe felt his faith in God would cover both him and his precious daughter. Here I have been moved to believe that in their last seconds of life, Kobe and GiGi were covered in the blood of Jesus Christ. In this salvific covering, they were both safely transitioned from the land of the dying earth to the land of the living heaven. Their new life, known to me as the everlasting, became their ever-present reality. Revelation 21:4 comes to mind, where John writes: "And God shall wipe away their tears from their eyes. There will be no more mourning or crying or pain, for the old order of things has passed away." Revelation 7:17 reads this way: "For the Lamb at the center of the throne will be their shepherd; he will lead them to springs of living water. And God will wipe away every tear from their eyes." This is the Old Testament equivalent of Isaiah 25:8: "he will swallow up death forever. The Sovereign Lord will wipe away the tears from all faces; he will remove the disgrace of his people from all the earth. The Lord has spoken." The prophet Isaiah teaches that death, the great swallower (Ps 49:14) will be swallowed up by our Sovereign Lord as "they are destined for the grave."

When I say that Kobe did not fear much of anything in life, I was also referring to the way he approached basketball in particular and life in general. When it came to basketball, Kobe had no fear. He did not fear incorporating new things into his game. He did not fear hard work, and he did not fear missing shots. Kobe did not fear getting hit by his defensive opponents, and he did not fear hitting them right back as the offensive aggressor. Most important, Kobe did not have a fear of being great and wanting to be a dominant player in the NBA. He was not afraid of the consequences. If being great at anything in his earthly life meant he had to give up his life, I am sure Bryant would have been more than willing to die. Kobe had the heart of champion and a hero. Although we are not actively rooting for this to happen, the truth is that champions and heroes die too.

Bryant's family had no way of knowing that Sunday morning would be the last time they would see him or hear his voice. But God knew.

One thing we know is Kobe's helicopter crashed, and nine people lost their lives. But that is not the whole story. There is another important fact about January 26, 2020 that seems to fall through the cracks of our thoughts. The first is that Kobe attended Catholic mass and took the sacrament of Holy Communion with his daughter GiGi. This is important to note because it helps us to understand Kobe's faith in God, not so much for the purpose of questioning Kobe and GiGi's place of eternal residence, but rather it gives us a glimpse of Kobe's religious affirmations.

The best article written about Kobe's faith is "Why Kobe Bryant Took His Catholic faith so seriously" by Tom Hoffarth and Steve Lowery of *Angelus News*. Hoffarth and Lowery factually blend the faith actions of Kobe with his overarching commitment to family, in addition to using the testimony of Kobe's pastor, Father Steve Sallot, to give a detailed account of the final hours Kobe's life. Kobe and his family were members of Our Lady Queen of Angels Church in Newport Beach, California.

In the immediate aftermath of Bryant's sudden death along with eight other people, including his 13-year-old daughter Gianna, in a helicopter crash on January 26th, it soon became known that Bryant stopped by Queen of Angels, located a couple miles from his Newport Coast home, for a few moments of reflection and prayer, leaving just 10 minutes after that 7am Mass started to head to John Wayne Airport. Father Sallot later confirmed to various local news outlets that he had seen Bryant after he had prayed in the chapel. While Bryant's presence in church did not play a role in the outcome the crash, it does show that he took his relationship with God seriously. It also shows that Kobe was a man of faith.

For Bryant, talking to a priest was his way of connecting with God. Whether it be confession, the reading of scripture or praying in the presence of God, Kobe knew that the ways and means in which he connected with God strengthened his relationship with God. In the simplest of ways, being in church for worship and communion with his family uplifted Bryant's spirits. It also showed Bryant the greater purpose of the church—to bring people closer to God in Christ Jesus by the power of the Holy Spirit.

The day after his last NBA game in 2016, one in which he scored a record 60 points, Bryant told an ESPN reporter that he celebrated by rising early, drinking a cup of coffee, and going to church. "It was me, alone,"[3] he said. This statement is abundantly apropos because most of

---

3. Hoffarth and Lowery, "Why Kobe Bryant Took," para. 11.

what Bryant did behind closed doors to develop himself into the greatest basketball player ever, he did it alone. Here the interpretation is that after 20 years of playing professional basketball at the highest levels, I think it was important for Kobe to give thanks to God.

> In 2001, Bryant married his wife, Vanessa, herself a Catholic, at St. Edward the Confessor Church in Dana Point. Father Sallot said that he and Kobe had chatted about his desire to receive the sacrament of confirmation in the future. Though all of this may have been surprising to some, it certainly wasn't to those at Queen of Angels who knew Bryant as a consistent and enthusiastic part of the faith community. . . . Bishop Freyer found out about the crash Sunday night in Rome . . . Ironically, priests assigned to that parish over the years had shared with Bishop Freyer how they've been inspired by Kobe's humility. "He would frequently wait until the entrance procession got . . . part of the way down the aisle and he would . . . come in and go into one of the back pews so . . . he wouldn't distract the people . . . He wanted people to focus on Christ's presence, not his."[4]

More reflections of theological importance in the life of Kobe Bryant.

> Sister Usselmann believes . . . such a loss can help people face the fear of death more honestly. "It is hard to grasp the 'why' in such a tragic death of a celebrity, but we believe . . . God has a plan. . . . The fact that he was at church not long before that flight is a great consolation that even in our mistakes of our past, God reaches out to us, longing to have us to himself and will take every opportunity for us to draw close to him. We just need to listen. Thankfully, Kobe listened."[5]

John 11:25 is extremely relevant to the conversation of Kobe Bryant's death (and his faith as well), particularly the second half of this verse: "even though he dies; and whoever lives and believes in me will never die. Do you believe this?" In this single verse of Scripture, Jesus is teaching us multiple lessons. Jesus was saying he gives both resurrection and life. In some way these (resurrection and life) are identified with him, and his nature is such that final death is impossible for him. Jesus is life (John 14:6; Acts 3:15; Heb 7:16). Jesus is not only life, but he is also the conveyor of life to believers so that death will never triumph over those who die (1 Cor 15:57).

---

4. Hoffarth and Lowery, "Why Kobe Bryant Took," paras. 13, 21–23.
5. Hoffarth and Lowery, "Why Kobe Bryant Took," paras. 39–40.

One fan, taking in the whole event, said he couldn't help but think of a passage from Matthew 25. The passage of Scripture this fan is pointing to is Matthew 25:32–33. It reads: "All the nations will be gathered before him, and he will separate the people one from another as a shepherd separates the sheep from the goats. He will put the sheep on his right and the goats on his left." Matthew 7:21–23 connects to Matthew 25:32–33 when Jesus says that "Not everyone who says to me, 'Lord, Lord' will enter the kingdom of heaven, but only he who does the will of my Father who is in heaven. Many will say to me on that day, 'Lord, Lord, did we not prophesy in your name, and in your name drive out demons and perform many miracles?' Then I will tell them plainly, 'I never knew you. Away from me, you evildoers.'" The word "Lord" seems to mean more than merely "sir" or "master" in view of the final act that Jesus is the one who makes the final decision about a person's eternal destiny. My interpretation is that whosoever does the will of the God the Father shall enter into the kingdom of heaven. This "doing" is the deciding factor as to who enters the kingdom. In the same theological vein, Matthew 13:40–43 declares

> As the weeds are pulled up and burned in the fire, so it will be at the end of the age. The Son of Man will send out his angels, and they will weed out of his kingdom everything that causes sin and all who do evil. They will throw them into the fiery furnace, where there will be weeping and gnashing of teeth. Then the righteous will shine like the sun in the kingdom of their Father. He who has ears, let him hear.

Daniel 12:3 summarizes that, "Those who are wise will shine like the brightness of the heavens, and those who lead many to righteousness, like the stars for ever and ever."

One fan thought it was appropriate to quote a passage from Matthew 25: "'So, Kobe was the GOAT . . . right?' he said. 'There is that Bible verse about how some day we will all be separated, sheeps from goats. Sheeps go to heaven, right? . . . But if Kobe was the GOAT, hey, maybe they can make a special case for him.'"[6] In Psalm 23:4, David proclaims "Yea, though I walk through the shadow of death, I will fear no evil. For thou art with me, thy rod and thy staff comfort me." David also says in Psalm 16:8, "I have set the Lord always before me. Because he is at my right hand, I will not be shaken." Not only is David praising the Lord, who counsels and keeps, but he is also affirming the abiding presence of

---

6. Hoffarth and Lowery, "Why Kobe Bryant Took," paras. 53–54.

God in his darkest moments. *He is at my right hand.* As the Sustainer and Protector of David, God is further described as the One who has made known to David the path of life, the One who will fill David with joy in God's presence, and the One who will fill David with eternal pleasures at his right hand (Ps 16:11).

Death, amongst other human realities, is a relevant part of the culture of sport. Just like common, everyday folk, professional athletes die in the most uncommon of ways, accidents included. I say that because while we continue to mourn deeply the death of Kobe Bryant, we find that he is not the first professional athlete to perish in an accidental manner. The 1955 Le Mans disaster is the deadliest, most tragic accident that ever occurred in motor sport history. Pierre Levegh, a forty-nine-year-old driver, was involved in a crash that caused large fragments of race car debris to fly into the crowd, killing eighty-three spectators and Levegh. An estimated 120 more were injured. According to the creepy reports, the hood of the car decapitated the tightly jammed spectators like a guillotine blade. Along the same lines, the Munich air disaster is undoubtedly one of the worst sports tragedies in British history, and one of the worst in European soccer. On February 6, 1958, British European Airways Flight 609 crashed on its third attempt to take off from a slush-covered runway at Munich-Riem Airport in West Germany, which caused the death of twenty of the forty-four passengers on-board. The injured, some unconscious, were taken to the nearest hospital where three more died, resulting in twenty-three dead, the vast majority of them players from Manchester United.

NBA players Dražen Petrović and Malik Sealy died in car accidents. Petrović was asleep in the passenger seat of his car when his girlfriend crashed the both of them into a truck. Sealy's sport utility vehicle was struck by a pickup truck traveling the wrong way down the highway. Major League Baseball greats Roberto Clemente, Thurman Munson, and Cy Young Award-winning pitcher Roy Halladay all died in accidental plane crashes. Clemente was carrying relief aid packages to Managua, the capital city of Nicaragua, when his plane crashed into the Atlantic Ocean off the coast of Isla Verde, Puerto Rico on December 31, 1972. Clemente's widow, Vera, mentioned that Roberto had told her several times that he thought he was going to die young. Halladay was flying his own plane when he crashed into the Gulf of Mexico. Undefeated heavyweight champion boxer Rocky Marciano and champion PGA golfer Payne Stewart also died in accidental plane crashes. Both Marciano and

Stewart perished alongside multiple passengers. National Hockey League star Pelle Linburgh, NFL player Jerome Brown, track and field star Steve Prefontaine, and professional boxer Salvadore Sanchez were all killed in car accidents. Brown's accident also killed his nephew.

Professional drivers Dale Earnhardt Sr. (NASCAR) and Ayrton Senna (Grand Prix) lost their lives in racing accidents. Hockey player Bill Barilko died in a boating accident. Swimmer Camille Muffat died in a helicopter accident. NFL player Joe Delaney died in a swimming accident. Even as Delaney could not swim, he jumped into deep waters trying to save two other people from drowning. He managed to save one of the drowning young people. DeLaney and the other young person did not make it out of the water. Famed cyclist Joaquim Agostinho died after he accidentally hit a dog at the end of a bicycle race. Baseball player Raymond Chapman died after he was accidentally hit in the head by a pitch. In 1999, a single stroke of lightning killed a whole soccer team in the eastern province of Kasai in Congo. Including Bryant, the two things that all of these people have in common is that they were professional athletes, and they were human beings created in the image of God. While I am sure God had a purpose and a plan for all of those athletes that have perished by way of an accident, perhaps Kobe Bryant is the greatest athlete in the history of sports to lose his life in an accidental way. One thing is for sure: Kobe Bryant did not fear death.

Just like it is difficult to separate Kobe the basketball player from Kobe the family man, it is very much irresponsible to talk about the death of Kobe and Gianna Bryant without including the other seven people who perished in the accident as well. As people who were created in the image of God, their beautiful names are spiritually etched into our hearts forever:

KOBE BRYANT
GIANNA BRYANT
JOHN ALTOBELLI
KERI ALTOBELLI
ALYSSA ALTOBELLI
CHRISTINA MAUSER
SARAH CHESTER
PAYTON CHESTER
ARA ZOBAYAN

Hebrews 2:14–15 says that "Since the children have flesh and blood, he too shared in their humanity so that by his death he might destroy him who holds the power of death—that is, the devil—and free those who all their lives were in slavery by their fear of death. According to the writer of Hebrews, Satan wields the power of death only insofar as he induces people to sin and to come under sin's penalty, which is death (Rom 5:12; 6:23). Being freed from the slavery of corruption is an act of God in Jesus Christ. This freedom will take place among those believers who shall sleep and be changed. Because Jesus Christ is the one who puts on incorruption and immortality, death is swallowed up in victory. Being freed from the sting of death and the power of sin is made possible through the resurrection of the body of Jesus Christ (1 Cor 15:51–57). In the Black religious experience, I have heard many preachers declare that death is not the end of life; rather, it is the beginning of a new life with God.

4

Vanessa Bryant's Eulogy and God's Knowledge of Human Life

I wanted to eulogize Kobe Bryant. As one who has eulogized a number of family members, friends, and other high-profile people, I understand what it means to combine the biblical text with factual reflections and other special revelations that God gives us to say to those who are still living. What we say about someone during the eulogistic moment has no bearing on their eternal residence. Whether the deceased goes to heaven or hell is not our decision. That is God's decision. Only God can decide the place where human beings spend eternity. As pastors, preachers, and ministers, we do not preach or eulogize people into heaven. Our words have no swaying power with God. The best we can do is preach what it means to have faith in Jesus Christ and be saved by grace through faith in the same. I believe people preach their own eulogy by the way they live their life. There is nothing that ordained clergy can say over the deceased body that will reverse or undo the way a person lived their life. Certainly, the truth of a person's life and faith in God is known by God and it shall come to fruition as God renders the final judgment. Even with all of this God-talk and Bible-talk in terms of what it means to speak the last words over someone who has transitioned from this earthly life, the eulogy still has a special purpose.

Vanessa Bryant's Eulogy and God's Knowledge of Human Life

A good eulogy has a way of putting things into a proper theological perspective, of revealing unspoken thoughts and making unknown information known. The eulogy is both a teacher of hope and a teller of truth. Of course, our primary task is to remain true to the word of God and keep the celebration moments as spiritual as possible, but the eulogy does even more than that. More than words of comfort or words of reflection, the eulogy speaks of both our relational connection to the deceased and God's knowledge of human life, lest we forget that Jesus was both 100 percent human and 100 percent divine at the same time. He was the Son of God and the Son of Man. He was a real human being, and he was God clothed in human flesh. Jesus is Lord of the sacred and Lord of the secular in that he sits high and looks low. God presides over heaven and earth. God is in control of everything seen and unseen in that he has the whole world in his hands. He is the master of the sea, and he is a rock in a weary land. Even in death, God is better than good. Here in my quasi-eulogistic moment, I am not sure the word *good* is a good enough word to describe the overarching goodness of God in our lives. Subsequently, the spiritual act of eulogizing someone we know and love is our way of simultaneously honoring God and honoring the memories of our loved ones.

Throughout the course of this very difficult time, and in the years that have passed since this tragic accident, Kobe's wife, Vanessa, has been the absolute rock of her family and of the world too. Vanessa has been the rock of the world in the manner in which she has conducted herself. As one who lost her husband and daughter in a senseless helicopter accident, Vanessa has shown enough inner fortitude to cover us all. If anyone has emerged a stronger, Godlier person in the wake of such a tragedy, it would be Vanessa. She has really been the star of stars. Similar to her husband Kobe, Vanessa has been an inspiration to us all. She has shown herself to be the supportive wife behind her superstar husband. On my read and watch of Mrs. Bryant, she has carried and conducted herself with such dignity, grace, and strength. She has been quiet when the situation called for her to be quiet. And when the situation called for her to speak publicly about her husband's posthumous achievements, she has risen to very single occasion. She has made the right decisions where her husband's business ventures and projects are concerned. She has followed the legal advice of her lawyers, and she has comforted her three daughters with the guiding vision of a queen. She has spoken out in search of justice for Kobe with respect to how the Calabasas police officers handled the scene of the crash. Vanessa Bryant and the other families affected by the crash settled a lawsuit against the helicopter company. The suit was brought by Mrs. Bryant and the family members of the other seven people who perished in the crash. Vanessa has been a bright spot for both her family and Kobe's fans amidst the darkest of times.

In terms of substance, I think Vanessa has been at her very best when she has been suffering the most. I knew she was a strong woman of God when I heard her eulogize her husband and daughter at their memorial service at the Staples Center on February 24, 2020. In front of a massive Staples Center crowd and the world abroad, Vanessa delivered an outstanding word to the people, many of whom were heartbroken over the loss of Kobe, Gianna, and the over seven people who lost their lives. Not only did Vanessa show her Godly strength, but she also revealed a sweet humanity about herself. She spoke with grace and fluency about what her husband and daughter meant to her. Kobe, Vanessa, and their four daughters were the first family of the Lakers organization and the Staples Center. The word that comes to mind is royalty. If the Staples Center is the house that Kobe built, then the Staples Center is also the house that Vanessa kept clean. Vanessa's eulogy was breathtakingly great. I was proud to hear what she had to say, considering the circumstances.

I was also nervous for Vanessa. I was nervous in general just watching the memorial service on television. I was filled with emotions, and I needed to hear a word from both the Lord and the person closest to Kobe—his wife. As a pastor and a scholar, I was interested in what Vanessa had to say. I did not expect Kobe and Gianna's memorial to be churchy and filled with religious symbolism. I did not expect to hear gospel music and church hymns from large choirs with matching robes. I did not expect people to shout, scream, and cry because they felt the Holy Spirit in their human spirits. I also did not expect people to openly worship God. The one thing I did expect is for people to be both transparent and honest. I expected those who were asked to speak to tell the truth about Kobe, even it meant contradicting their own thoughts about Kobe. In the wake of memorializing Kobe and Gianna and celebrating the greatness of their respective lives, Vanessa Bryant stole the show. Still reeling from their death, Vanessa mustered up enough strength to speak from her heart in eulogizing Kobe and Gianna Bryant. Vanessa spoke approximately ten minutes before she began to theologize her husband and daughter. Vanessa stated in her eulogy that, "Even though Kobe and GiGi were up in Heaven, she still had the best team down here on Earth"[1] with her and their three other children. Then Vanessa made the statement that changed the molecules of Kobe and Gianna's memorial service. She said that "*God knew they couldn't be on this Earth without each other,*"[2] speaking of Kobe and Gianna. "He (God) had to bring them home to Heaven together." Now speaking to her late husband with the faith that he could clearly hear what she was saying to him, Vanessa said: "Babe, you take care of our GiGi, and I got Nani, BB and Coco. We love and miss you Booboo and GiGi. May you both rest in peace and have fun in Heaven. Until we meet again. We love you both and miss you. Forever and always. Mommy."[3]

For the purpose of theological reflection, I want to park the conversation on Vanessa's words "*God knew.*" Whether we are referring to the knowledge of God, or God's knowledge, we are still talking about the omniscience of God. This theology of God's unfathomable knowledge gives perspective and reasoning to the unfathomable nature of God's omniscience. It claims first that God's knowledge is an extension of God's perfection. God is perfect and God's knowledge is perfect in that God (literally and figuratively) knows everything about everything. God knows things that are beyond everything we include in the term "all things." Divine omniscience is predicated on God's observational dependence upon himself. In mentioning the presence of divine essence (the presence of God) with the act of divine knowledge (the power of God) as the theological by-product of divine omniscience (the knowledge of God), Roman Catholic theologians hold true to God's knowing of all created objects and their finite and contingent mode of being. Here God's infinite knowledge covers all that is finite in creation. Put another way, God is omniscient. But what does the Bible say about the omniscience of God?

There is evidence of God's omniscience in the Old Testament. First Kings 8:39 says, "then hear from heaven, your dwelling place. Forgive and act; deal with each man according to all he does, and since you know his heart for you alone know the hearts of men." When the writer of this text says that God "will forgive and act and render to each according to all of his ways", he is teaching us that this instruction is not to be viewed as a request for retribution for the wrong committed (forgiveness and retribution are mutually exclusive) but as a desire for whatever discipline

---

1. Andrew, "Read Vanessa Bryant's Speech," paras. 26–27.
2. Andrew, "Read Vanessa Bryant's Speech," para. 26 (emphasis mine).
3. Andrew, "Read Vanessa Bryant's Speech," para. 27.

God, in his infinite wisdom, may use to correct his people and to instruct them in the way in the way of the covenant (1 Kgs 8:40; Prov 3:11–12; Heb 12:5–15).

"Remember the former things, those of long ago; I am God, and there is no other; I am God, and there is none like me. I make known the end from the beginning, from ancient times, what is still to come. I say: My purpose will stand, and I will do all that I please" (Isa 46:9–10). *Former things.* Isaiah 41:22 says "Bring in your idols to tell us what is going to happen. Tell us what the former things were, so that we may consider them and know their final outcome." The former things refers to God's earlier divine predictions or accomplishments. Here God takes the Babylonian nations and their idols to court. In his perfect knowledge, God's purposes and plans regarding Babylon and Israel transcend the plans they have for themselves.

"Who has understood the mind of the Lord, or instructed him as his counselor? Whom did the LORD consult to enlighten him, and who taught him the right way? Who was it that taught him knowledge, or showed him the path of understanding?" (Isa 40:13–14). With God already knowing the one answer to all of the spiritual inquiries, rhetorical questions are used to persuade, deliver, strengthen, and restore his people. God's perfect knowledge has both saving power and persuasive power. Romans 11:34 reads, "Who has known the mind of the Lord? Or who has been the counselor?" Paul's praise to God, whose infinite wisdom and perfect knowledge brought about his great plan for the salvation of both Jews and gentiles, is an authentic expression of thankfulness. Paul writes 1 Corinthians 2:16 this way: "For who has known the mind of the Lord that he may instruct him? But we have the mind of Christ." Lastly, Isaiah 9:6 says, "For to us a child is born, to us a son is given, and the government will be on his shoulders. And he will be called Wonderful Counselor, Mighty God, Everlasting Father, Prince of Peace." When Isaiah says *a son is given*, he is referring to a royal son, a son of David. In Hebrew, each of the four names of the Messiah consists of two elements. "Counselor" points to the Messiah as a king (see Mic 4:9) who determines and carries out a program of action (see Isa 14:27 for "purposed" and Ps 20:4 for "plans"). As Wonderful Counselor, the coming Son of David will carry out a royal program that will cause all the world to marvel. What that program will be is spelled out in Isaiah 11, and more fully in Isaiah 24–27 (see Isa 25:1). *Marvelous things* means that things have already been planned (counseled) long ago or in earlier times. In Isaiah 28:29, the same two Hebrew words underlying "Wonderful Counselor" describe the Lord as being "wonderful in counsel" (Judg 13:18). The words *Mighty God* refers to God's divine power as a warrior and protector of his people. *Everlasting Father* says God will be an enduring, compassionate Provider and Protector. In God being the *Prince of Peace,* this means his rule will bring wholeness and well-being to individuals and to society. In other words, God has a plan and a purpose for the whole world.

"Would not God find this out? For he knows the secrets of the heart" (Ps 44:21). The writer affirms that God is our witness that his people have not turned to another god. "O LORD, you have searched me, and you know me. You know when I sit and when I rise; you perceive my thoughts from afar. You discern my going out and my lying down; you are familiar with all my ways. Before a word is on my tongue you know it completely, O LORD" (Ps 139:1–4). Psalm 139 is a prayer that is written by David. It is a prayer for God to examine the heart and see its true devotion. Like Job, the author firmly claims his loyalty to God. Nowhere (outside of Job) does one find expressed such profound awareness of how awesome it is to ask God to examine not only one's life but also one's soul—God, who knows every thought, word, and deed, from whom there is no hiding, who has been privy even to one's formation in the dark concealment of the womb. God's searching and knowing begins and ends within his infinite knowledge. The reason why God knows us perfectly is because God's knowledge is perfect. God knows our every action, our every undertaking, the manner with which we pursue those undertakings, our uncrystallized thoughts, and our not-yet-uttered words. In his infinite knowing, God perceives our wishes, desires, and plans from afar (Ps 139:1–6). God knows and sees everything there is to know and see about his creation.

> My frame was not hidden from you when I was made in the secret place, when I was woven together in the depths of the earth. Your eyes saw my unformed body; all the days ordained for me were written in your book before one of them came to be. How precious to me are your thoughts, God! How vast is the sum of them! Were I to count them, they would outnumber the grains of sand—when I awake, I am still with you. (Ps 139:15–18)

Secret place . . . depth of the earth. The womb is called "the secret place" because it normally conceals and shares with the "depths of the earth's" (2 Sam 12:12; Ps 30:1) associations with darkness, dampness, and separation from the visible realm of life. Moreover, both phrases refer to the place of the dead (Ps 63:9; Job 14:13; Isa 44:23; 45:19) with which, on one level, the womb appears to have been associated, as humans come from the dust (Ps 90:3; Gen 3:19; Eccl 3:20; Ps 12:70) and the womb is the "depth"-like place where they are formed (Isa 44:2, 24; Jer 1:5). All the days of life are ordained by God. The span of life sovereignty in God determines the book of our lives. The heavenly register of God's decisions is found in the purposes of God. God knows what is best for God's creation (Ps 56:8).

God's thoughts are not ours, and our human thoughts are not God's. *When I awake.* The sleep of exhaustion overcomes every attempt to count God's thoughts/works (Ps 63:6; Ps 119:148) and waking only floods his soul once more with the sense of the presence of this God. On the other hand, reference may be to awaking from the sleep of death, as in Psalm 17:15. If so, the psalmist extends the sphere of God's presence to beyond the "gates of death" (Job 17:16). Along the same lines, Psalm 147:4–5 says "He determines the number of the stars and calls them each by name. Great is our Lord and mighty in power; his understanding has no limit." God's knowledge has no limits in that his limitless power knows what human beings could never know. God knows the number of grains of sand and the stars in the sky. Just as they are a part of God's creation, God knows them by name.

"And you, my son Solomon, acknowledge the God of your father, and serve him with wholehearted devotion and with a willing mind, for the LORD searches every heart and understands every desire and every thought. If you seek him, he will be found by you; but if you forsake him, he will reject you forever" (1 Chr 28:9). Even as David was preparing for his final succession and preparing for the temple, God knew that David would ascend to the kingdom of Israel. God not only searched the hearts of David and Solomon, but he also searched—and searches—the heart of every human being. In his infinite knowledge, God understands every desire and every thought of every single person.

"Do you know how the clouds hang poised; those wonders of him who has perfect knowledge?" (Job 37:16). God is perfect in knowledge because God is, in essence, perfect knowledge. He contains a perfect knowledge of all things past, present, and future, a knowledge that is infinite in its far-reaching depth. Psalm 36:4 says "Be assured that my words are not false; one perfect in knowledge is with you." *Perfect in knowledge.* Here Elihu applies the phrase to himself, while in Psalm 37:16 he applies it to God—thus appearing to make himself equal to God. But the

Hebrew for "knowledge" is not quite the same here as in Psalm 37:16. Elihu is probably referring to his ability as a communicator, i.e., he claims perfection in the knowledge of speech (Job 32:6, 10, 17). "From heaven the LORD looks down and sees all mankind; from his dwelling place he watches all who live on earth—he who forms the hearts of all, who considers everything they do" (Ps 33:13–15).

There is also evidence of God's omniscience in the New Testament. "Oh, the depth of the riches of the wisdom and knowledge of God! How unsearchable his judgments, and his paths beyond tracing out!" (Rom 11:33). This particular doxology helps to end this section of Romans. It is the natural outpouring of Paul's praise to God, whose wisdom and knowledge brought about his great plan for the salvation of both Jews and gentiles. "Nothing in all creation is hidden from God's sight. Everything is uncovered and laid bare before the eyes of him to whom we must give account" (Heb 4:13). Existing as one of the major reasons for giving serious attention to the exhortation of Hebrews 4:11, the author of Hebrews associates the activity of the word with the activity of God as though they are one and the same, which, in a spiritual sense, they are.

"Indeed, the very hairs of your head are all numbered. Don't be afraid; you are worth more than many sparrows" (Luke 12:7). God's numbering signifies our creative connection to God. Not only is God perfectly familiar with us, but as God's creation we are of value to God. As human beings, God has placed value in and on us. All lives matter because we are all created in the image of God (Gen 1:26). Creation, familiarity, and faith (which is the opposite of fear) are all parts of God's perfect knowledge of everything and everybody in the world and on the earth. "For whenever our heart condemns us, God is greater than our hearts, and he knows everything." (1 John 3:20 ESV). *God is greater than our hearts.* An oversensitive conscience can be quieted by the knowledge that God himself has declared active love to be the evidence of salvation. He knows the hearts of all; he knows whether or not, in spite of shortcomings, they have been born of him (John 3:9).

"Are not two sparrows sold for a penny? Yet not one of them will fall to the ground apart from the will of your Father. And even the very hairs of your head are all numbered" (Matt 10:29–30). God cares deeply for his creation. He even cares for little birds, sold cheaply for food. "And they prayed and said, 'You, Lord, know the hearts of all men, show which one of these two You have chosen'" (Acts 1:24). God knows the inner hearts and inner thoughts of human beings. He knows things before they happen, and he knows our words before they come out of our finite mouths. In the biblical text, God knew Matthias would be chosen to replace the betrayer Judas. After Jesus was taken up to heaven, the lots cast fell to Matthias (Acts 1:26). God's intervening in this very important decision preceded the Holy Spirit coming at Pentecost. Again, God's perfect knowledge of all that is within was on full display. As they prayed, the disciples asked God, the knower of all hearts, to show them which of the two candidates God would have chosen to replace Judas in the apostolic ministry (Acts 1:25). And God, in his perfect knowledge, did what they asked him to do. Certainly, God knows what is best for us.

A biblical theology of God's omniscience affirms that God is an all-knowing God. Because God is greater than our hearts, he forms the hearts of all men. God knows the hearts of all men and the sons of men. Here God has an intergenerational knowledge of human beings and the families they belong to. God knows the hereditary secrets that are associated with the knowledge of families. God knows the secrets of the heart because he searches every heart. In the same vein, God determines the number of stars and calls them by name. Infinite in his understanding of creation, God knows our worth as human beings and he considers all we do. In his knowing of all things, God sees everything in all of creation. God has a deep and perfect knowledge and watches all who live on earth. God is mighty in power and is present with all of creation in its awakenings. God has searched us all and knows us completely. In having an unfathomable knowledge, God knows everything from the beginning of time to the end of time. God is the God of history (the past), the God of today (the present), and the God of tomorrow (the future). God has a perfect knowledge of the past, present, and the future because he knows the finite proceedings within each human dimension. God knows the particulars and the generalized statuses of our human existence. He also knows the collective needs of society and the individual desires of each human heart. God knows how much his people can bare, and because of this he will not put on us more than we can possibly bare. We are all human beings, one race of people, created in the image of God. We are all created in the infinite wisdom and knowledge of God. In both the preincarnation of Jesus Christ and the ministry of the incarnate Jesus, God knows all and sees all. The Spirit of God that hovered over the waters of creation and the Holy Spirit that gives life in saving us from eternal death are both the Spirit of Christ. In knowing all there is to know about God's creation (and even more than we could ever fathom), Jesus Christ is God clothed in human flesh. Jesus Christ is the Son of God and the Son of Man. Jesus Christ and the Holy Spirit are both omniscient.

Meanwhile, down here on this imperfect earth, Vanessa Bryant lovingly mourns and grieves the loss of all nine human beings with courage and strength. And while she is not doing it for fanfare or for someone to compliment her or lift her up in any way, Vanessa continues to fight for justice where her husband is concerned. She believes with her whole heart that heaven is a real place. According to Vanessa, it was God's mission to bring Kobe and Gianna home together to heaven. Not that God had to bring them home to heaven, but God lovingly decided to bring them together home to heaven. Vanessa speaks to Kobe as if he could hear every word she was saying to him. Vanessa acts as if there is a certain type of microphone on earth that one can use to get in contact with a loved one in heaven. Vanessa then instructs Kobe to take good care of Gianna in heaven, while she will do the same and take good care of their other three daughters on earth. It seems as if Vanessa and Kobe's parental collaboration on earth will now continue on in two separate places—heaven and earth. In other words, what Vanessa and Kobe achieved in life will be achieved in heaven. The continuation of their work in their earthly life will take place in Kobe and Gianna's afterlife. Even though Vanessa is hurt to the core of her being, she still has faith and confidence that Kobe, herself, and their four daughters are still the best team. It is almost as if Vanessa has embodied Kobe's attitude of being the best at whatever they put their minds to. Just as the Bible says that nothing in this life shall separate us from the love of God that is found in Jesus Christ, nothing shall separate Vanessa from the love of her life—Kobe Bean Bryant. Not even death. As a way of breaking more of the grieving ice, Vanessa calls Kobe and Gianna by their nicknames (Boo-Boo and GiGi). For Vanessa, loving someone means we are missing their presence in the abiding sphere of God's love for us. And when we miss the ones we love, we are actually using love as a way of covering as much of the distance lost (in death) as possible. Vanessa then says to Kobe and Gianna: rest in peace and have fun in heaven.

Exodus 33:14 reads, "The Lord replied, 'My Presence will go with you, and I will give you rest.'" The literal interpretation of "My presence" is "My face." The Lord will not "hide" his face from his people but will cause it to "shine" on them (Num 6:25; Ps 13:1; Exod 33:12). Matthew 11:28 says, "Come to me, all you are who are weary and burdened, and I will give you rest." *Weary and burdened.* This is probably a reference to the "heavy loads" the Pharisees placed "on men's shoulders" by insisting on a legalistic interpretation of the law (Matt 23:4). Hebrews 4:9 says, "There remains, then, a Sabbath-rest for the people of God." *There remains, then, a Sabbath-rest.* God's rest may still be entered by faith in his Son. Since the pre-Christian Greek translation of the OT (the Septuagint) that the author and his readers knew well made no verbal distinction between the Sabbath "rest" and the condition of "rest" that Israel, if faithful, was to experience every day in the promised land, the writer associates these two in a way that suggests he saw in the weekly Sabbath-rest a sign and pledge of the promised life of rest. The fact that neither the Hebrew nor the Septuagint made any verbal distinction between God's rest in Psalm 95:11 and his "resting place" in Psalm 132:14 or Isaiah 66:1 (Ps 132:8) may have reinforced this striking conceptual association. Resting in peace could mean one resting in the peace of death or in the peace that only death can bring.

While it is true that Kobe Bryant, his daughter, and seven others passed away on a Sunday morning, we cannot assume their deaths were God's way of giving them rest from their experiences in life thus far or the stressful things they would have experienced later on in life. My faith in God tells me that God knew what was best for all nine passengers. God had a purpose and a plan for each life lived and all of those yet to be lived in eternity. The words "Until we meet again" represent a statement of Vanessa's faith in the fact that they will one day be reunited in heaven. Heaven is a place of reunion and being together. First Thessalonians 4:13–18 is helpful as the apostle Paul talks about those believers who have gone on to a greater glory:

> Brothers, we do not want you to be uninformed about those who sleep in death, so that you do not grieve like the rest of men, who have no hope. We believe that Jesus died and rose again, and so we believe that God will bring with Jesus those who have fallen asleep in him. According to the Lord's own word, we tell you that we who are still alive, who are left until the coming of the Lord, will certainly not precede those who have fallen asleep. For the Lord himself will come down from heaven, with a loud command, with the voice of the archangel and with the trumpet call of God, and the dead in Christ will rise first. After that, we who are still alive and are left will be caught up together with them in the clouds to meet the Lord in the air. And so we will be with the Lord forever. Therefore encourage each other with these words.

Those who fall asleep. For the Christian, sleep is a particularly apt metaphor for death since death's finality and horror are removed by the assurance of the resurrection. Some of the Thessalonians seem to have misunderstood Paul and thought all believers would live until Christ returns. When some died, the question arose, "Will those who have died have part in that great day?" *Who have no hope.* Inscriptions on tombs and references in literature show that first-century pagans viewed death with horror, as the end of everything. The Christian attitude was in strong contrast (1 Cor 15:55–57; Phil 1:21–23). *Died.* Paul does not say that Christ "slept," perhaps to underscore the fact that he bore the full horror of death so that those who believe in him would not have to. *Rose again.* For the importance of the resurrection (1 Cor 15:14, 17–22), it is important to note that Christ defeated sin, evil, and death once and for all. *Those who have fallen asleep in him.* What this verse means is that believers who have died trusting in Jesus Christ are the ones God knows fell asleep in Christ. *According to the Lord's own word.* The doctrine mentioned here is not recorded in the Gospels and was either a direct revelation to Paul or something Jesus said that Christians passed on orally. *We who are still alive.* Those believers will be alive when Christ returns. "We" does not necessarily mean that Paul thought he would be alive then. He often identified himself with those he wrote to or about. Elsewhere Paul says God will raise "us" at that time (1 Cor 6:14; 2 Cor 4:14). *Will certainly not precede.* The Thessalonians had evidently been concerned that those among them who died would miss their place in the great events when the Lord comes, and Paul assures them this will not be the case. *The Lord himself* (Acts 1:11). *Archangel.* The only named archangel in the Bible is Michael (Jude 9; Dan 10:13). In Scripture, Gabriel is simply called an angel (Luke 1:19, 26). *Will rise first.* Before the ascension of believers mentioned in the next verse (1 Thess 4:17). *We who are still alive* represents those will be alive when Christ returns. *Caught up.* The only place in the New Testament where a "rapture" (from the Latin Vulgate rendering) is clearly referred to. Some hold that this will be secret, but Paul seems to be describing something open and public, with loud voices and a trumpet blast. *In the clouds* (Acts 1:9). With the Lord. Being with the Lord is the chief hope of the believer (1 Thess 5:10; John 14:3; 2 Cor 5:8; Phil 1:23; Col 3:4). *Encourage each other.* The primary purpose of 1 Thessalonians 4:13–18 is not to give a chronology of future events, though future events are a part of vision of the Lord's coming. The true purpose of Paul's ministry efforts was to urge the people to encourage one another (1 Thess 4:13).

At the end of her moving eulogy of Kobe and Gianna, Vanessa referred to herself as a third-person mommy. She mustered up as much self-encouragement (and encouragement for her trio of daughters) as possible in creating a beautiful balance of eulogistic topics. In addition to being the wife of Kobe Bryant, Vanessa understood her place in the life of her four beautiful daughters. Her being a mom to Natalia, Gianna, Bianka, and Capri, included her being a great wife to Kobe. Jeremiah 1:5 says, "I knew you before I formed you in your mother's womb. Before you were born I consecrated you; I appointed you as a prophet to the nations." *I formed you* (Isa 49:5). God's creative act (Gen 2:7; Ps 119:73) is the basis for this sovereign right (Jer 18:4–6; Isa 43:21) to call Jeremiah into his service. *I knew you.* In the sense of making Jeremiah the object of his choice, God gives him some important information. The Hebrew verb used here is translated "chosen" in Genesis 18:19 and Amos 3:2. *I set you apart.* I consecrated you (Judg 13:5; Isa 49:1; Rom 1:1; Gal 1:15). *I appointed you.* The Hebrew for this verb is not the same as that in Jeremiah 1:10, but both refer to the commissioning of the prophet. *Prophet.* The word "prophet" literally means "one who has been called" to be God's spokesman (Exod 7:1–2; 1 Sam 9:9). *Nations.* Although Judah's neighbors are probably the main focus (Jer 25:8–38; chapters 46–51), Judah herself is not excluded.

And what about accidents? Does God care about those who are in accidents? Does God's infinite knowledge include him knowing when and where accidents will take place? According to many Bible scholars, there is no such thing as accidents or luck or happenstance. Things do not happen in life by chance. According to Mark Altrogge, the pastor of Sovereign Church of Indiana, Pennsylvania, there are no accidents with God:

> Tony Evans tells this story: "Our God is sovereign. That means there's no such thing as luck. Anything that happens to you, good or bad, must pass through His fingers first. There are no accidents with God. I like the story of the cowboy who applied for health insurance. The agent routinely asked him, 'Have you ever had any accidents?' The cowboy replied, 'Well no, I've not had any accidents. I was bitten by a rattlesnake once, and a horse did kick me in the ribs. That laid me up for a while, but I haven't had any accidents.' The agent said, 'Wait a minute. I'm confused.

A rattlesnake bit you, and a horse kicked you, Weren't those accidents?' 'No, they did that on purpose.'

God's sovereignty is his complete and absolute rule, control, and power over all things. God has decreed all that has ever happened and ever will happen and ultimately brings about all things he has purposed. "He has total control of all things past, present, and future. Nothing happens that is out of His knowledge and control. All things are either caused by Him or allowed by Him for His own purposes and through His perfect will and timing.... He is the only absolute and omnipotent ruler of the universe and is sovereign in creation, providence, and redemption (from www.GotQuestions.org)."[4]

Artrogge's main point is that there are no accidents with God. And God in Jesus Christ, by the power of the Spirit, has perfect timing for everything he does. "Remember the former things of old; for I am God, and there is no other; I am God, and there is none like me, declaring the end from the beginning and from ancient times things not yet done, saying, 'My purpose will stand, and I will do all that I please'" (Isa 46:9–10).

Further, why does God allow Christians to die in accidents? According to the United Church of God, "One of the most difficult aspects of following God is when we see something bad happen to people that we love. When suffering or tragedy strikes close to home and people whom we know love God and follow him die in a sudden, unexpected or tragic way—it can cause believers to question where God was and why he did not intervene."[5] Scripture tells us that God "will never leave us nor forsake us" (Deut 31:6). Moses begins this particular verse by stating: "Be strong and courageous. Do not be afraid or terrified because of them, and you must divide it among them as their inheritance." This is the Lord's exhortation, often through his servants, to the people of Israel (Josh 10:25), to Joshua (Josh 10:7, 23; 1:6–7, 9, 18), to Solomon (1 Chr 22:13; 28:20) and to Hezekiah's military officers (1 Chr 32:7). By trusting in the Lord and obeying him, his followers would be victorious in spite of great obstacles. *He will never leave you nor forsake you* (Deut 31:8; Josh 1:5; 1 Kgs 8:57; Gen 28:15). This particular clause is quoted in the first-person in Hebrews 13:5, and it is applied to God's faithfulness in providing the material needs of his people.

---

4. Altrogge, "There Are No Accidents with God," paras. 1–2.
5. United Church of God, "Why Does God Allow?," para. 1.

The Bible teaches that, "God is our refuge and our strength, and a help in time of trouble" (Ps 46:1). This one verse represents a triumphant confession of fearless trust in God. Jerusalem's total security is found in the protection of God. "The Lord is my shepherd, I shall not want" (Ps 23:1 ESV). Very similar to Psalm 46, Psalm 23 is a profession of joyful trust in the Lord as the good Shepherd-King. In affirming the psalmist's total security in God, David professes his full faith and confidence for the future—a confidence grounded in the Shepherd-King's faithful covenant love. Psalm 23 is framed by the first and last couplets, each of which refers to God as "the Lord." So if the word of God is true in all it says about the perfect knowledge and supreme love and protection of God working in the lives of those who believe in God and serve God, how do we rectify God allowing people to die in accidents and God being Protector through his abiding presence? One the one hand is the absolute truth of God's divine protection and provision, and on the other hand is the fact that our Christian brothers and sisters sometimes die in sudden, unexpected and tragic ways. As a Christian theologian, my only answer to these probing questions is that God is omniscient in wisdom, power, and glory. He knows all, sees all, creates all, and is present with those who love him and believe in him. In allowing people to die in accidental ways, I hold fast to my belief that God has a plan for us who are living on earth, and he has a plan for those who perish and transition from this life to eternal life with God. God's infinite and perfect knowledge of all things includes his knowledge of accidents and the deaths that result from them. While some argue against this theological view in terms of accessing the reality and facts that surround accidents, still the best way to be informed is through Scripture. What does the Bible say about accidents? Here are some select pieces of Scripture to ponder:

> Exodus 22:2-3—"If a thief is caught breaking in, and is struck so that he dies, the defender is not guilty of bloodshed; but if it happens after sunrise, he is guilty of bloodshed. If the sun be risen upon him, there shall be blood shed for him; for he should make full restitution; if he have nothing, then he shall be sold for his theft." According to Moses, an act of self-defense in darkness does not produce blood guilt.
>
> Romans 12:19—"Do not take revenge, my friends, but leave room for God's wrath, for it is written: 'It is mine to avenge; I will repay, says the Lord.'" Deuteronomy 32:35 says that "It is mine to avenge; I will repay. In due time their foot will slip; their day

of disaster is near, and their doom rushes them." This particular text is quoted in Romans 12:19 to affirm that avenging is God's prerogative, not ours.

Romans 13:4—"For he is God's servant to do you good. But if you do wrong, be afraid, for he does not bear the sword for nothing. He is God's servant, an agent of wrath to bring punishment on the wrongdoer." *He is God's servant.* In the order of divine providence, the ruler is God's servant (Isa 45:1). *Good.* Rulers exist for the benefit of society—to protect the general public by maintaining good order. *Sword.* The symbol of Roman authority on both the national and international levels. Here we find the biblical principle of using force for the maintenance of good order.

First Timothy 5:8—"But if anyone does not provide for his relatives, and especially for this immediate family, he has denied the faith, and is worse than an unbeliever." *The faith.* First Timothy 3:9 states, "They must keep hold of the deep truths of the faith with a clear conscience. They must first be tested; and then if there is nothing against them, let them serve as deacons." This Pauline text refers to apostolic teaching (1 Tim 4:1, 6; 6:10, 12, 21; 2 Tim 4:7; Titus 1:13; 1 Cor 15:3; 2 Thess 2:15). Apostolic teaching emphasized social responsibility. *Worse than an unbeliever.* Even in the pagan world of that time, people generally took care of their family members.

Luke 10:27—"He answered: 'Love the Lord your God with all your heart and with all your soul and with all your strength and with your mind; and love your neighbour as yourself.'" Luke's main teaching point from this popular piece of Scripture is that total devotion (of heart, of soul, of strength, of mind) is demanded in the living out of our faith in God and love for God. Love is both the only way and the most important way. Most notably, love is the greatest commandment.

John 14:26—"'But the Counselor, the Holy Spirit, whom the Father will send in my name, will teach you all things and will remind you of everything I have said to you.'"

Acts 4:28—"They did what your power and will had decided beforehand should happen." *Decided beforehand.* Not that God had compelled the believers to act as they did, but he willed to use them and their freely chosen acts to accomplish his saving purpose (Acts 2:23).

Matthew 4:1–7—"Then was Jesus led by the Spirit into the desert to be tempted of the devil. After forty days and forty nights, he was hungry. The tempter came to him and said, 'If you are the Son of God, tell the stones to become bread.' Jesus answered, 'It is written: "Man does not live by bread alone, but on every word that comes out of the mouth of God."' Then the devil took him up into the holy city and had him stand on the highest point of the temple. 'If you are the Son of God,' he said, 'throw yourself down. For it is written, "He will command his angels concerning you, and they will lift you up in their hands, that you will not strike your foot against a stone."' Jesus answered him, 'It is also written, "Do not put the Lord your God to the test."'"

Even as Jesus being tempted by Satan would seem like an accidental occurrence, it was not. Things happen for a reason under the will of God. The question is: How are we to respond to the things that come our way? Accidental or not, God is still in control of the situation. Jesus was confronted by the tempter with a real opportunity to sin. Although Jesus was the Son of God, he defeated Satan by using a weapon that everyone has at their disposal: "the sword of the Spirit, which is the word of God" (Eph 6:17). The earthly Jesus met all three temptations with scriptural truth (Matt 4:4, 7, 10) from the Old Testament book Deuteronomy.

There are two main takeaways from these eight Bible verses. First, there are events that God plans, prevents, prohibits, and permits. Events which God plans are events that have to happen because they are a part of God's purpose, and they are predestined. They cannot not happen. The cross is the best example of God's plan and purpose. It was planned before the world was created, for God could not create such a high-risk human being, capable of choosing to sin and thus fall away from him, without also giving human beings the opportunity to be redeemed and restored. The cross was the most necessary event in history. In one way or another, God's plans for us will end up being our plans for us. God's plan and purpose for humanity includes his preventing, prohibiting, and permitting things that are both good and bad. These plans, preventions, prohibitions, and permissions are founded in the perfect knowledge and will of God. For every action, there is a reaction. God transcends both action and reaction because his infinite knowledge shows he knows what it best for us. God knows what we are going to do before we do it, and his perfect will demonstrates his plan for our individual and collective lives.

And second, in loving God and trusting God with our body, heart, soul, spirit, and mind, we understand that God's thoughts are not ours. The ways of God are the ways of human beings. What we consider to be accidents, God may view differently. God's infinite knowledge transcends our finite existences. God knows certain things, deep things. The deep knowledge of God is a knowledge we could never comprehend. The Bible says we are to trust in the Lord with all thine heart and lean not onto our own understanding (Prov 3:5). While we cannot lean on our own knowledge, the love of God says we can lean and depend on his word for the purpose of his producing the outcome and/or result he deems appropriate. So I would say the tragic reality of people dying in what we consider to be accidents are inclusive of God's omniscience. When we say God has knowledge of all things, accidents are included. Accidents and accidental deaths are examples of all things known to God. God wants us all to trust and believe that all things work for the good of those who love him and are called according to his purpose (Rom 8:28).

Away from the truth of Scripture, it seemed as if everybody with some form of media outlet and other social media platforms had something to say in response to Kobe's untimely death. From sportscasters to commentators to fellow players to politicians to ordained clergy, it felt like people from all walks of life took a stab at eulogizing and judging Kobe. I will say more about this epidemic in the final chapter, but several different personalities from different professions and cultures took a swing at giving words of comfort along with their memories and thoughts of Kobe. Interestingly enough, those who were on the program at Kobe and Gianna's memorial celebration tried to speak on the life and career of Bryant. They all attempted to eulogize Kobe in the form of song, poetry, jokes, stories, memories, acknowledgments, compliments, and other forms of oral communication. Everybody wanted to render their body of knowledge in terms of explaining their existential connection to Kobe and Gianna. Not that Kobe and Gianna's memorial celebration became a contest to see who could speak about them the best, because that was not the purpose of the massive gathering. But the truth is that while most everyone did a decent job of expressing their thoughts about Kobe and Gianna, Vanessa's eulogy was easily the most outstanding display of courage, strength, and faith.

Vanessa Bryant's poignant words about Kobe and Gianna demonstrated her faith in God, Jesus Christ, and the Holy Spirit. Vanessa was humble and transparent in her incredible unpacking of Kobe and Gianna's legacy. In her eulogizing of Kobe and Gianna, Vanessa gave the world an intimate description of what it meant to be a part of their family. Not only did Vanessa speak from the heart, but she also expressed herself from the spiritual standpoint of faith. Her presence was a demonstration of faith. Her words flowed from the reality of her faith in God. Everything she did and said was an extension of what she believed about God, Kobe, and Gianna. Although she made it look easy, I know her eulogy of Kobe and Gianna was the most difficult and most painful thing she has ever had to do. More important than anything, Vanessa showed herself to be a woman of faith. As Kobe's wife and Gianna's mother, Vanessa was the strongest soul in the room. She made the world proud. My question is: Was Vanessa articulating her personal views of what it means to have faith in God or was she attempting to follow the tenets of Roman Catholic theology?

Catholics believe that the death and resurrection of Jesus have changed the meaning and the effects of human death. Death is no longer the end of individual human identity because the soul continues on after death. The Catholic Church teaches that a soul may go to heaven, purgatory, or hell, depending on the quality of a person's life on earth, and that "heaven is the ultimate end and fulfillment of the deepest human longings, the state of supreme, definitive happiness."[6] In heaven one experiences the beatific vision. In terms of the afterlife and salvation, Catholic Christians believe that,

> All of human history is geared toward salvation. Humans are trapped by their own sinfulness in bondage to death, but God became incarnate in Jesus and broke the bondage, allowing those who believe in Christ to be saved from their fate of death. Salvation is a gift from God, given not as payment for good actions but as freely given grace.[7]

With the understanding that Kobe Bryant was a man of faith, we also recognize his wife Vanessa as a woman of faith, as one who was willing to give glory to God for Kobe and Gianna's life publicly and privately. The fact that Kobe and Gianna attended Catholic Mass and took communion on the morning of their death only means that they were partaking in the real present body of Jesus Christ. In receiving the Christ's body and blood, Kobe and Gianna took the sacrament of holy communion as a sign

---

6. *Catechism of the Catholic Church:* Second Edition, para. 1024. http://www.scborromeo.org/ccc/para/1024.htm.

7. "Religion Library," para. 1.

of God's grace being present in their lives. The taking of communion has no salvific implications. Kobe and Gianna were saved by grace through their faith in Jesus Christ. Most important, Catholics believe that holy communion (or, the holy Eucharist) is the actual body and blood of Jesus Christ. This is one conviction that sets Catholicism apart from other Christian religions. When Catholics receive communion, they believe Christ is actually within them, so they observe certain practices of reverence. Catholics believe the Eucharist, or communion, is both a sacrifice and a meal. We believe in the real presence of Jesus, who died for our sins. As we receive Christ's body and blood, we also are nourished spiritually and brought closer to God. The holy Catholic Church also teaches that at the moment of the consecration of the mass, the bread and wine on the altar truly become the body, blood, soul, and divinity of Jesus Christ. The bread and wine cease to exist, though the appearances and properties of bread and wine remain.

The way that Vanessa has conducted herself since Kobe and Gianna's untimely death lines up with the tenets of Roman Catholic theology. One can tell she is a woman of faith. One can also tell that Vanessa is committed to teaching her three daughters what it means to be women of faith. In experiencing the deepest pains of her life, Vanessa has demonstrated to the world a strong spirituality. Her daughter Natalia was absolutely correct when she stated that her mother was the strongest woman she knows. I would follow that by saying that Vanessa is the strongest woman in the world. The all-out strength that she has demonstrated during the most horrible time of her life is worth writing about. Vanessa's comments on Kobe's impending NBA Hall of Fame enshrinement were ones befitting of a family that was both heartbroken and proud. Vanessa promoting Kobe's new book showed her to be one who supported her husband's gift for writing and creative literary narratives. Vanessa shouting out her and Kobe's wedding anniversary shows that she still takes their matrimonial vows seriously. She still loves her husband. I will chime in here to give a big shout-out to Kobe's ex-teammate, Pau Gasol, for sending Vanessa red roses from Kobe on their anniversary. Such a class act. Vanessa posting old pictures of herself, Kobe, and their lovely daughters demonstrates her undying love of family. Her finding of one of Kobe's old love letters symbolizes his abiding presence in her life and the life of their daughters. Vanessa also demonstrates a prophetic courage in demanding that the police officers who shared pictures of the crash scene be identified and brought to justice.

Nobody said it would be easy for Vanessa and her daughters to get on with their lives. Nobody said there would not be any difficult moments to ponder and painful memories to get over. Nobody said the tears would stop flowing or the images would stop appearing. Nobody ever said life would be easy, because we all know it is not. But it is totally understandable for Vanessa to feel a certain way about life. Vanessa's statement that "life truly isn't fair"[8] is her way of lamenting in words her mourning and grieving the loss of her husband and daughter. She never intended to live this life in completion without Kobe and Gianna. Her statement does not mean life is not worth living, because it is. While they did not live as long as we would have hoped, Kobe and Gianna both lived their lives to the fullest while they were able, all of which is layered in Vanessa's greatest wish—for Kobe and Gianna to be physically present with her in her life and in the lives of their three living daughters.

The Bible teaches that life is, in essence, a gift from God that is directly connected to our faith in the Jesus Christ. Jesus Christ is both the LORD and the Savior of our lives. We have been given the gift of life because God, Christ, and the Spirit live within us. The Bible says even more about the goodness of life:

> Genesis 2:7—"Then the Lord formed the man from the dust of the ground and breathed into his nostrils the breath of life, and the man became a living being." *Breath of life.* Humans have the breath of life within them (Gen 1:30; Job 33:4). *The man became a human being.* The Hebrew phrase here translated "living being" is translated "living creatures." Human beings have received the gift of life at the moment in which they were created in the image of God (Gen 1:26).
>
> Isaiah 40:31—"but those who hope in the Lord will renew their strength. They will soar on wings like eagles; they will run and not grow weary; they will walk and not be faint." Here God's strength is designed to aid and empower us to live our lives to the fullest. Such spiritual acts as soaring, running, and walking are both forms of grace and the living inspiration of God giving us life. Not growing weary and not fainting are also forms of grace. God's grace is God's unmerited favor. Here, God does things for human beings; things he knows we do not deserve. God's mercy is a form of grace that withholds from us that which we deserve.

---

8. Hearon, "Vanessa Bryant Says."

John 6:35—"Then Jesus declared, 'I am the bread of life. He who comes to me will never go hungry, and he who believes in me will never be thirsty.'" *The bread of life.* This title of Jesus may mean "the bread that is living" and/or "the bread that gives life." Either way, God specializes in giving his believers the life needed for them to live their lives. Life is worth living because life is a gift of love from our Creator God.

John 10:10—"The thief comes only to steal and kill and destroy; I have come that they may have life and have it to the full." *Thief.* The thief's interest is in himself. Christ's interest is in his sheep, whom he enables to have life to the full (John 1:4).

John 11:25-26—"Jesus said to her, 'I am the resurrection and the life. He who believes in me will live, even though he dies; and whoever lives and believes in me will never die. Do you believe me?'" Here Jesus was saying more than he gives resurrection and life. As resurrection and life are associated with Christ, his nature is such that final death is impossible for him. Christ is life (John 14:6; Acts 3:15; Heb 7:16). Jesus not only is life, but he also conveys life to believers so that death will never triumph over them (1 Cor 15:57). Death cannot destroy the life Christ gives.

Philippians 4:13—"I can do everything through him who gives me strength." *Him who gives me strength.* Jesus Christ is the one who gives Paul (and all other believers) the strength to deal with various situations in life. Union with the living, exalted Christ is the secret of being content (Phil 4:12) and the source of Paul's abiding strength (2 Cor 12:9-10; John 15:5; Eph 3:16-17; Col 1:11).

Romans 8:28—"And we know that in all things God works for the good of those who love him, who have been called according to his purpose." *Good.* That which conforms us "to the likeness of his Son (Rom 8:29). *Called.* Effectual calling: the call of God to which there is invariably a positive response.

John 14:6—"Jesus answered, 'I am the way and the truth and the life. No one comes to the Father except through me.'" *The way.* To God. Jesus is not one way too many, but the only way (Acts 4:12; Heb 10:19-20). In the early church, Christianity was sometimes called "the Way" (Acts 9:2). Jesus being the way to God is a key emphasis in the Gospel of John (John 1:14). *The life.* The notion of life is one the greatest concepts in the Gospel of John. The Greek word for "life" is found thirty-six times in John, while no other New Testament book uses it more than seventeen times. Life is Christ's gift (John 10:28), and he, in fact, is "the life" (John 14:6). The Old Testament link between life and light is found in Psalm 36:9: "For with you is the fountain of life; in your light we see light." Here, God provides the water of life through Jesus Christ (John 4:10, 14). *Light.* Life in its fullness, as it was created by God to be. For the association of light with life, read Psalm 49:19; 56:13; Job 3:20; 33:28; and Isaiah 53:11.

The two takeaways from these eight pieces of Scripture are: 1) God created us in his image and gave us life for the purposes of us hoping in him and being strengthened by him, and 2) those who believe in Jesus Christ shall receive the blessings of God. These blessings come with both a purpose for our lives and a promise that God will give us his life in the living of our lives. While life is not fair at times, life is certainly worth living. Life is worth living because the Spirit gives us life and hope that we might discover ways to live on and do the best we can in life. Vanessa was absolutely correct about life when she lamented that it is not fair. But life in God, Jesus Christ, and the Holy Spirit is better than anything we could ever hope for in this earthly life.

In my spirit, I believe Kobe and Gianna would want Vanessa and the girls to live their lives to the absolute fullest. This living of their lives includes Vanessa making smart executive decisions in regards to their family's business ventures. Vanessa renaming Kobe's sports complex the Mamba and Mambacita was most appropriate. In making sure that the other people who died alongside Kobe and Gianna got their just due, Vanessa did her due diligence in celebrating the beautiful lives of the other seven human beings in the helicopter. Her planning Kobe and Gianna's public memorial on 2/24 (February 24, 2020) was creatively wise. Coming off of the heels of Kobe and Gianna's private funeral and burial, and Vanessa filing a wrongful death suit against the company that employed the pilot of Kobe's helicopter, that took real courage. And all while still mourning and grieving the painful loss of Kobe and Gianna. What this says to me is that Vanessa knows God. She is still in the process of responding to adversity in a Godly way, and I am sure she is listening to the LORD, her spiritual advisors, and her pastor. Just like her husband, Vanessa has a competitive streak. She likes competing and she desires to win. She desires to be successful in whatever she strives to do in life. Her kids mean everything to her, she values her privacy, and she has experience dealing with tragedy. Vanessa is steadfast in her faith as she gives thanks to God for her daughters, other family members, and close friends.

I conclude this important chapter by stating that it is a sinful shame that Vanessa Bryant had to find out about her husband and daughter's death on a social media platform. Like human beings, social media are a sinful, destructive part of this fallen world. Social media have a demonic outreach of growth that make it addictive to those whom are already struggling with various issues. As the undisputed leader of the Bryant family, Vanessa does not need a psychological evaluation. She is very much a sane human being. What Vanessa Bryant and the Bryant family need is legal and infrastructural accountability, and open and honest confessions from the Los Angeles County Sheriff's Department about how they broke laws and rules in their idolatrous acts of intentionally not securing the helicopter crash site for the purpose of unnecessary tomfoolery. The police officers who failed to secure the crash site are the ones who need a psychological evaluation. The fact that there could be pictures of the crash scene circulating in public domains presupposes the demonic presence of evil and the work of Satan. The only things Vanessa Bryant and the entire Bryant family need are justice, prayer, privacy, and respect. By faith, I can proclaim that the presence of God is still with the Bryant family.

5

It's Time to Dance
The Effect of Michael Jackson's Artistic Genius

IN FORTY-SEVEN YEARS OF living on this earth, I have met my fair share of celebrities. Some were sweet. Some were arrogant. Some were humble and gracious. Others thought they were God's gift to the world. I mastered the art of meeting celebrities in person and not giving too much attention to who they were. I mean, I knew who they were, and I had observed them on television as they demonstrated their God-given ability to act, sing, and entertain. But I refused to participate in the act of worshiping any of the celebrities I was privileged to meet. I found them to be no different from me. I recall having a conversation with one particular celebrity who lived in Los Angeles. I asked him had he ever met Michael Jackson in person. His eyes got really big, and he turned red in the face. He told me that he met Michael Jackson one time in his life. And then he said, "I'll never forget that night as long as I live." In great excitement he went on to say that there was something different about meeting Michael Jackson. While he could not quite put it in proper words, I could tell by his mannerisms that he was taken aback in a good way. According to the celebrity I spoke with, when other famous people meet Michael Jackson in person, the molecules of the environment changed. In other words, Jackson's presence carried both a sense of godliness and a sense of worldliness. He said that Michael was all colors, races, and genders, to all people, all at the same time. He was not like everybody else. Michael was not only the greatest entertainer of all time, but he was also one's of God's children. And he carried himself in that fashion. By way of unpacking his thoughts about Jackson, Bryant described Jackson as a spirit. He said Jackson was the hardest working celebrity God had ever created. He also said Jackson was one of God's greatest creations in any field of study or profession. Nobody was greater than Michael Jackson.

Michael Jackson taught Kobe Bryant the teenager what it meant to be both a great leader and a great winner. What Bryant figured out in his later years was that leadership and winning defined what it meant to be successful in the NBA. Bryant understood that being a great leader and a great winner were the developmental results of him being committed to his craft. Jackson taught Bryant the fundamentals of success: 1) study the materials that are relevant to your craft; 2) work hard at developing your physical strength; and 3) commit yourself to doing whatever it takes to be the best. While the teenage Kobe could not grasp the totality of what Jackson was trying to teach him, it seemed like Kobe got the message. For Kobe, to be in the presence of Jackson at a young age was a godsend. To be in conversation with the greatest celebrity in the world was most beneficial for Bryant:

> We would always talk about how he prepared to make his music, how he prepared for concerts. He would teach me what he did: How to make a 'Thriller' album, a 'Bad' album, all the details that went into it. It was all the validation that I needed—to know that I had to focus on my craft and never waver. Because what he did—and how he did it—was psychotic. He helped me get to a level where I was able to win three titles playing with Shaq because of my preparation, my study. And it's only all grown.[1]

Bryant describes Jackson as more of a theoretical mentor than a life teacher. The greatest teachers have a unique way of teaching up specific types of lessons. These taught lessons are normally received as materialized inspiration. The greatest mentors, on the other hand, are gifted in the area of leading people deeper into their respective calling/purpose. Readers, notice that I did not say leadership. I used the word "leading." Teachers inspire us to become great leaders in the realm of greater achievement. Mentors lead us into the direction of developing a specific talent. While I am sure Michael Jackson was both a mentor and a teacher to Kobe Bryant, I am not so sure if we can fully measure the qualitative totality of what Jackson sowed into Bryant. I say that because success

---

1. Sharp, "Kobe Bryant Learned Game from MJ," para. 3.

comes in many different shapes and sizes. I guess the real question is: In what way did Jackson connect with the young Bryant in terms of helping him to see that he was already on his way to the greatness he envisioned for himself? In introducing new names, new movies, and new books to Bryant, I imagine Jackson introduced a new language to Bryant. New language means a new of communicating one's hopes and dreams, a new way of talking about what the future might look like for someone with aspirations. Most importantly, Jackson also introduced Bryant to a new way of thinking. This new way of thinking would give Bryant the tools to transcend the sport of basketball, while helping him to become the master of his sport. Bryant confesses: "That's the mentality that I have—it's not an athletic one. It's not from Jordan. It's not from other athletes. It's from Michael Jackson."[2]

Michael Jackson guided Bryant's way of thinking into the realm of greater possibility. He helped Kobe to see it was possible for him to achieve all of his goals as a basketball player and as a human being. Even more than Michael Jordan, Michael Jackson showed Kobe the path to greatness at an early age, and not just greatness in a professional sport, but greatness in all facets of life. Michael Jordan showed Kobe what being obsessed with winning NBA Championships looked like. Michael Jackson showed Kobe what being obsessed with developing into one of the greatest human beings ever looked like. While both required a lot of hard work and a multitude of sacrifices, Bryant understood the difference between the two in terms of compartmentalizing his creative knack for performing. What Michael Jackson and Kobe Bryant had in common was fourfold, as they both: 1) understood greatness as the journey toward something even greater; 2) were obsessed with the artistic greatness of performance; 3) dared to be different in terms of figuring out the path to maximum achievement; and 4) had an insatiable appetite for acquiring knowledge, in that both superstars possessed a curiosity that made others question reality. As a theologian and a scholar, I saw more Michael Jackson in Kobe Bryant than I did Michael Jordan. I saw the music concert greatness of Michael Jackson in Kobe's creative genius on the basketball court. Part of the reason why Kobe's teammates called him Showboat was because they thought he was more committed to creating a new flashy way of playing the game than he was mastering the fundamentals of the game. What they learned later was that Kobe was committed to both.

---

2. Mathur, "How Michael Jackson Inspired Kobe Bryant," para. 5.

Even if it meant going against the advice of Jerry West, the executive that traded for Bryant, Kobe remained true to the identity of his otherworldly basketball talent.

Bryant says that preparation is one of the main things he learned from Jackson. Kobe prepared harder than anyone in the NBA. Jackson had that same type of work ethic. The amazing part of Jackson's tutelage of Bryant was that he taught Kobe about himself. "Your curiosity is your greatest gift,"[3] Jackson told Kobe. "Use it to expand your scope. Ordinary people won't understand your insatiable thirst for excellence. They won't bother to keep striving because it's too onerous, too difficult."[4] Kobe admits he "asked a ton of questions. I was curious."[5] The primary reason why Kobe was so curious was because he wanted to use the knowledge of information, situations, and philosophies to create the best version of himself. Kobe never intended to be a copycat of anyone. He only wanted to be Kobe Bryant. In doing so, Kobe asked questions to find the answers needed for him to grow as a professional basketball player and perform at the highest level possible. Bryant says "A lot of people appreciated my curiosity and passion. They appreciated that I wasn't just asking to ask, I was genuinely thirsty to hear their answers and glean new info. Some people, meanwhile, were less understanding and gracious. That was fine with me. My approach always was that I'd rather risk embarrassment now than be embarrassed later, when I've won zero titles."[6] Here Bryant believed that knowledge and wisdom in the form of helpful information could lead him to his ultimate goal: winning as many NBA Championships as possible.

Michael Jackson challenged Kobe to be a great student in terms of discovering ways to learn even more. "You've got to study all the greats. You've got to learn what made them successful and what made them unsuccessful."[7]

Bryant learned another thing from Jackson: life isn't about making money. Bryant wanted to be the best at what he did, not the highest paid. Jackson wanted to be the best performer; Bryant wanted to be remembered as a winner and not a brand name. Kobe's life seemed to embody some of Jackson's more popular songs. From the outside looking in, some

---

3. MacMullan, "Jordan, Russell, Kareem," para. 13.
4. MacMullan, "Jordan, Russell, Kareem," para. 13.
5. Bryant, *Mamba Mentality*, 40.
6. Soni, "Mamba Mentality Key Takeaways," para. 11.
7. MacMullan, "Jordan, Russell, Kareem," para. 16.

people would say that Kobe was "Living Off the Wall" of what people expected him to be in life. With Kobe's aggressive nature in terms of the way he played the game of basketball, it seemed like he "Want(ed) to Be Starting Something" with whomever wanted to take on the challenge of guarding him or playing him one-on-one. Jackson's hit song "You Are Not Alone" puts me in the mind of Bryant's isolation and how those close to him might remember his life and legacy. This particular R&B ballad demonstrates Jackson's retaliation against the injustice and isolation he felt and directs his anger at the media.

I am sure there were times in Bryant's career when he felt alone. I am also sure Bryant knew in his heart of hearts that we was never truly alone. He had God, his family, and the game of basketball. Both Bryant and Jackson were alone throughout their storied careers. Always taking the high road to train alone as a teenager and an up-and-coming NBA superstar, I am sure Kobe had to say goodbye (or no) to a lot of people, places, and situations. In being a loner, and aloof to some degree, Kobe oftentimes felt far apart from those around him. It was known that Bryant's journey to basketball immortality was a lonely journey. The collaborative totality of Kobe's twenty years in the NBA says he spent way more time alone than he did in the presence of other human beings. Ultimately, I believe Bryant's death showed him he was never alone in his earthly life, and he will not be alone in the afterlife. "You Are Not Alone" was considered by many to be a love ballad. The music video showed images of Jackson and his wife, Lisa Marie Presley—the daughter of Elvis and Priscilla Presley. Like Kobe, Michael Jackson was great at doing things that carried some type of historical importance.

Jackson's hit song "Human Nature" was a softer, more soulful ballad from the 1982 *Thriller* album. The track was produced by Quincy Jones and performed by members of Toto, with Jackson providing vocals. It was originally written by keyboardist Steve Porcaro, based on a conversation he had with his young daughter Heather after a hard day at school. "Human Nature" was one of seven Top 10 songs from the *Thriller* album. At that time Michael's seven Top 10 songs from the same album was a record. Because I affirm Kobe's Bryant's humanity by consistently referring to him as a normal human being, Jackson's song "Human Nature" hits home for different reasons. I am sure Bryant had many conversations with his daughters after they had difficult days at school or hard times in the sports of basketball and volleyball.

In being a human being created in the image of God, Bryant was affected by human nature, and he affected the nature of other human beings. The question "Why?" always arises when people are displeased with the outcome, or they do not get their way. This is when folk begin to play judge and jury over people's lives. Also, with Kobe waking up early in the morning to train and work out, I am sure he looked over the city's sunrise and listened to the heartbeat of Los Angeles. Sometimes choosing to work out alone in the gym would take away from Kobe's time with his family. It is clear to me that Kobe was an aspirational dreamer, and the communities, gymnasiums, outdoor courts, and streets of Los Angeles were the canvases upon which he painted inspirational pictures on.

If there is one Michael Jackson song that describes the way Kobe Bryant played basketball, it would be "Thriller." Kobe was an absolute thriller on the basketball court. I referred to him as a walking video game and a basketball record-breaker. *Thriller* was the record-breaking, self-titled album that ended up being arguably the greatest album in the history of music. *Thriller* sold over 66 million albums worldwide. Kobe stated that he had always been a fan of Jackson. Kobe was one of the 66 million people worldwide who purchased the *Thriller* album. The video for the song "Thriller" changed the culture of music videos. MTV and VH1 have both named "Thriller" one of the greatest music videos in the history of entertainment. "Thriller" also sealed MTV's position as a major cultural force, helped to dismantle racial barriers for black artists, revolutionized music video production, popularized the making of documentaries, and drove rentals and sales of VHS tapes.

Many of the NBA commentators who called Kobe's games referred to him as a killer because he showed no mercy to his opponents. He approached winning with a mindset that he would do whatever it took to win the game. Bryant played basketball with a "no failure, no surrender" mentality. He played the game with courage and vision. Others would call Bryant a killer because of the way he ripped out the hearts of his opponents with his ability to dominate the game on both ends of the court and hit game-tying/game-winning shots in clutch moments. Commentators also referred to Bryant as a killer because of his ability to make shots with hands in his face. While Kobe's natural abilities showed him to be a killer and have a killer-mindset, I saw Kobe as an absolute thriller with his array of offensive moves and the variety of ways he finished at the rim. Kobe also thrilled us with both his perimeter shooting and the many times he dunked on an opposing player. Kobe was the classic combination of both killer and thriller.

Michael Jackson was one of Kobe Bryant's greatest muses—perhaps his greatest influence. In being a great source of inspiration to Kobe, Michael Jackson left his imprints on Kobe's life. One of the great things Jackson and Bryant had in common was their commitment to performing at a high level in front of crowds. Whether it was the NBA arenas for Kobe's basketball games or the sold-out stadiums for Jackson's concerts, both were entertainers who referred to themselves as artists. In performing a prearranged musical script or a prearranged game plan, both Jackson and Bryant understood the importance of entertaining the masses to the point of educating them on the nuances of cultural artistry. Bryant evolved from a player that wanted to do it all himself to one that wanted to make others around him better. With the vision of winning championships in mind, Michael Jackson taught Kobe that leadership and winnership went hand in hand.

Just as Michael Jackson felt the need to pursue a solo career separate from his famous brothers, Kobe felt the need to establish himself as the unquestioned leader of the Los Angeles Lakers. Jackson needed to move beyond the group setting of the Jackson 5 or the Jacksons, and Kobe needed to move beyond being Shaquille O'Neal's little brother superstar sidekick. Even as both Jackson and Bryant were considered little brothers, their individual talents showed them to be much greater than the contexts they grew up in. Jackson and Bryant's pursuit of greatness in their respective professions is what bonds them together in history. Both took good risks and gained great rewards for their risk-taking. Both were also accused of crimes. Let us not forget the accusations of Jackson's overnight guests and the accusations of the young lady in Eagle, Colorado. Neither Jackson nor Bryant were beyond reproach. Both were human beings created in the loving image of God. After we are done critiquing their human imperfections, let us begin to acknowledge Jackson and Bryant as the greatest ever in music entertainment and professional basketball, respectively. Critique them as human beings and then crown them as geniuses in their respective fields of study.

Not only did Jackson help Bryant to understand the importance of knowledge and intellectualism within their respective careers, he also introduced the concept of world knowledge to Bryant. Jackson believed that one's knowledge of the world would inspire one's greatness in the world. Jackson taught Bryant that if you want to be the greatest at anything in life, you must be willing to study the greatness of those who came before you. You must be willing to research and ask questions about the greatness of those whom you desire to move past. For Bryant, this meant that his growing greatness in the game of basketball had to be matched by his inspirational greatness in the world abroad. Put another way, Kobe's basketball greatness in the United States foreshadowed his overall greatness throughout the world. Although it took years for Kobe to embrace the totality of Jackson's mentorship, he eventually grew into what Jackson envisioned for him. Bryant figured out what it meant to transition his vision in life from basketball savant to world-changer.

Bryant believed Jackson understood the transition of being a child prodigy to becoming a serious artist. He credited Jackson with opening up his mind to a whole new world of inspirational names, ideas, and sources. Bryant did not leave Jackson's presence the same way he entered it. He felt inspired, empowered and emboldened in the pursuit of basketball greatness. Jackson talked to Bryant about his commitment to music entertainment. He told Bryant he would practice dancing until his legs and hips pained him to the point where he couldn't stand up. Dancing was to Jackson what conditioning and running were to Bryant. Singing and making good music were to Jackson what scoring and winning were to Bryant. In my research, I found that Kobe's greatest takeaway from Michael Jackson was a personal one. At the end of the day, Bryant believed if he could approach the game of basketball the way Jackson approached music, he would be doing pretty well. From Jackson, Kobe learned the importance of development. In focusing more on how hard work develops one's talent (and not the other way around), Kobe realized he had been blessed by God with the opportunity to be the greatest player in the history of the NBA.

Kobe considered himself an artist on the basketball court. People forget that Kobe was a child prodigy when he was drafted into the NBA at the tender age of seventeen, having been in the national limelight throughout his high school years. Being that he began his professional career in music at an incredibly young age, Michael Jackson could relate to Kobe in a number of ways. He was qualified to teach Bryant the various disciplines needed to achieve greatness. Here I am assuming Michael Jackson affected Bryant in a way that Michael Jordan did not. While we can attempt to compare Michael Jordan to Kobe Bryant on the basketball court, we could never compare Michael Jordan to Michael Jackson in terms of world influence. Jordan was limited in what he could teach other basketball players because he felt his particular realm of greatness was created just for him. In the mind of Bryant, Jordan's inability to inspire others revealed him to be a muse of lesser significance. The older Bryant got, the more he embraced the teachings of Michael Jackson. Jordan may have taught Bryant the secret to a few of his moves and answered his questions about branding and business, but Michael Jackson schooled Kobe on what it really meant to be the greatest at whatever he put his mind to. Jackson taught Bryant how to be obsessive in his work ethic. Jackson's message to Bryant was that the sky is the limit, and the earth provides the clues necessary to rise up out of its ordinariness.

Jerry West, one of Kobe's first mentors, commented on Bryant's basketball skills and work ethic:

> It was something inside of him. Some people have it, some people don't. Kobe was so talented, even at a young age, and it was pretty evident when you watched him as a seventeen year-old kid, he was an extraordinarily gifted athlete. Anyone could have seen that. But he was more gifted as a young skilled player. A lot of young players are terrific athletes, but they don't have the skill level he did. Honestly, a lot of veteran players don't have the skill level he did. But he combined two elements, regardless of the skill level you have, regardless of their physical gifts that you have: one, his work ethic was second to none, and two, his competitive desire was second to none. That really separates the men from the boys. . . . He was the most talented player I had seen in a long time. You can have great skill set, but if you do not have the work ethic you are not going to accomplish anything in your life. I do not care what you're doing. He was an exceptionally gifted young man. When he was born, he was a prodigy kid, and he just needed to find his own niche. His niche happened to be basketball, and he found it. But the work ethic he showed was exceptional. You can have great skill, but if you don't have work ethic, you are just going to tease everybody about what your potential is. Anyone who is great at anything has a work ethic— and really, there are a lot of players who have a great work ethic but did not have the skill Kobe Bryant had. The combination of those two made him what he was.[8]

Around the time Kobe entered the NBA (1996–97), he began to absorb training-wheel lessons from Jackson. If Kobe was already committed to working out his mind and body for the grind of professional

---

8. Deveney, *Remembering Kobe Bryant*, x.

basketball, then Jackson's wisdom forced Bryant to an even deeper level of obsessive preparation. Bryant's workouts often took place in the early a.m. hours. Bryant claimed his midnight workouts had become a thing of legend. One of the lessons Michael Jackson taught Kobe was that most legends are obsessed with their craft or field of study. Whether it be in music or sports, obsession is what ultimately creates legends. Bryant's legend was developed during the time when most people were sleep. For Kobe, those grueling early morning workouts served the dual purpose of developing him as a professional basketball player and developing him as a family man. Both purposes were equally important to Bryant in that basketball and family were his full-time jobs. Having those two jobs meant Bryant had to put in the necessary work to be successful in both realms. He lived in the present, knowing each moment, each opportunity, might be his last. He trained like a rookie and prepared like a bench-warmer wanting true minutes. According to Pat Mixon,

> No one views more tape than Kobe. He watches current players and studies the legends from eras past, always with an eye for gaining the slightest edge. And nothing gets by him. Kobe trains like a real Gladiator, pushing his work ethics beyond anything the NBA has ever seen. He is more than dedicated, owing his grit to become a legend. He is at times a solo hero, a James Bond or Jason Bourne, fighting against all comers. And, Kobe has his own motivations for feeling this way.[9]

Michael Jackson taught Kobe that hard work within one's commitment to learning would eventually lead to success. For Kobe, success in the game of basketball meant winning NBA Championships, and so what this means is Jackson found a way to connect with Kobe in the realms of leadership and winning. Kobe understood that if hard work led to success, then hard work would also lead to winning. Because winning is the embodiment of success, Jackson believed that hard work would help Kobe to discover his ability to learn. Hard work would also separate him from the rest of the pack. Just as Jackson's talent and his commitment to work tirelessly on his craft separated him from other entertainers, Kobe took Jackson's message of commitment to heart. Kobe not only embraced hard work as a way of life, but he also critiqued those who did not put in the work as he did.

9. Mixon, *Kobe Code*, 28.

For Bryant (and I believe this as well), the major reason for Jordan and Pippen's basketball dominance throughout the 1990s was founded in their contemporaries' lack of commitment to the game. Outside of Jordan, Pippen, and Hakeem Olajuwon, we would be hard-pressed to mention one NBA player in the 1990s that put in the work necessary to achieve ultimate greatness. Just as Jordan critiqued Bryant's generation of competitors, Kobe also critiqued the greatest players of Jordan's era. According to Bryant, none of them put in enough gym work to stand eye-to-eye with Jordan. They were either afraid to compete with Jordan on the basketball court, or they were afraid to try hard and work even harder in the privacy of their own basketball development.

Kobe knew there was a reason why Jordan dominated a debased NBA (both talent-wise and effort-wise) in the 1990s. None of those teams the Bulls defeated in the NBA Finals compared to the best Lakers, Celtics, 76ers, and Pistons teams of the 1980s. I am sure Dr. J, Magic, Bird, and Kareem would attest to the fact that the 1983 76ers, the 1986 Celtics, the 1987 Lakers, and the 1989 Pistons were all much better than those teams. In this vein of thought, Michael Jackson's mentorship helped Kobe to understand the importance of performance history. Bryant grew in his understanding of developmental systems and individual production. This is what made him the most dominant basketball player of the 2000s—his deep knowledge of the difference between the 1980s and the 1990s. Michael Jackson inspired Bryant to study the history of the game he so desired to master.

I also believe Michael Jackson taught Bryant how to deal with adversity. I say that because, similar to Bryant's situation in Colorado, Jackson was also dragged into court for different types of allegations. Even though it seemed like showing up for court was a total embarrassment, Jackson still showed up. Even when he was not feeling or even looking his best, Jackson showed up for court for what ended up being the most humiliating experiences of his life. When he was able, Jackson showed up for his press conferences and answered the questions posed to him. Like Bryant, Jackson knew the public wanted him to be guilty of the alleged charges. He knew he was being targeted because of his fame and his money. In his darkest hours, Michael Jackson remained humble and strong in facing his charges. I saw that same humility and strength in Kobe when he had to show up for court proceedings. Even as he was embarrassed and hurt, having to answer the allegation of sexual assault, Kobe did what he had to do. With his mentor Jackson watching from a distance, Kobe stood up to the charges and maintained his innocence. While not the admission the world had hoped for, Kobe's admission of committing adultery was a show of strength. I was personally proud of him. As a follower of his basketball journey, I wanted to see how Bryant would respond to the enduring darkness of adversity.

Just as Jackson had taught him, Bryant dealt with his legal troubles with humility and strength. There were times when Bryant had to fly from California to Colorado for court appearances and then fly right back to California just in time to make it for a scheduled home game. I recall one particular time when Kobe had to fly back to California from court in Colorado for a game against the Denver Nuggets. Talk about irony! Not only did Kobe make it to the game on time, but he played well enough to lead the Lakers in scoring and make the game-winning shot. I recall Karl Malone was the first one to celebrate with Bryant after he made the shot over the outstretched hands Brent Barry. While I am sure Malone supported Bryant during his court appearances in Colorado, I am also sure he made a pass at Vanessa. I am also sure Malone was offended when Bryant waved him and his screen away during the 1998 NBA All-Star Game in New York. At the age of nineteen, this was Bryant's first All-Star Game. I do not know how well an aging Malone took to Bryant being the number-one option in the Lakers triangle offense during the 2003–04 season. I did not think it was Shaq and Kobe's responsibility to win an NBA Championship for Malone. If he was not able to get over the championship hump in Utah, where he played for eighteen years, then surely winning in Los Angeles would be a challenge for everybody. Unlike Malone, at least Lakers teammate Gary Payton won an NBA title with the Miami Heat in 2006.

It was around this time in 2006 that Kobe embraced what he called the Mamba Mentality. As the self-proclaimed Black Mamba, Bryant figured out an effective way to compartmentalize his various responsibilities, while at the same time giving energy and attention to all facets of his busy life. In his book, *Kobe Bryant: The Inspirational Story of One of the Greatest Basketball Players of All-Time!*, Patrick Thompson lays out the contours of Kobe's Mamba Mentality:

> But to Kobe, it's a philosophy that pushed him to do great things, not just in basketball, but also in other aspects of life. It's the blueprint to which he elevated his game to get the best possible outcome—win multiple championship rings.[10] The Mamba Men-

10. Thompson, *Kobe Bryant*, 31–32.

tality is the mentality that enables a person to constantly become the best version of himself/herself. It's a mindset of continuous improvement. It is a legacy that he wanted to leave to the younger generations so that they could achieve their goals and dreams. It emphasizes on the never-ending question for answers to questions that could improve one's self. It promotes the mentality of infinite curiosity. It is not hinged on other people's opinions.[11]

Other variables that do not contribute to one's improvement are just noise that can be disregarded. The focus is on being in the moment and constantly improving, no matter how small the progression is. As long as you emerge better than you were yesterday, there's no need to worry about the end result. The Mamba Mentality is what defined Kobe's colorful 20-year career in the NBA, and it continues to characterize his attitude and approach to self-improvement beyond basketball. It promotes the mindset of always performing at a high level and giving a hundred percent maximum effort. Nothing is wasted when you know that you gave your all in what you do.[12]

Put simply, Kobe referred to the Mamba Mentality as an organic mindset. It was not a catchy hashtag he started on Twitter. The Mamba Mentality is something witty and memorable. Metaphysically speaking, Kobe explains the Mamba Mentality in three pneumatic words: Mastering the Craft.[13] The words "master" and "craft" are important when it comes to describing Michael Jackson's mentoring of Kobe Bryant. Jackson mastered the craft of music entertainment, and he believed Bryant was called to do the same in professional sports. For Kobe, his craft was basketball. Bryant broke down his desire to master the craft of playing basketball into eight phases: Balance, Pressure, Leadership, Footwork, Handwork, Contact, Defensive fundamentals, and Playing through injuries.

As a young player in the NBA, Kobe thought he was off-balance quite often. In terms of defensive posture and maintaining a certain center of gravity at all times, Bryant felt he had to improve his balance. He wanted to learn how to stand straight from the waist up and not lean in either direction. This would help him to be more balanced and centered in his body movements. This development would not only help him have more control of his body, but it would also help to balance out his overall game

11. Thompson, *Kobe Bryant*, 32.
12. Thompson, *Kobe Bryant*, 33.
13. Bryant, *Mamba Mentality*, 195.

on both ends of the floor. After noticing his bad posture in a photo, Bryant corrected his balance and made it more difficult to operate against him in the post. This correction was made over time through strength-building and practice. Speaking of balance, Kobe was much more than an offensive genius. He was also one of the greatest defensive players of all-time.

As one who made over thirty career, game-winning shots (six of them during the Lakers' 2009–10 championship season) and many other clutch buckets in the waning moments of close games, Kobe Bryant was never moved by the pressure. Instead of the "big shot" being the biggest shot of an NBA player's career, Kobe believed a big shot was just another shot.[14] Clearly, Bryant knew how to perform in the clutch moments. He knew how to get the ball into his hands and do whatever he had to do to win the game. In being a master of sizing up the defender, Kobe understood that all the fundamentals in the world could not make the shot go in the basket. As one who mastered the fundamentals of shooting, Bryant was undoubtedly the greatest clutch player in the history of basketball.

In terms of connecting the Mamba Mentality to the effectiveness of Kobe's leadership abilities, I was led back to a Lakers home game at the Staples Center in 2003. The Lakers were playing against the Houston Rockets. This was to be Kobe's sixth straight game (on his way to a record nine straight games) of scoring forty or more points. Further, Kobe found himself in a position where he had to be the leader of his team. Kobe went on to score fifty-two points in a double-overtime win. This was also the game where Kobe went around two defenders toward the left baseline and dunked on the 7'6" Yao Ming. For Kobe, leadership was about the timely appropriation of courage and power. Coach Phil Jackson knew he had to utilize Kobe as the primary leader of the team during their three-peat era. This was because Kobe's mental approach to the game showed he was worthy of the responsibility. Leadership was a substantive part of Kobe's journey toward basketball immortality.

In continuing the conversation of Kobe paying great attention to Michael Jackson's footwork, I now turn my attention to the genius of Kobe's footwork. In the mind of Bryant, offensive footwork was all about efficiency. Having great footwork meant one was efficient in his or her movements on the basketball court. Kobe believed he could move with both his body and his feet, depending on what the situation called for. Bryant had a unique ability to keep his head pointing straight forward while his feet

---

14. Bryant, *Mamba Mentality*, 98.

veered in another direction. Footwork fed Bryant's needs in terms of how he envisioned attacking an individual defender. In other words, footwork served a particular purpose.

Bryant learned the various approaches to basketball footwork when he was living in Europe. For Bryant, his immediate goal was to point his foot, either left or right, in the direction he wanted to go—a few dribbles to the right or left for a mid-range jumper. If Kobe wanted to cut the corner and go to the basket, he would rotate his toes to apply more torque. For Kobe, handwork was just as important as footwork. He believed God gave us two hands for a particular reason. As a right-handed basketball player, Kobe made it a point to work on strengthening his left hand. By brushing his teeth and writing his name with his left hand, he began the processes of turning discomfort into strength. Kobe viewed his performance on the basketball court that way too. In the NBA, hands were used for a plethora of reasons. Hands were used to grab jerseys, hold players in place, pull and shove the opponent, or block a player's court vision and position the defender for a steal. Quick hands could swipe at the basketball and eventually knock it away. Active hands could disrupt the offensive player, and hands in the face of the shooter could hinder their efficiency.

According to Bryant, "Hands are weapons"[15]—especially on the defensive end of the court. Whether one is using their left hand to hold the opponent's right arm down, or using their right hand to pick on an active arm to prohibit their opponent from dribbling or pulling up for a short-range jump shot, the work of hands in the sport of basketball is important. Kobe had left-handed efficiency on the offensive end of the court as well. He often shot with his left hand from close-range and he even made some three-point jump shots with his left hand. Most notably, Kobe was a master at finishing at the rim with his left hand. He was fundamentally sound to the point of where he could lay the ball up off the glass and dunk ferociously with this left hand. Bryant's combination of excellent footwork and active handwork made him lethal on the offensive and defensive ends of the court.

Kobe viewed contact as both a natural part of the game and as a mental challenge. While he does not get enough credit for how strong his body was, Kobe relied greatly on his physical strength to endure the contact of playing professional basketball. Even though Kobe developed into a phenomenal perimeter shooter, his main goal was to get to the

---

15. Bryant, *Mamba Mentality*, 106.

basket and absorb the contact of defenders. In the name of contact on the basketball court, Kobe also loved posting up and backing down bigger defenders such as LeBron James, Kevin Durant, and Carmelo Anthony. Bryant embraced the physical contact because his body and mind were prepared for it. He also loved the contact associated with boxing out the taller centers and power forwards because it represented a form of contact within the competitiveness of playing the game.

Kobe enjoyed defending the team's best player just as much as he enjoyed torching the team's best defender on the offensive end. This was because unlike most great offensive perimeter/wing players, Kobe mastered the fundamentals of defense. While there are several different principles one can apply in defending the opposing team's best player, Kobe kept his defensive strategy simple and plain. He did not try to reinvent the wheel, nor did he act as if he was God's gift to defensive basketball. Kobe studied his opponents by watching film, completed his homework during practice, and worked tirelessly on being in the right position to defend. For Bryant, the key to being a fundamentally sound defender was to mentally and physically gain the upper hand every single time, regardless of what the situation looked like. Bryant understood defense as a bodily strategy. He would do such things as use his left forearm to put pressure into the offensive player's back and put his left leg behind him to further negate any opportunity he had to spin off him. Simultaneously, Bryant would use his right leg to cut off his opponent's angle to drive directly. If his opponent seemed like he wanted to make a mistake with the ball, Kobe's right hand was there to flick it away and take advantage of the error.

Bryant's reputation as a supreme on-the-ball defender was earned, as he made it a point to put turnover pressure on the opposing team's perimeter threats. Bryant enjoyed defending some of the bigger small forwards and smaller power forwards in the paint area. As an all-world competitor, Kobe was also a great team defender, as he would often rotate over to help his teammates and block the shot. As a shooting guard, Kobe loved blocking the opponent's shot.

Lastly and most impressively, Kobe always found a way to play through painful injuries. Not only was Bryant a tough guy on the court, but he was also a durable player whose body did not have to be 100 percent healthy for him to play the game. Bryant believed that one's ability to play through and with injuries was a critical part of leadership. When Bryant's knee would swell up the size of a melon, he found a way to play. When he was having a lot of problems moving his body, Bryant played anyway. When Bryant's body was sore heading into back-to-back games, Bryant always played in both games. When he would twist his ankle or fracture his finger, Bryant oftentimes played despite the pain. When he dislocated his shoulder or cracked his knee cap, Kobe got his normal treatment, put protective gear on his injured parts, and played through his injuries. For Bryant, putting the team on your back sometimes means playing through injuries and with injuries.

Kobe once had a serious finger injury that required taping before every game. To be specific, his finger was fractured. According to his trainer Gary Vitti, the finger was not going to get better. It was fractured beyond repair. As a result, Kobe played in the games with his injured finger wrapped in a splint, a hard cast, and some spongy elastic tape. Kobe's finger was injured to the point of him being forced to change his shooting form. Bryant played through the pain of injury with a strong mental toughness. He believed that, with adjustments and alterations, he could still dominate the game while enduring the pain of injuries. Bryant's competitive spirit and determination inspired him to play on the game's biggest stage with injuries. He played injured during his first NBA Finals (2000) and his last NBA Finals (2010). While playing in pain, Bryant still found a way to lead the Lakers to victory during both sides of the decade.

In being committed to playing through and with painful injuries, Bryant was also committed to doing all the things he needed to do to prepare himself to play. Kobe was religiously faithful to taking his medicines, showing up for treatment, taping his ankles, wearing sleeves on his fingers, and wearing braces on his knees, elbows, shoulders, and shins. He followed the instructions of the team doctors, therapists, and trainers.

Maybe Kobe's Mamba Mentality was the creative result of both his personal trials and his continued pursuit of basketball immortality. Maybe the Mamba Mentality was something Bryant learned from his developmental time with Michael Jackson. Maybe the Mamba Mentality was someone Kobe was forced to create within himself as the result of him being ridiculed and made an outcast by his teammates, coaches, and fellow opponents. Maybe it was all of the above. Maybe the Mamba Mentality was one of Bryant's many myths. Either way, history and mythology suggests Kobe did exceedingly well in all areas of his life.

Mike Krzyzewski, the legendary former head basketball coach of Duke University and the U.S. Men's national team, refers to Bryant as one of the greatest players he has ever been around. According to Coach K, what made Bryant so great was that he was the best at preparing himself to win and be successful. Coach K knew that Kobe was prepared to lead Team USA to victory. Subsequently, Bryant's abiding commitment to preparation is what made him an all-time great. In his book, *Sports Theology: Finding God's Winning Spirit*, Greg Smith believes that "Christian athletes have prepared well because they know what is required and where they are going. In 2 Timothy 4:2 we are told, 'Preach the word; be prepared in season and out of season; correct, rebuke and encourage—with great patience and careful instruction.'"[16] Smith explains his train of thought:

> We have all heard it said that 90 percent of athletic excellence is mental. That may sound true, but I do not believe most athletes would agree. If this were true, why do athletes spend so much time in physical preparation? I think it would be safe to say that a professional golfer has spent some time on the range, an Olympic swimmer has spent some time in the pool and the all-pro quarterback has taken a few reps. The point here is that a large part of any athletic success comes from dedicated preparation. How many times have you heard a football player credit the hard off-season workouts for the team's success? I would think that practice accounts for more than 10 percent of any given athletic outcome. Joe Paterno once said, "To win is important, but the will to prepare is vital." . . . Most athletes will tell you that there is a lot more time spent in preparation than in actual competition. these same athletes will also tell you that they would rather play than train. Who can blame them? Months or even years before competition, there are endless hours of jumping rope, miles on the treadmill or countless repetitions in the gym, all requiring dedication and perseverance.[17]

Smith's important statements in regards to an athlete's commitment to preparation would be music to Kobe Bryant's ears. Bryant's claim to fame is that he was both the most purely talented basketball player ever and the hardest-working player ever. Bryant not only trained his body in the basketball gymnasiums, weight rooms, and other significant venues, but he also took the time to train and develop his mind. Bryant was a stickler for in-season practice and off-season training. The interconnected combination of practicing and training his body and mind is what set Bryant apart from his contemporaries. In my opinion, the rare combination of

---

16. Smith, *Sports Theology*, 8–9.
17. Smith, *Sports Theology*, 9.

Kobe's work ethic along with his natural ability is what made him the greatest basketball player ever.

As Michael Jackson taught Kobe how to be successful in both basketball and life, let us not forget that Jackson himself was pretty successful in the music industry. Jackson was inducted into the Hollywood Walk of Fame in 1980 as a member of the Jackson 5, and in 1984 as a solo artist. He also won the World Music Awards Best-Selling Pop Male Artist of the Millennium, the American Music Awards' Artist of the Century Award, and the Bambi Pop Artist of the Millennium Award. Jackson was inducted to the Rock and Roll Hall of Fame as a member of the Jackson 5 in 1997, and again as a solo artist in 2001. In 2002, he was added to the Songwriters Hall of Fame. In 2010, Jackson was the first Pop and Rock'n Roll performer inducted into the Dance Hall of Fame, and in 2014 he was posthumously inducted into the Rhythm and Blues Music Hall of Fame. In addition to being inducted to various hall of fames, Jackson won hundreds of awards, more than any other popular music recording artist. His awards include many Guinness world records (eight in 2006 alone), including Most Successful Entertainer of All Time, Grammy Awards, the Grammy Legend Award, and the Grammy Lifetime Achievement Award, and a record twenty-six American Music Awards (including the "Artist of the Century" and "Artist of the 1980s"), thirteen number-one singles in the US in his solo career—more than any other male artist in the Hot 100 era—and estimated sales of over 350 million records worldwide, making him one of the bestselling artists in music history. Jackson received an Honorary Doctorate of Humane Letters from Fisk University in 1988. On December 29, 2009, the American Film Institute recognized Jackson's death as a moment of significance.[18] With Bryant always wanting to learn from the best, who better to teach the young Bryant the contours of success than the great Michael Jackson?

In teaching Bryant the fundamentals of success, Jackson connected the talents of such artists as Fred Astaire and James Brown to the game of basketball. During Michael Jackson's memorial service in 2009, Kobe described yet another facet of Jackson's greatness: his humanitarian side. In addition to holding numerous records of greatness in the music industry, Bryant stated that Jackson holds the record for the most charities supported by a pop star. Bryant iterated that as much as Jackson gave on

---

18. "Michael Jackson," paras. 80–83.

stage in performances and concerts, he gave even more to charities as part of his work off stage.

The day after the special *Motown 25: Yesterday, Today, Forever* aired in 1983, Jackson received a phone call from his lifelong idol, Fred Astaire, who told him, "You're a hell of a mover." Michael wrote, "It was the greatest compliment I have ever received in my life and the only one I had ever wanted to believe. For Fred Astaire to tell me that meant more than anything."[19] Fred Astaire's phone call to Jackson reminds me of Jackson's phone call to Kobe Bryant. While the phone calls were different in nature, both were outreaching compliments of admiration and interest. Just as Fred Astaire was Jackson's favorite idol and muse, Jackson himself was one of Bryant's most inspirational muses. Commenting on Michael's superiority as a gifted performer, his oldest brother Jackie stated that,

> Tito, Jermaine and I started the group. We were just fooling around on guitar and bass and then one day Michael joined us, playing bongos on a Quaker oatmeal box. He played them so well we thought he should be a part of the group. As soon as we did that, he started dancing up in front, doing his James Brown thing. Michael always watched James Brown on television, and Jackie Wilson, too. Also the Temptations and the Four Tops. He would copy what they were doing. That's when we realized how much showmanship he had, and we thought maybe he should be up front, singing lead. Michael was a little kid at the time but he was very professional.[20]

James Brown, Jackie Wilson, the Temptations, and the Four Tops were muses for the young Jackson—they were the musical acts he tried his best to emulate. Jackie Jackson goes on to say about his megastar brother: "Michael was a genius. He would dance every day. He was always studying the craft. He was a talented writer who created great melodies. Some people just have it, and he was one who had it."[21]

Even though Bryant wanted to make sure his footwork was as flawless as that of his basketball idol, Michael Jordan, I am sure Kobe kept a keen eye on Michael Jackson's footwork as well. There is a substantive reason why coach Mark Jackson and other basketball commentators used the word "dance" or "dancing" to describe the defender's interaction with Bryant on the offensive end of the court. Jackson was one of

---

19. The Jacksons, with Brunson, *Jacksons*, 159.
20. The Jacksons, with Brunson, *Jacksons*, 19.
21. The Jacksons, with Brunson, *Jacksons*, 239.

the greatest dancers in the history of music entertainment. What Kobe wanted to do on the basketball court, footwork-wise, Jackson had already perfected on stage. Both Bryant and Jackson understood the art of footwork as the key to performing in the moment. Performing in the moment meant being fundamentally sound and entertaining the crowd through precise execution.

For every Michael Jackson leg swipe, there is a Kobe Bryant pump-fake up-and-under move. For every Michael Jackson anti-gravity lean, there is a Kobe Bryant post-up, arching his back into the defender, drawing him off balance. For every Michael Jackson circle slide, there is a Kobe Bryant crossover dribble from right to left. For every Michael Jackson side slide, there is a Kobe Bryant move over to his far right side to shoot in the face of a defender whose covered his entire left side. For every Michael Jackson spin, there is a Kobe Bryant spin move in traffic to free him for his close-range jump shot. For every Michael Jackson kick, there is a Kobe Bryant offensive jab step toward his defender with the ball in his hands. For every Michael Jackson toe stand, there is a Kobe Bryant catching the ball in triple-threat position freezing his defensive opponent in preparation for shooting, passing, and dribbling. For every Michael Jackson robot dance, there is a Kobe Bryant pump-fake on his mid-range jump shot to get his defender off his feet. For every Michael Jackson *Dangerous* move, there is a Kobe Bryant spin back the other way, going right and then spinning left into the lane. For every Michael Jackson moonwalk, there is a patented Kobe Bryant baseline fade-away jump shot. In the final analysis, Michael Jackson was dangerously great with his genres of musical entertainment and Kobe Bryant was the most unstoppable noncenter offensive force in the history of the NBA.

Lastly, in Jackson teaching Kobe what it meant to be successful within and beyond the game of basketball, he introduced Bryant to the greatness of leadership and winning. In terms of hard work and obsessive preparation, Kobe internalized the inspiration of Jackson's lessons in phases over the course of time in the following ways:

1. Greatness begins with an unwavering commitment to working hard.
2. In pursuit of greatness, the most talented player works as if he is the least talented player.
3. As the result of hard work, an obsession is birthed out of a growing interest in the craft.

It's Time to Dance

4. A growing interest for the craft means absorbing more knowledge about the craft (curiosity).
5. The curiosity that is associated with moving in the direction of greatness means the journey has officially began.
6. One's personal development toward mastering the craft is what defines the journey.
7. One's transition into leadership means that the journey has transcended the craft itself.
8. More experience in leadership presupposes one's commitment to perfecting the craft.
9. In perfecting one's craft, he or she will find that leadership on the court is the supreme art of performance in clutch situations.
10. Success comes in the form of winning NBA Championships. Perfection is winning multiple championships.

In the final analysis, Kobe did his absolute best to embody the teachings of Michael Jackson. Even as Jackson spent time with Bryant the teenager, those early lessons stuck with Bryant throughout the course of his adult life.

I would argue that a major reason Kobe spent time with Jackson was because he wanted to be just as great in basketball as Michael was in the music industry. Kobe needed and wanted to soak up as much information from Jackson as humanly possible. For Kobe, being the Michael Jackson of basketball meant being the greatest basketball player ever. As I iterated earlier, Jackson helped Bryant to connect the proverbial dots of hard work, obsession, leadership, and winning. I would suggest that in order for Bryant to digest the totality of Jackson's teaching, he himself would have had to have some of that "greatness juice" working in his system. In order for Kobe to grasp the full creativity of Michael Jackson, he would have had to be familiar with the creative genius within himself. As a child prodigy Kobe was already on the road to greatness. What Michael Jackson did for Kobe was akin to Proverbs 27:17: "As iron sharpens iron, so one man sharpens another." This select Old Testament proverb contains an object of the sharpening action. The spiritual act of sharpening iron is an example of developing and molding the other person's character for the purpose of excellency and greatness.

Within this particular text, there is a principle of motivation. One person can be used by God to help the other. The incentive here was to be mutually beneficial. Both pieces of iron must work together to accomplish the desired intent. That was the motivation. Both items needed sharpening. This leads us to a valuable component of growing close, personal relationships with other people. Relationships are never to be a one-way street. God-honoring, interpersonal connections are designed to help both parties grow in Christlike maturity. Again, this process is not just pointing out perceived weaknesses in someone else. This sharpening must come with a heartfelt desire to help the other person, and in the process receive some input that leads to personal improvement as well. God used Michael Jackson to help Kobe Bryant. Jackson and Bryant's interaction was mutually beneficial. Both Jackson and Bryant worked together to accomplish the desired intent. I am sure Jackson and Bryant found a way to relate to one another as friends who have something in common and as competitors who loved to compete against those who dared to challenge them.

It is no secret that 2003 was a difficult year for both Jackson and Bryant. It was the year in which Jackson was hit with child molestation charges and Bryant was charged with sexual assault. While both were acquitted of all charges, the time they spent in court damaged them to some degree. Even as Jackson and Bryant were used to being in the spotlight, many people believe their legal problems tarnished their reputation as superstars. I do not share their sentiments. What I believe is that both Jackson and Bryant were judged guilty by the public before they even appeared in court. In the same way they were beloved for being masters of their crafts, Jackson and Bryant were hated for what many considered to be indiscretions and human flaws. I was proud of the way both superstars handled themselves in the face of so many human judges.

The Bible teaches that only God can judge human beings. God is the only Law-giver and Judge. Those who judge others shall be condemned while being judged themselves. I will leave that statement right where it is. As Bryant went through an exceedingly difficult time in the middle of 2003, the beginning of 2003 saw him move into the peak years of his basketball career. In February 2003, Kobe averaged 40.6 points per game for the entire month (2003 was the year Kobe scored 40 or more points in a then-record nine straight games). During the 2002–03 season, Kobe averaged 30.0 points per game, 5.9 assists, 6.9 rebounds, 2.2 steals, and 1 block per game. He shot 45 percent from the field, 38 percent from

3-point range, and 84 percent from the free-throw line.[22] Two thousand three was the year Kobe saw the opponents' top dog and never backed down from any challenge. It was also the year Kobe carried the load for the Lakers from both a scoring and emotional perspective.

With Bryant claiming that the Lakers needed to surround him with enough talent to compete for NBA titles, keep in mind that Shaquille O'Neal was still on the Lakers roster. O'Neal gave witness to Kobe's groundbreaking 2002–03 season. And the Lakers were one year removed from winning three straight titles. Whether Kobe wanted to continue playing alongside Shaq or not, it was apparent he was looking beyond the present moment. Kobe saw himself as one who was destined to win more championships.

Much has been said about Michael Jordan's guiding impact on Bryant the basketball player, and rightfully so. During his interview on Jordan's documentary, *The Last Dance*, Kobe reminded the world that what the world got from him basketball-wise, it came from Jordan. Without Jordan's influence, Kobe admits he does not win five NBA Championships. But when it comes to gauging who has had the greatest overall impact on Bryant, the worldwide inspiration, we may have unintentionally referenced the wrong MJ.

---

22. Basketball Reference, "2002–03 Los Angeles Lakers Roster and Stats."

6

Twenty-four Claims and the Polarization of Otherworldly Greatness

As one who thrived intellectually while doing interviews, Bryant's mental approach to the game of basketball was critical to his success on the court. By way of connecting his mental preparation to the reality of zeroing in on what was needed at various moments of competing, Bryant's Mamba Mentality possessed a strong commitment to process. For Bryant, getting into his zone was about concentration, focus, meditation, and energy.

I am sure that prayer by way of connecting to God was a part of Kobe's process Phil Jackson helped Bryant to understand the importance of mental and spiritual preparation. Bryant also learned the importance of preparation from his Team USA coach, Mike Krzyzewski. According to Bryant, "You could sense [Coach K's helping to instill national pride and personal motivation into Team USA] in the way he had us playing, in the intensity we showed."[1]

Going back to our conversation on how Kobe's obsession with details was founded in his commitment to preparation, I realized his watching of film included his reading of books. Kobe oftentimes read books while he took baths. For Bryant, reading was both a preparatory activity and a fundamental practice. The act of reading was about being able to

1. Bryant, *Mamba Mentality*, 80.

interpret what was needed to win the situational battle. Kobe not only read the NBA officials handbook, he also read the offensive and defensive schemes of the opposing team. Described by his teammates as a mind-reader, Kobe always found a way to remain one step ahead of his opponents. Part of what made Kobe such an inspirational figure in both sports and life was his ability to prepare for the critical moments that lay before him. Bryant realized that in order for him to inspire others to a greater level of achievement, he had to draw upon a divine inspiration that would keep him focused on achieving his own goals.

I understand Vanessa Bryant's statement about there being a purpose behind a professional athlete's time away from their respective families. Here Vanessa believed that if an NBA player spends a considerable amount time away from his or her family training their bodies, developing their talents, and working on their craft, then the end result should come in the form of him winning the NBA Championship. Embracing the winning mindset of her husband and missing him when he was away, Vanessa believed that one's decision to work hard and develop their athletic abilities should produce rings and titles. In other words, the end result should justify the means of time sacrificed. With the notion of winning multiple championships in mind, let us take a look some of the myths that were attached to Kobe Bryant.

Claim #1: Kobe, the little brother, could never eclipse those who claimed to be his big brother

Kobe fulfilled his full potential as a professional basketball player. In winning five NBA titles (2000, 2001, 2002, 2009, 2010), I believe that Kobe, the "little brother," eclipsed big brothers Michael Jordan and Shaquille O'Neal. Kobe surpassed them both.

Claim #2: Kobe was not liked among his NBA peers

While I am not sure if his peers liked Kobe or not, I am sure it was not his goal to be liked by anyone. According to the way Kobe conducted himself over the course of twenty years, it seemed that winning and being respected took precedence over being liked. He may not have been liked by many of his peers, but he was certainly respected by many of them for his ability to play basketball at the highest level.

Claim #3: Kobe was a selfish basketball and human being

Being considered a selfish ballplayer does not equate to one being a selfish human being. Kobe's skill set, work ethic, and mindset propelled him into the realm of unprecedented greatness in the game of basketball. He had faith in himself as a leader of men, a supreme scorer, and a supportive teammate. As a human being, Kobe was far from selfish. He helped many people in many different ways.

Claim #4: Kobe was a rapist because he was accused of rape

Kobe was accused of rape. In the court of law, we are all considered innocent until we are proven guilty. I think many people wanted Kobe to be found guilty of rape in court. But it never happened because the charges were dropped. The two parties settled out of court, which is all the accuser wanted in the first place. Because many people, in their ignorance, felt a certain way about Kobe the basketball player, they wanted him to have a criminal past. Andrea Peyser's *New York Post* article summed up Kobe's situation in Denver this way: We all know that "Kobe was no rapist."[2] Gale King's after-the-fact critique of Kobe was totally uncalled for.[3] It was yet another form of hate and anyone who attempted to support King in her efforts was out of bounds as well.

Claim #5: Kobe's greatness was limited to the sport of basketball

Kobe was gifted in a number of pertinent areas. He spoke multiple languages. He could read, write, and conceptualize. He was a gifted public and motivational speaker. He was into fashion and shoes. Away from the game of basketball, he was a supreme intellectual. To say that Bryant was more than a basketball player would be an understatement—Kobe was a great human being. Basketball was just one way he showcased his greatness. There was nothing remotely limited about the greatness of Kobe Bryant. He had no limits.

---

2. Peyser, "Kobe Bryant Was No Rapist," para. 1.
3. Welk, "Gayle King 'Is Mortified.'"

Claim #6: The only reason Kobe was a great basketball player was because his father was a former NBA player

Yes, Kobe's father, Joe Bryant, was once a professional basketball player. But many other NBA players' fathers have preceded them in playing in the NBA, and none of them came close to being the player Bryant was. Kobe was the greatest basketball player ever, and his father also played in the NBA. Joe is not the only reason Kobe became an all-time great. Kobe was physically gifted, mentally driven, highly skilled, fundamentally sound, and he was an all-time great on both ends of the floor. Kobe was also considered by many to be the hardest-working player in the history of the game. He was committed to be the best player he could possibly be, most of which had nothing to do with his dad playing in the NBA.

Claim #7: Kobe abandoned his family responsibilities during his basketball playing career

This myth is not true at all. Kobe embraced the responsibility of being a husband to his wife and a father to his daughters. As a professional athlete, Kobe was not always present at home with his immediate family, but he still took care of them emotionally and financially.

Claim #8: Kobe was the lower-level superstar sidekick to Shaq during the Lakers' three-peat

While Shaq referred to Kobe as his little brother, the truth is that Kobe was just as much of an NBA superstar as Shaq was. There were times when Shaq was the alpha dog of the team, and there were times when Kobe was the alpha dog. There were times when both Shaq and Kobe were the alpha dogs together. They played in four NBA Finals and numerous All-Star Games together. They were both alpha males—higher-level superstars playing for the same team.

Claim #9: Kobe could not win an NBA Championship without Shaq because he carried Kobe to their three titles together

While Shaq won one NBA Championship as a member of the Miami Heat after leaving the Lakers, Kobe won two NBA Championships without Shaq as a teammate. Shaq ended his NBA career with four total rings while Kobe had five.

Claim #10: Kobe did not make his teammates around him better

With a total of 6,306 career assists (approximately five assists per game), Kobe led the Lakers to seven NBA Finals appearances and five championships. While not known as an assists guy, Kobe led the Lakers in assists per game nine times during the decade of the 2000s, including each of their four NBA championship runs during that decade. During the Lakers three-peat from 2000 to 2002, Kobe served as point guard as he was charged with initiating the Triangle offense from the top of the key. In being an all-around basketball player, Kobe was one of four players in NBA history to amass at least 25,000 points, 6,000 assists, and 6,000 rebounds (Oscar Robinson, John Havlicek, LeBron James being the other three).

Claim #11: Kobe would never be as great a basketball player as Michael Jordan

This is an old myth—one that remained a hot-button conversation throughout the course of Kobe's twenty years in the NBA. While I believe Kobe eclipsed Jordan in the game of basketball, many others believe Jordan is still the greatest ever. I think it depends on how one defines greatness or being the greatest. As I explained in chapters 1, 7, and 8, Kobe surpassed Jordan when he won multiple NBA Championships without Shaq from in the 2008–09 and 2009–10 seasons. Jordan never won titles without his superstar sidekick Scottie Pippen.

Claim #12: Because of Kobe's preoccupation with himself, he couldn't inspire others to human greatness

Despite experiencing some difficult moments throughout his NBA career, Kobe managed to be one of the greatest inspirers of people that has ever walked this earth. Kobe's self-confidence ended up being his greatest asset—one that moved him into the realm of being a master teacher of inspiration. Kobe inspired people of different sports, backgrounds, fields of study, and abilities. Kobe destroyed this particular myth both during and after his NBA career.

Claim #13: Kobe wanted to die young and be immortalized as the greatest basketball player ever

Tracy McGrady's words are poignant. McGrady and Bryant had been friends for a long time. Both are NBA Hall of Famers. Both played the two-guard position with excellence. Both were great scorers. McGrady could have very easily been Kobe's best friend in the NBA. If any anybody knew Kobe in that way, it would have been McGrady. However, saying at a young age that one wants to die an early death is something totally different from someone actually wanting to die. Bryant was nowhere close to being suicidal, and he had way too much going for him in his post-NBA years to desire to die.

Claim #14: Kobe was anti-social because he thought he was above or better than his teammates

In his early years of playing in the NBA, Kobe was very anti-social. He did not spend much time with his teammates outside of playing basketball. Bryant's anti-social manner did not take place because he thought his teammates were not on his level as human beings. Kobe was anti-social because he spent tens of thousands of hours working on his game, practicing his craft. Kobe's legendary work ethic and inner drive did not allow him to be as social as people thought he should have been.

Claim #15: In his prime years, Kobe established himself as one of the greatest pure scorers the game has ever seen

I agree with this myth. I could name numerous instances where Bryant did the unthinkable on the offensive end of the court. But I will settle on the fact that in 2007, Kobe averaged an astronomical 49.8 points per game over a twelve-game period. During this stretch, Bryant scored 60 or more points twice, 50 or more points five times, 40 or more points three times and 30 or more points twice.

Claim #16: During the Lakers three-peat in the early 2000s, the NBA Finals was the most competitive part of each championship runs

I agree with this myth. Where the Los Angeles Lakers were concerned, I believe certain rounds of the Western Conference playoffs (2000 to 2002) were far more competitive than those NBA Finals series with the Pacers, Sixers, and Nets. The Lakers had to get past the likes of the Trail Blazers, Spurs, Kings, and Suns—all of which were talented teams. During the early 2000s, it was much more difficult to win in the Western Conference than it was to win the Eastern Conference. In winning two NBA Finals games (2000), the Indiana Pacers gave the Lakers their toughest challenge.

Claim #17: Jordan was a better basketball player than Kobe Bryant

From what I have seen and heard in my time as a fan of basketball, more people have declared Jordan as the greatest ever. But I have not asked every single basketball fan in the world their choice of greatest ballplayer. I have only lived in the states of Kentucky, Ohio, and Illinois. I have not been exposed to what other NBA fans are saying in other parts of the country. One thing is for sure, though: the more I heard fans, commentators, and media pundits calling Jordan the better player, the more I began to think deeper about what it actually means to be the greatest basketball player—other than hearing one's biased opinion. NBA Hall of Famers Wilt Chamberlain, Bill Russell, Kareem Abdul-Jabbar, Julius Erving, Jerry West, Elgin Baylor, Walt Frazier, Oscar Robinson, and others have not crowned Jordan as the greatest ever. They have not crowned Bryant as the GOAT either. But everyone is entitled to their respective opinion.

Claim #18: Kobe is the second-greatest shooting guard behind Michael Jordan

This myth was started by television commentators, media pundits, and those who felt Jordan represented their generation (the 80s and 90s) of playing and watching the game of basketball. Obviously, I believe Kobe Bryant to be the greatest shooting guard we have ever seen. One of the major reasons I say that is because Bryant was a better perimeter shooter or shooting guard than Jordan. His mid-range jump-shot, three-point shot, and free-throw shooting were all better than Jordan's. In my opinion, Kobe was the greatest shot-maker in the history of the game. Kobe's athleticism was on par with Jordan's. Jordan had bigger hands, but in my humble opinion, Kobe had the bigger overall game.

Claim #19: Michael Jordan was the original and Kobe was the remix

According to Jalen Rose, this was the case. Just as Jordan thought Kobe had stolen all of his basketball moves, I believe there was a plethora of things Kobe did better than Jordan. I am certain Kobe surpassed Jordan as the greatest basketball player ever. Myth or not, both were transcendent athletes.

Claim #20: Kobe was one of the greatest tough-shot makers in the history of the NBA

This myth is 150 percent true. This particular myth is also a part of the Kobe Bryant-Michael Jordan G.O.A.T. debate. In Corey Hansford's 2014 article "Lakers News: Grant Hill Says Kobe Hit More 'Tough Shots' than Jordan," it is affirmed that Bryant is one of the greatest tough-shot makers in league history. Hansford's article includes the following quote concerning statements from Hill: "Kobe hit more 'tough' shots than Jordan and got more 'star treatment' in his view. Jordan more efficient in mid-range."[4] For Hill, Kobe was the most difficult defensive assignment of his NBA career.

Claim #21: Certain NBA coaches sat Kobe on the bench to teach him a lesson

To some degree, this particular myth could have some factual merit, especially where Kobe's first two years in the NBA are concerned. In addition, I believe George Karl intentionally benched Kobe for an extended period of time during the second half (including the entire 4th quarter) of the 1998 NBA All-Star Game at Madison Square Garden. I feel like that was done to teach the young Showboat a lesson about respect and to keep

---

4. Hansford, "Lakers News: Grant Hill Says," para. 3.

Kobe from winning Jordan's All-Star Game MVP. When the nineteen-year-old Bryant went to the bench, he was the game's leading scorer.

Claim #22: Kobe deserved to be punished because of the Denver situation

Totally untrue. I have heard this statement so many times over the years. The truth is that only God can judge human beings. Sinful, imperfect people have neither the power nor the knowledge to judge others. Nobody can say that anybody, including Kobe Bryant, deserves to be punished for any reason under heaven. That is God's decision and God's decision only. I believe human beings are at their absolute worst when they attempt to play God. Kobe Bryant is a child of God, and he will forever be in the hands of the loving God who created him in God's image.

Claim #23: Kobe won an unprecedented Oscar because of his basketball fame

As an intellectual par excellence, Kobe won an Oscar because he was a great thinker, writer, and poet. His creative genius, along with his unique ability to write on paper what his imagination revealed to him, won him the highest honor and greatest award possible in the film world. His Oscar win was more about his ability to write than it was his ability to play basketball.

Claim #24: Kobe did not have a good working relationship with legendary coach Phil Jackson

This myth could not be further from the truth. It took some years for Phil and Kobe to come to an understanding of what their union would become. The working relationship they had when Kobe was twenty-one (2000) was something totally different from the working relationship they had when Kobe was thirty-three (2012). They learned to love, respect, and accept each other for who they were. I believe Phil and Kobe learned a lot from each other. Obviously, they had a good working relationship. They won five NBA titles over an eleven-year period.

After winning four NBA titles in the decade of the 2000s and a fifth title in 2010, most onlookers thought Kobe Bryant's basketball talent had died when he tore his Achilles heel in 2013 in a nationally televised game against the Golden State Warriors. They thought his career was over. Ever the tough-guy warrior, Kobe tried to put the ruptured Achilles back in place with his hands. Realizing that he could not repair the Achilles with his bare hands, Kobe rose from the Staples Center floor and walked to the free-throw line on his own strength. With tears welling up in his eyes, Kobe swished two free throws with no lift in his legs. Kobe's display of strength was phenomenal. It was also different from Kevin Durant's episode in the 2019 NBA Finals. While the injuries were the same, the way both players dealt with it was different. While Durant needed help to get up and walk back to the trainer's room, Kobe walked back to the locker room on his own. Understanding that his basketball season was over, Kobe cried throughout the postgame interviews. With head coach Mike D'Antoni, Steve Nash, Dwight Howard, Metta World Peace, and Pau Gasol on the roster, Kobe had once again led the Lakers to the playoffs. Due to his ruptured Achilles, Kobe did not get a chance to participate in the 2013 playoffs. By all accounts, Kobe's seventeenth season was one of his best. He averaged 27 points, 6 assists, 6 rebounds, and 1 steal per game. The ultimate competitor, Bryant was confident that his Lakers could compete for an NBA Championship, regardless of their seeding in the playoffs.

Without Bryant in the lineup, the Lakers were swept by the San Antonio Spurs in four games. Obviously, the Achilles injury was heartbreaking for Bryant. It meant a year of grueling rehabilitation and it also meant another transitioning of the Lakers roster. The Lakers lost Nash, Howard, World Peace, and Gasol. What this meant for Kobe was that he had to start all over again in his eighteenth year in the NBA. Even as his body was slowing down in his final years, Kobe still had the desire to compete at a high level. He still loved battling and participating in the wars for basketball supremacy.

The fact that Kobe scored 60 points in his last game is both legendary and otherworldly. It was downright unbelievable that yet again Kobe brought his team back from the jaws of defeat and hit the game-winning shot. A student of Greek mythology, Kobe was similar to the Greek hero Achilles. I say that because Achilles was known as one of the greatest warriors and heroes in Greek mythology. He was a major character in Homer's *Iliad*, where he fought in the Trojan War against the city of Troy. Achilles's father was Peleus, king of the Myrmidons, and his mother was Thetis, a sea nymph. After Achilles was born, his mother wanted to protect him from harm. She held him by the heel and dipped him into the River Styx. In Greek mythology, the River Styx was located in the Underworld and had special powers. Achilles became invulnerable everywhere but at his heel where his mother held him.

Because Achilles was a half-god, he was extraordinarily strong and soon became a great warrior. However, he was also half-human and was not immortal like his mother. Like most people, Achilles knew he would get old and die someday. He also knew he could also be killed. When the Trojan War began, Helen, the wife of the Greek king Menelaus, was taken by the Trojan prince Paris, and so the Greeks went to war to get her back. Achilles joined the battle and brought along a group of powerful soldiers called the Myrmidons. This scene reminds me of Kobe Bryant and the Los Angeles Lakers. During the Trojan War, Achilles was unstoppable. Much like Kobe's dominance in the NBA, Achilles defeated many of Troy's greatest warriors. However, the battle involving Achilles raged on for years. Many of the Greek gods were involved, some helping the Greeks and others helping the Trojans.

Just like Kobe refused to shoot the basketball in Game 7 of the 2007 Western Conference Playoffs against the Phoenix Suns, Achilles refused to fight at times. At one point during the war, Achilles captured a beautiful princess named Briseis and fell in love with her. However, the leader of the Greek army, Agamemnon, became angry with Achilles and took Briseis from him. Achilles became depressed and refused to fight. With Achilles not fighting, the Greeks began to lose the battle. The greatest warrior of Troy was Hector, and no one could stop him. Achilles's best friend was a soldier named Patroclus. Patroclus convinced Achilles to lend him his armor. Patroclus entered the battle dressed as Achilles. Thinking that Achilles was back, the Greek army was inspired and began to fight harder. Just when things were improving for the Greeks, Patroclus met up with Hector. The two warriors engaged in battle. With the help of the god Apollo, Hector killed Patroclus and took Achilles' armor. Achilles then rejoined the battle in order to avenge his friend's death. He met Hector on the battlefield and, after a long fight, defeated him.

Achilles continued to battle the Trojans and it seemed like he could not be killed. However, the Greek god Apollo knew his weakness. When Paris of Troy shot an arrow at Achilles, Apollo guided it so that it struck Achilles on the heel. Achilles eventually died from the wound. Today, the term "Achilles' heel" is used to describe a point of physical weakness that could lead to one's downfall. One story tells of how Thetis disguised

Achilles as a girl in the court of King Skyros in order to keep him from war. Another Greek hero, Odysseus, traveled to Skyros and tricked Achilles into giving himself away. Subsequently, the Achilles tendon that connects the heel to the calf is named after the hero Achilles. With courage, he fought and killed Penthesilea, the Queen of the Amazons. After Achilles's death, the heroes Odysseus and Ajax competed for Achilles's armor. Odysseus won and gave the armor to Achilles's son.

Like Achilles during the days of Greek mythology, Kobe Bryant was one of the most polarizing figures in the history of the NBA. I have often thought about what exactly made him so polarizing. What was it about Kobe that inspired people to love and hate him simultaneously? Was it his self-confidence? Or was it his pursuit of perfection? Was it those last-second shots that broke the hearts of other teams' fans? Was it the Denver situatio? Maybe the break-up with Shaquille O'Neal? Or could it have been that people found Kobe to be polarizing because he was great in so many different ways? Whatever the reason, Kobe taught us all about the polarizing quality of greatness. A huge part of Kobe's polarizing greatness was found in his ability to lead others. Kobe was thrust into a leadership position during the Lakers three-peat years for two reasons. First, Kobe's basketball talent and otherworldly skill set demanded that he lead his teammates. And second, Kobe wanted to be put in a leadership position for both the present time and for the future. Kobe felt he could be an effective team leader and the team needed him to be a leader both on the and off the court. The tugging that Bryant felt from both ends of the pendulum (internal and external) made his promotion into leadership with the Lakers a natural fit. The transition was smooth in that Kobe was physically and mentally prepared to help lead his team to the promised land. The narrative of Kobe's leadership abilities was different from that of Magic, Bird, and Jordan. While they led their respective teams with an equal balance of verbal direction and on-the-court execution, Kobe led the Lakers by exemplifying what he wanted his teammates to be and by verbally challenging them to be better. Kobe's unmatched work ethic was the blueprint for how he wanted his teammates to be. His historical knowledge of the game and his deep familiarity with his teammates is what gained him their respect.

For Kobe, leadership meant scoring and winning championships. Mythologically, I believe Kobe polarized the world with his unique ability to score in the most unfathomable of ways. Kobe reached the offensive zenith of his basketball greatness on the night he scored a career-high 81 points. Over the years, we have all borne witness to Bernard King scoring 60 points in one game, Larry Bird's 60 points, Shaquille O'Neal's 61 points, Carmelo Anthony's 62 points, Stephen Curry's 62 points, Michael Jordan's 69 points, and David Robinson's 71 points. The Phoenix Suns' Devin Booker scored 71 points on March 24, 2018. All of these performances carried some type of historical significance in terms of what it meant to dominate a game through scoring. Outside of the still-young Booker, all of the aforementioned names are NBA Hall of Famers for sure. They are all great players and great scorers in their own right. We still get excited when someone in the NBA scores 50 points. However, what took place on January 22, 2006, inside the Staples Center, can only be described as mythical. The reason I used the word mythical is because myths are defined as stories. Usually when people tell you a story, you do not know if it is true or not. We normally struggle with whether or not to believe someone who tells us a story. The story could be true or untrue. Either way, myths and stories can have powerful consequences when used in the right context.

Do not get it twisted. Kobe Bryant scoring 81 points in one game is not a cultural myth. It is a true story. Kobe put on the greatest scoring performance in NBA history. I know many of you are now beginning to reflect on the great Wilt Chamberlain's 100-point night on March 2, 1962. I know you are thinking of how Wilt's historic night compares to Kobe's masterpiece. In my humble opinion, I believe that Kobe's 81 points was a greater achievement than Wilt's 100 points. With all due respect, I say that because Kobe played guard and Wilt played center. Kobe's performance was more creative and dynamic because he scored points in a variety of ways. While the majority of Wilt's points were accumulated in the paint area or closer to the rim, Kobe scored in an assortment of ways. Kobe made three-point jump shots, two-point jump shots, lay-ups, dunks, and free throws. Both Wilt and Kobe took advantage of the opportunity to shoot free throws, but Kobe's offensive display was more versatile, and it took up a great amount of his energy. Shooting that many jump shots can drain a player. I would like to think that when Kobe walked off the Staples Center floor on that historic night, he was exhausted. Kobe was everywhere. He played great defense too. Which brings me to my main point. Kobe's historic night must have been great in a polarizing way because he received both universal praise and local criticism.

One of Kobe's contemporaries, Vince Carter, thought Kobe's 81-point game was bad for basketball. Carter believed Kobe's offensive displays on the court set a bad example for young people who were just beginning to play organized basketball. Kobe's performance was deemed the wrong way to play the game. Kobe's idol, Michael Jordan, chimed in on Bryant's historic night as well. Jordan said something to the effect that if he were playing in a Toronto Raptors uniform, he would have used all six of his personal fouls in defending Bryant. Jordan's generational comments took shots at both Bryant's offensive prowess and the Raptors' defensive miseries. Both critiques, Carter and Jordan's, reeked of jealousy. I never heard anyone negatively critique Carter's 51 points against the Miami Heat in 2005 or Jordan's 69 points against the lowly Cleveland Cavaliers in 1990. The truth is that Kobe was offensively superior to both Jordan and Carter. LeBron James was absolutely correct when he stated that Bryant had no weakness on the offensive end of the floor. He could shoot from any distance (close up, free throws, mid-range, and three-point range) at any given moment, dribble with an *And 1* streetball handle, drive to the basket from any position on the court, post up with an unlimited array of moves, finish at the rim from various perspectives, split the screen and roll and then dunk over his opponent in a half-court set, and make the most impossible of shots look routinely simple.

What many did not understand about Kobe's historic night was that the Lakers needed all 81 of Kobe's points to win the game. The Lakers had lost the previous game and needed a win. The young Lakers were out of sync and Kobe's body was extremely sore from playing so many minutes. But Bryant treated the Raptors game as a must-win. Kobe was obsessed with winning. He would have done anything that would lead to a much-needed victory. Most important, the Lakers were struggling and needed a win. As much as people attempted to make light of his performance, the truth is Kobe's desire to win the basketball game motivated him to score 81 points. He did for the purpose of winning. Not to place another notch in his basketball belt. Of the 1,280 games Kobe played in, this was his greatest performance. The Los Angeles Lakers star shot an incredible 28-of-46 from the field (61 percent), including an even more impressive 7 of 13 from the three-point line (54 percent). In twenty free throw attempts, Bryant missed just two (90 percent). What most commentators and pundits forget is that the Lakers were trailing the Raptors by 18 points in the early parts of the 3rd quarter. At that moment in the game, Kobe completely took over, scoring 55 points in the second half alone (27 points in the 3rd quarter and 28 in the 4th), leading his Lakers to a 122–104 win. Again, Kobe's 81-point night was more about the Lakers needing a win than it was Kobe's individual performance. And to top it all off, Jalen Rose, a member of the 2006 Toronto Raptors, testifies that Kobe did not say one word to him and the Raptors throughout the course of the game. There is a reason why Bryant believed that Wilt Chamberlain, Jordan, and himself were the three greatest scorers of all time.

When his critics reflect upon Kobe's highest-scoring games, their first argument is that Bryant was a selfish basketball player. What the pundits and commentators never expound on is that in the majority of those games which he scored a massive number of points, Kobe's Lakers won. When he scored 81 points against the Toronto Raptors, 65 against the Portland Trailblazers, 62 points in three quarters against the Dallas Mavericks, 61 against the New York Knicks, 60 against the Memphis Grizzlies, and again against the Utah Jazz, the Lakers won the game. You see where the analysis is taking us. We are now moving into the collaborative conversation of how Kobe's quality of scoring and his quantity of winning went hand in hand. In the 29 games that Kobe scored 50 or more points, the Lakers won 21 of those games (72 percent). In the 26 games that Bryant scored between 45 and 49 points, the Lakers won 20 of those games (77 percent). Even as he accumulated enough points to become the fourth-leading scorer in NBA history and the fourth-leading scorer in NBA Playoffs history, Bryant's otherworldly scoring abilities were motivated by his desire to win games.

In his NBA career, Kobe Bryant registered a large number of great moments—moments that either blew your mind or dropped your jaw. Kobe was the first NBA basketball player that reminded me of a video game. Kobe was a real-life, walking video game because he did things on the basketball court that defied logic. If Jordan defied gravity with his basketball athleticism, then Kobe defied all sense of human logic and practical reason with his basketball skill. This is what I was thinking as I watched Kobe's magnificent display of basketball magic in Game 6 of the 2010 Western Conference Finals. Allow me to give you some important context. Kobe and the Shaq-less Lakers were on their way to winning back-to-back NBA titles (Kobe's fourth and fifth titles). They were facing the Phoenix Suns in a critical road game. With the chance to advance and face their longtime rivals, the Boston Celtics, in the NBA Finals for the second time in three years, the Lakers were hoping to end the series in six games. It seemed ironic that Kobe was back in Phoenix, the place where the Lakers were shamefully eliminated from the playoffs in 2007. On top of that, Kobe was playing opposite Steve Nash. Even though he never won

Twenty-four Claims and the Polarization of Otherworldly Greatness 129

an NBA title, Nash was a two-time MVP. In both 2006 and 2007, Nash had bested Bryant for the league's top regular season honor. To add some intrigue to the narrative, Kobe was also facing his nemesis Raja Bell, and one the great wing men of the era in Grant Hill. The stage was set for Kobe Bryant to perform, and the hated Celtics were waiting in the wings.

For the most part, the game was nip and tuck as the Lakers consistently maintained a five-to-ten-point lead. As usual, Kobe got what he wanted on the offensive end. Phoenix did not have an answer for Bryant as he was one his way to another 35-plus-point night. I was not paying much attention to the score because I was sure the Lakers would somehow leave Phoenix with a victory. I mean, the Lakers were supposed to win because they had the greatest closer in history on their team. However, predictable as it was, what stuck out to me was the way in which Kobe shut the door on the Suns. As he was being guarded by Hill and anyone else who dared to switch out on him, Bryant made every perimeter shot known to man. He hit jump shots from every angle possible. He hit one from behind the goal. He hit a tough one-hander from beyond the free-throw line. He hit shots off one foot, and others off two feet. The last shots that Bryant hit were one where he reversed back the other way against two defenders, and the other a deep two-point jump shot with Hill's hands squarely in his face after he had pump-faked Hill twice in front of the Suns bench. Both clutch jump shots were amazing for two reasons. First, Grant Hill and his Suns teammates knew Bryant was taking those shots, so they defended him as if they knew what the Lakers had drawn up. And second, while not actual three-point shots, those two off-balance jump shots were deep enough to say that Bryant was awfully close to the three-point line. Both shots were heartbreaking to the Suns and their heckling fans. Heck, those shots broke my heart, and I was rooting for the Lakers to win. Bryant put on a shooting display for the ages on his way to playing in his seventh NBA Finals.

In terms of gauging the polarizing greatness of Kobe Bryant, the NBA legend, it is fitting to give an overview of what he had to overcome in a truly short period of time. Between the years of 2003 and 2007, Kobe was faced with an array of difficulties. The Los Angeles Lakers were no longer NBA champions. The working relationship between Shaq and Kobe was worsening by the day, as both superstars blamed each other for their losing to the San Antonio Spurs in the 2003 playoffs. Bryant continued to believe Shaq was lazy and did not put the time in the gym to keep himself in basketball shape. O'Neal missed the first 12 games of the

2002–03 season recovering from toe surgery. He was sidelined with hallux rigidus, a degenerative arthritis issue in his toe. He waited the whole summer until just before training camp for the surgery and explained, "I got hurt on company time, so I'll heal on company time."[5] O'Neal debated whether to have a more invasive surgery that would have kept him out an additional three months, but he opted against a more involved procedure. The Lakers started the season with a record of 11–19. At the end of the season, the Lakers had fallen to the fifth seed and failed to reach the Finals in 2003. Things were not going well for the Lakers and things were worsening between Shaq and Kobe.

In preparation for the 2003–04 season, the Lakers decided to bolster their roster by adding perennial All-Stars Gary Payton and Karl Malone. Even as Kobe was now playing with three aging superstars, his overall basketball game was still on the rise. Just as he had done over the course of his seven years with the Lakers, Kobe improved his basketball skills by way of summer workouts and practice. By the looks of things, the new-look Lakers were playing the game with a renewed sense of urgency. The "Big Four" seemed to be in sync. Even though the Shaq-Kobe feud brewed around the team's goal of winning a fourth NBA title in five years, the Lakers looked the early-season favorites to win it all. Lurking in the dark shadows of what could have been a historic season for the Lakers was Kobe's sexual assault charge. I am not saying that the situation in Denver ruined the Lakers season. Kobe still performed at a high level in the regular season and the playoffs. What I am saying is that the combination of the assault charges, which led to serious marital issues, an ever-growing tension with Shaq, and the pressure of winning another title, was, to say the very least, a lot for Bryant to deal with. Even as history records that the assault case in Eagle, Colorado was dropped because the accuser did not want to testify, the damage that situation caused was unmeasurable. During a fourteen-month span in 2003 and 2004, Kobe's life as a free man, his professional basketball career, and his marriage were all in limbo.

Obviously, things did not go as planned when the Lakers lost to the Detroit Pistons in the 2004 NBA Finals. The Shaq-Kobe feud had reached an all-time high as both superstars underperformed on the game's highest stage. Shaq and Kobe failed as individuals and as one of the most dominant duos in NBA history. It also did not help that starting power forward

---

5. McT, "Shaq vs. Kobe," para. 33.

Karl Malone was injured and could not help the team much. Malone was an important part of the Lakers squad. If Malone had been healthy during the NBA Finals, the outcome might have been different. There was no way on God's green earth that the Pistons were supposed to beat the Lakers. Watching Kobe and Shaq walk off the Pistons' home court in separate areas, I knew then that the Shaq and Kobe era was over in Los Angeles. Unfortunately, the level of disgruntlement between the two superstars grew over time. The 2003–04 NBA year would be Shaq and Kobe's last year as teammates. Shaq was traded to the Miami Heat and Kobe signed a long-term contract extension with the Lakers. As expected, Kobe was blamed for the superstars' break-up. The rumor was that Kobe went to the Lakers ownership and demanded that Shaq and himself be split up, either by trade or some other type of executive decision. The truth is that the Lakers' brass decided to keep the younger Bryant and make a basketball commitment to the upside of his basketball potential. Even Bryant claims that while his skill set had reached its zenith in 2004, his overall basketball game had yet to reach its full potential. The Lakers knew that Kobe's best years were in front of him.

During the 2004–05 season, the Lakers starting five consisted of Bryant, Chucky Atkins, Caron Butler, Lamar Odom, and Chris Mihm. The Lakers replaced nine-time title-winning coach Phil Jackson, with two-time title-winner Rudy Tomjanovich. Tomjanovich had guided the Hakeem Olajuwon-led Houston Rockets to back-to-back titles in the NBA's Jordan-less years of 1994 and 1995. The deprived Lakers amassed a dismal 33–49 regular season record. They did not make the playoffs. Statistically speaking, Kobe had a decent year. He averaged 28 points, 6 assists, 6 rebounds, 1 block, and 1 steal per game. By Kobe's standards, these are acceptable numbers. The problem for Kobe was the 49 losses and not making the playoffs. Another disappointing part of the season took place of Christmas Day as the Lakers lost a close game in overtime to the Miami Heat. Because this nationally televised game represented the first volume of Shaq-versus-Kobe, it was the most hyped regular-season game in NBA history. Kobe scored a game-high 42 points, Shaq fouled out in the 4th quarter, and the Heat edged the Lakers by two points. Kobe missed a last-second three-point shot that would have won the game. Kobe got a little personal revenge on Dwyane Wade in 2009 when he hit a last-second game-winner over his outstretched hands in a game between the Lakers and the Heat in Los Angeles.

Again, I was always looking to see how the great Bryant would respond to adversity. He seemed like he was made to take an earthly licking and keep on spiritually ticking. I remember when Dwyane Wade accidentally broke Kobe's nose during the 2012 NBA All-Star Game. Kobe made a quick move past Wade and Wade grabbed him from behind as he was ascending to score the basketball. I thought the play was dirty and unsportsmanlike, especially for an All-Star Game. Kobe did not say one word about the incident with Wade. Whether he was offended by the hard foul or not, he never said a word. Unlike Kobe, Wade was not known for competing hard in All-Star Games. Wade openly criticized Bryant after the 2011 All-Star Game in Los Angeles, stating after the game that he could tell Kobe really wanted to win the MVP. Following the incident with Wade in 2012, Kobe had to wear a face mask for eleven games. Over that stretch, Kobe averaged 31.1 points per game. Perhaps his most impressive game came against Wade and the star-studded Miami Heat. The game took place at the Staples Center. Scoring 32 points despite matching up with Wade, Shane Battier, and LeBron James, Kobe led the Lakers to a convincing victory over the Heat. Although the Heat ended up winning the NBA Championship that year, Bryant put on a shooting clinic against his rivals. With a sense of curiosity and revenge, Kobe relished the opportunity to compete against the three-headed monster of Wade, James, and Chris Bosh. Most important, Kobe responded to the adversity of having a broken nose by playing at a remarkably high level while wearing a protective face mask. This was not an easy endeavor. He responded like the warrior-champion he was.

Speaking of Bryant being a warrior-champion, I recently read where Hall-of-Fame guard Gary Payton stated that Michael Jordan was a better scorer and a greater player than Bryant.[6] While I am not sure why a defensive-minded point guard who played in his prime during the 1990s would make a comparison between Jordan and Bryant, I am sure that people are entitled to their own opinion about anything that is relevant to them and their context in life. Payton played against Jordan in the 1996 NBA Finals, and he played with Bryant during the 2003–04 NBA season. While I do not agree with Payton, I respect his basketball opinion. As a historian of the NBA, I would like to list the reasons why I believe Bryant eclipsed and surpassed Jordan.

1. Bryant scored more career regular-season points than Jordan.
2. Bryant scored more career All-Star-Game points than Jordan.

6. Mehdi, "Jordan Is a Better Scorer."

3. Bryant's highest scoring game of 81 was 12 points better than Jordan's highest-scoring game of 69.
4. Bryant was a much better perimeter shooter than Jordan.
5. Bryant was a better ball-handler than Jordan.
6. Bryant had more career assists than Jordan.
7. Bryant made more All-NBA Teams than Jordan (First, Second, Third, and All-Defensive Teams combined).
8. Considered by many to be the most skilled player in the history of the NBA, Bryant was superior to Jordan in overall skill set.
9. Bryant was a better free-throw shooter than Jordan.
10. Bryant played in more All-Star Games than Jordan.
11. Bryant had more 60-point games than Jordan.
12. Bryant worked harder at his craft than Jordan did.
13. Bryant played against greater competition at the two-guard and small forward positions than Jordan.
14. Bryant played against a greater array of athletic shooting guards and small forwards than Jordan. And he surpassed them all.
15. Bryant was more creative on the offensive end and a greater shotmaker than Jordan.
16. Bryant was a greater clutch player, hitting more game-winning shots than Jordan did.
17. Even as both led their teams to two Olympic gold medals, Bryant played in a more competitive Olympic environment than Jordan did.
18. Bryant was a much better three-point shooter than Jordan.
19. Bryant had better offensive footwork than Jordan.
20. Whereas Jordan never won an NBA Championship without his superstar sidekick Scottie Pippen, Bryant won multiple NBA Championships with *and without* multiple superstar sidekicks.

7

Kobe's Sixth Championship Ring
Inspiring the World and the Lakers

IF KOBE DID NOT achieve his goal of winning eight NBA Championships, he would have been OK with matching Jordan's six rings. He desperately wanted to achieve his second three-peat with a new crop of Lakers teammates, but he fell short in the 2011 NBA Playoffs as the Lakers were swept in four games by the Dallas Mavericks in the 2011 Western Conference Semifinals. After winning five championship rings as a player, I believe Kobe won another type of championship ring. I call this ring THE WORLD INSPIRATION RING. Kobe inspired the world in ways known and unknown. As I stated in the introduction, I would place Bryant alongside Muhammad Ali in terms of gauging the type of effect Kobe had on the world. Like Ali and every other human being who has walked this earth, Bryant was not perfect. Like Ali in the sport of boxing, Kobe did not have a perfect record in basketball. But very much like Ali, Kobe found a way to inspire millions of people with both his work ethic and his philosophical worldview. Towards the end of his NBA playing days, Kobe seemed to have a change of heart in regards to his life's goals.

Whereas he once was hell-bent on surpassing Jordan to become the world's greatest-ever basketball player, Kobe now began to focus more on helping and caring for people. He used the word "fickle" to describe his desire to be the greatest basketball player ever. I wonder what led him to the revelation of wanting to inspire the world in life over against being called the greatest basketball player ever. Maybe he realized that winning his fifth NBA title was more than enough to declare him the GOAT. Outside of Bill Russell during his tenure with the Celtics, no other NBA superstar had won multiple titles with different star sidekicks. Maybe Kobe began to see the proverbial light at the end of his NBA career tunnel. Maybe in some privatized kind of way, Bryant began to catch glimpses of his own mortality. Lest we forget, Kobe had a personal relationship with his Creator God.

Just as Kobe inspired the world with his work ethic and the way he lived his life, in his death he inspired the 2020 Los Angeles Lakers to win their seventeenth title. Under the leadership of LeBron James and Anthony Davis, the Lakers won four consecutive playoff series in an isolated location in Florida. While I do question the wholehearted legitimacy of playing games with no fans away from the traditional home/visitor playoff format, my heart rejoices at the fact that the Lakers drew enough inspiration from Kobe to help propel them over the top. Again, it seemed like the whole season was dedicated to the life and legacy of Bryant. But it was not easy. Whether you are a diehard Lakers fan or a diehard Kobe Bryant fan, it was downright difficult to process the game of basketball in Los Angeles. The city, the fans, and the keynote organization in the NBA had just lost their greatest basketball player.

At times emotions took over the Lakers organization and roster, but the players acted as if Bryant's spiritual presence was with them during their championship run. LeBron and AD consistently made references to Kobe being in the building. Bryant's presence in the Lakers' building only meant that the entire organization carried Kobe's spirit with them as they tried to emulate what Kobe would have done. I recall Anthony Davis hitting the game-winning shot in Game 2 of the Western Conference Finals against the streaking Denver Nuggets. After hitting the clutch shot and falling to the ground, Davis shouted, "We know he's looking down on us. I know Vanessa is proud of us, [Kobe] was a big brother to us. We did it for him."[1] After winning the NBA Championship, I noticed several Lakers crying. I am sure their tears were ones of joy (winning) and mourning (pain). I read where images of Kobe were included in the state-of-the-art championship rings that were given to the players and members of the Lakers organization. I would like to think the inspiration of Kobe Bryant helped push the Lakers over the Miami Heat in the 2020 NBA Finals. During the 2020 championship celebration, LeBron James said,

1. Brow, "Anthony Davis Dedicates NBA Finals Win," para. 2.

"It's always special to represent someone that meant so much, not only to the game but obviously to the Lakers organization for 20-plus years. . . . For us to honor him, being on the floor, this is what it's all about."[2]

Even today, over two years removed from the helicopter accident, millions of people continue to mourn Kobe's death because of his greatness. Being better was not Kobe's goal. Greater greatness as founded in the embodiment of more forms of helping people and inspiring people was his ultimate goal. It is amazing to me how the very people who claim to know Bryant or be his "big brother" are the very ones who wrongly interpret the most important passions in his life. We sometimes forget that Kobe grew as a person and in his world stature. He went from being fickle in terms of wanting to match Jordan, to being a man of purpose in terms of wanting to inspire others to greatness. Kobe realized he had a far greater purpose beyond the game of basketball.

Speaking of big brother's words, whoever said that the little brother could not eclipse the big brother? Who wrote the rulebook stating that the little brother could not be better than the big brother? In a conversation with a friend of mine, I asked him why he did not think Kobe was better Jordan at basketball. My friend's reason? "Kobe looked up to Jordan." My response: "Is that it?" He said "Yeah" and walked out of the room. What cultural constitution includes the statement that the student cannot eclipse the teacher? More important, who said God is not able to create a basketball player who is better than Michael Jordan, the one who has been universally lauded by those in his generation as the best ever? Lest we forget, Jordan, the little brother himself, eclipsed his big brother Larry Jordan in many ways as they grew up together in New York and North Carolina.

While I do not agree with the claim of Jordan being the single best player ever, I do understand the importance of generational greatness. I understand how the game has evolved from one generation to the next. Another word for generation is "decade." But in order for us to pick and choose who is the single greatest of all the generations, the argument must be more factual than opinionated. The "little brother" identification seems more like a cultural death sentence that insinuates that the little brother will never ascend to the level of the big brother. Kobe was the bridge between Michael Jordan and LeBron James. He challenged both players on the court and played well against both generational talents. I

---

2. Brow, "Anthony Davis Dedicates NBA Finals Win," para. 4.

believe Jordan got what he wanted because his opponents feared him. Kobe had to be creative in the totality of his offensive splendor. I also believe "little brother" Kobe surpassed "big brother" Jordan in terms of the totality of Bryant's on-the-court splendor. But there's no question about it: both were the absolute best players of their respective decades.

One of most powerful ways Kobe Bryant inspired his NBA colleagues was through his unique ability to respond to life's most difficult moments. The best thing we can say about Kobe is he inspired the world. The worst thing we can say about Kobe is he was an imperfect human being. Kobe redefined what it meant to wear the purple and gold by playing for the organization for twenty consecutive years. In other words, you do not let the best-ever talent in the game go to another team and win championships. There is a good reason why the Lakers' brass saw fit for Kobe to be a lifelong Laker. In their wildest dreams, they could not imagine Kobe doing for other teams what he did for the Lakers.

While I was aware of the legendary Hall of Famers that had worn the Lakers uniform in the past, I confess I did not become a Lakers fan until they drafted Kobe Bryant. I was a Philadelphia 76ers and a Detroit Pistons fan. I think the 1983 Philadelphia 76ers, the 2001 Los Angeles Lakers, and the 1989 Detroit Pistons are the greatest basketball teams in NBA history. The 1996 Chicago Bulls, 1986 Boston Celtics, and the 1987 Los Angeles Lakers are also all-time great teams. Kobe's connection to the first tier of organizations is that he lived in Philadelphia at age fourteen, helped to defeat the Sixers in the 2001 NBA Finals, and he won his first NBA All-Star Game MVP in Philadelphia. Kobe was a member of the NBA champion Lakers that posted an NBA-record fifteen consecutive wins in the 2001 playoffs. Lastly, the Detroit Pistons were a thorn in Kobe's side as they handed him his first NBA Finals loss in 2004. What I realized over the years in watching professional basketball was that the greatest teams are the ones that inspired other teams to championship greatness. One example of this philosophy is the Detroit Pistons referring to Larry Bird's Boston Celtics as teachers. Inspiration comes in many different forms.

Not only did Kobe inspire the world, but he was also an inspirational teacher. His actions and words taught people how to be inspired. He taught people what it meant to be inspired. He showed what inspiration looked like. Most importantly, Kobe inspired people by the way he played basketball. To me, Kobe's scoring 60 points in his last game was more inspirational than his 81-point game in 2006. Despite the twenty-one-point difference, I would choose Kobe's 60-point night because nothing was at stake, or so people had thought. The Lakers were out of playoff contention. Obviously, everybody wanted to attend Kobe's last game in a Lakers uniform. Kobe's final game was the best final game for any athlete in NBA history. It was also the hottest ticket in the world at that time. If you did not purchase a ticket online, stand in line at the Staples Center days in advance, or pour out an unfathomable amount of money just to see the game from lower-tier seats, then you had to watch it on television. The fact that Kobe found inspiration within himself and drew inspiration from the crowd was surreal. In the shadows of Kobe's historic performance, four amazing things happened on that night. First, Kobe's family got to see him turn back the hands of time. They got to see him play at a high level one last time while celebrating his historic career. Second, Kobe scored 60 points in his last game. No athlete in history has ever scored as many points in their last career game as Kobe did. Third, as he did numerous times throughout his career, Kobe took over the game in the 4th quarter and hit the game-winning shot.

Kobe inspired the NBA and the world when he led the Lakers back from a thirty-one-point deficit to beat the Dallas Mavericks in a game that took place in 2002. Kobe scored 21 of his 27 points in the 4th quarter. Kobe hit the game-winning shot that gave the Lakers a 105–103 victory. The Lakers were down by 27 points at the start of the 4th quarter. It was the greatest comeback in Lakers history. As Kobe walked back to the bench at the game's end, Coach Phil Jackson look like he was in a state of disbelief. Kobe and Phil gave each other a victorious high-five as they headed into the Lakers' tunnel. When it came to basketball, Kobe specialized in the miraculous. While he was not the author of miracles (that would be God Almighty), Kobe seemed to always be in the middle of those miraculous moments where the Lakers would somehow find a way to win the basketball game. Bryant often led the Lakers back from deficits. Not only was Bryant one of the greatest clutch players in the history of the game, but he was also passionate about playing well when the stakes were highest.

As one who cried every time I lost a basketball game, I was inspired when Kobe and Derek Fisher cried like brokenhearted children after they lost to the San Antonio Spurs in 2003 Western Conference Semifinals, ending their run of three straight NBA Championships. I could tell they both were deeply wounded as those two, more than any of the other Lakers, were motivated to win a fourth straight NBA title. Kobe cried when the Lakers lost to the Detroit Pistons in the 2004 NBA Finals, and he cried when his Lakers lost to the Boston Celtics in the 2008 NBA Finals. Kobe also cried at the press conference, on stage with Vanessa, addressing the Colorado fiasco. After all, Kobe was a human being. I was always inspired when Kobe demonstrated his passion for winning in both basketball and life. I was especially inspired when the Lakers played passionate basketball during the playoffs. Most of the time Bryant's on-the-court greatness was the inspirational source of that passion, which normally led to the Lakers winning NBA Championships.

In 2006, Bryant's passion was on full display again when he went on yet another historic scoring run against the Mavericks. This time the Lakers jumped on the Mavericks from the tip as Kobe started off hot and remained hot throughout the 3rd quarter. At the end of the 3rd quarter, the score was 97–61. The Lakers seemed determined to send the Mavericks a message. Led by Bryant's offensive genius, the Lakers blew out the hapless Mavericks in a game that was never really close. Mavericks head coach Avery Johnson could not come up with a game plan to stop Kobe. They put their most athletically gifted defenders on Bryant, but to no avail. Jerry Stackhouse, Marquise Daniels, Josh Howard, Keith Van Horn, Devin Harris, and Jason Terry all attempted to guard Bryant at various points in the game. Dirk Nowitzki ended up guarding Bryant a few times as well. Again, to no avail. Kobe's first head coach in the NBA, Dell Harris, was an assistant coach with the Mavericks. I am sure Harris's presence on the Mavericks' bench added intrigue to the game and extra motivation for Bryant. During the early years of Bryant's career, Harris did not give him much playing time. Bryant described those years under Harris as the toughest years of his NBA career. Similar to what then-Seattle SuperSonics head coach George Karl did to Kobe in his first All-Star Game in 1998, Harris benched Kobe for different reasons. Kobe never forgot about the tough lessons of playing under a coach who did not believe in him. With Harris in mind, Kobe took that game versus the Mavericks a little more serious than usual. In leading the Lakers to an insurmountable lead, Kobe himself outscored the entire Mavericks team 62 to 61. Kobe rested during the 4th quarter. Who knows what Bryant's point total would have been if he had played the last quarter.

I also recall Bryant inspiring the NBA and the world in his 65-point game against the Portland Trail Blazers at the Staples Center in 2007. This particular game was his highest-scoring game within the four straight games in which he scored 50 or more points. In tying the record of the great Wilt Chamberlain, Bryant was exceptionally proficient in his field-goal shooting. He hit 23 of his 39 shot attempts, 8 of his 12 three-point shots, and 11 of his 12 free-throw attempts. Obviously, Kobe was on fire in terms of his offensive efficiency, but what stuck out to me about the game was Bryant's otherworldly ability to make tough shots. Brandon Roy was assigned as Bryant's primary defender. The array of moves that Kobe put on Roy and the other Blazers defenders defied description. Bryant's shot selection was not the greatest, but he wanted to win the game so darn bad. Even in taking difficult shots with multiple hands in his face, balanced and off-balance, it seemed as if Bryant willed those shots into the basket.

Down late in the game, the Lakers needed Bryant to play hero ball just so they would have a chance of winning. And as he had done so many times in his illustrious career, Kobe delivered. He delivered in such a way that the broadcasters were at a loss for words in trying to describe Bryant's performance. The one play I see clearly in my mind is the one where Bryant was pinned deep in the right corner in front of the Lakers bench. Kobe took the pass. He then spun one way, only to be cut off by a Trail Blazers defender. This is where the miraculous took place. With very little space to maneuver his body, Kobe somehow found a way to spin back toward his right shoulder and raise up for a deep jump shot. Not only did Bryant find a way to walk a tight rope in making sure his feet were behind the three-point line, but his eyes did not find the rim until after the ball had left his hands. Bryant made an impossible shot look normal, as if he was supposed to make the shot. Watching the game on television, I was rendered both dumbfounded and speechless. As usual, Bryant led the Lakers to an overtime victory. I wondered what mythological universe Bryant was operating from on that mystical night. Bryant scored 33 of his 65 points in the 4th quarter and overtime.

Bryant's 61-point masterpiece at Madison Square Garden was one of his most spectacular scoring efforts on the road. I recall Bryant starting the game with a hot hand. He hit the majority of his 1st-quarter shots from the perimeter. Ever the shooting guard, Bryant made jump shots from all over the court. The famed Garden was put into a fan frenzy from the beginning of the game. Oftentimes veering away from the organized Triangle offense, Kobe played 1-on-1 with whomever ended up guarding him. He made shots with and without hands in his face. He made layups, dunks, and free throws in the 1st half. It did not take a rocket scientist to figure out that Kobe was headed toward the record books. Kobe was efficient as ever from the field as he scored close to 30 points in the first half. This was nothing new to Kobe. He was known for having mind-boggling scoring explosions. He could explode on the offensive end of the court at any given time. What struck me about his 61-point night in New York was the way Kobe was received by Knicks fans. The fans would either respond with the usual, high-toned ooohs and aaahs, or they would simply chant "MVP!!! MVP!!!" when Kobe would make one spectacular play after another. I was blown away at Kobe's creativity on the offensive end. He scored with flair. He scored when it seemed like the shooting angles were blocked. He scored from mid-range areas, and he scored from beyond the three-point arc. Long-time Knicks fan Spike Lee was beside himself. Sitting in his usual front-row seat, Spike was animated to no end. In preparing to shoot his documentary entitled *Kobe Doin' Work*, Spike was most pleased to see Kobe erupt for 61 points in person. Bryant was the type of basketball player that Knicks fans had dreamed about. They would have loved to have him play for the Knicks.

The climactic moment of Bryant's offensive show took place midway through the 4th quarter. Bryant captured the ball ten or so feet from the left corner of the free-throw line. Right in front of Spike Lee, Bryant then took two dribbles (one a stutter-step dribble) in a straight line up toward the free-throw area, pump faked his defender into the air, and quickly spun back left to free himself. With a dazzling display of basketball footwork, Kobe rose up for a smooth free-throw-line jumper. As Bryant was inching closer (passing Jordan in the process) to breaking Bernard King's record for the most points scored in the Garden by any player (61), the crowd went into yet another loud frenzy. Spike Lee rose up out of his seat in euphoria. He was celebrating the greatness of Bryant in both admiration and humor. That particular move was one for the ages. After the game, coach Phil Jackson told Kobe to let him know the next time he felt inspired to score a massive amounts of points.

As a watcher of the game of basketball, I was always enamored with how other teams' fans would respond to Kobe's unstoppable displays of offensive superiority. My favorite place to watch Kobe play, away from the Staples Center, was in Atlanta. Atlanta is the melting pot of Black people in the South. With the Atlanta Hawks being an Eastern Conference team, Kobe would normally play one game a year in Atlanta. In watching the highlights of some of Kobe's more animated games in Atlanta, I saw the Hawks' fans lose their everlasting minds (literally and figuratively) in response to Kobe's scoring genius. Kobe's basketball genius was Broadway entertainment to them, theater almost. With Atlanta being a party town made up of socialites and club-hoppers, they would normally drink alcohol while watching Hawks games. For Hawks fans, there was no greater show in the NBA than Kobe Bean Bryant and the Los Angeles Lakers. When the Lakers came to Atlanta, it was the hottest ticket in town. In the midst of absorbing Kobe's razzle and dazzle, I saw Hawks fans slap hands with one another in admiration, laugh frantically in disbelief, rise to their feet with their drinks in hand every time Bryant touched the ball, and shout to the heavens when Kobe would score. Like most NBA fans, the Hawks would have rather seen Kobe miss a shot than see other Lakers make a shot. Kobe's games in Atlanta were like after-hours parties. People dressed as if they were going out for an important social occasion. And as usual, Kobe always performed at a high level for those who were in attendance. In knowing that the fans were there to see him, Kobe tried his best to never let anyone down. The atmosphere was always electric when Kobe visited Atlanta. I am sure it was like that in other NBA cities as well. The Kobe show was the greatest show in the world of basketball.

There was one particular game in 2000 where the Lakers were playing the Houston Rockets on the road. Kobe led all scorers that night with 45 points. Kobe was red-hot from the field, and he abused the Rockets perimeter defenders. He shot 20 for 26 from the field. Kobe allowed the Triangle offense to flow through his jump-shooting prowess. He did not seem interested in getting the basketball down low to Shaq. I am sure there were numerous times when Shaq and Kobe would decide who was going to carry the offensive load. During the course of an eighty-two-game season there were ample opportunities for both superstars to shine. Kobe seemed to enjoy establishing himself as the first option in the Lakers' Triangle offense. Even though the goal was to get the ball down low to the dominant O'Neal, Kobe always managed to take his fair share of shots. During this particular game, Bryant was making shots from every angle. Even though it might have frustrated coach Jackson and O'Neal, there was nothing either of them could say with Kobe hitting shots at a high clip.

However, what really caught my basketball attention was the play-by-play analysis of former Rockets great Phil Ford. I was familiar with the young Bryant's ability to take over games. What I was not familiar with was Ford's enthusiastic way of calling games. Ford consistently praised Kobe for his play on both ends of the court. With Bryant carrying the Lakers' offense during this particular game, it allowed the boisterous Ford to both lament the Rockets' defense and celebrate the young Bryant. At the end of the 4th quarter, the game was extremely close. With the game on the line, Ford knew the ball would end up in Kobe's hands. He was hoping Cuttino Mobley could do a better job of defending Bryant. Bryant caught the ball at the top of the foul line. The shot clock was running down, and the Rockets were not double teaming Bryant. To Ford's dismay, he begin yelling out to the Rockets bench that, "He (Mobley) gonna need help. He gonna need help. He's gonna need help!" Kobe took two dribbles to his left and raised up over Mobley. To the dismay of Ford on the sidelines, Kobe calmly nailed the jump shot. Ford was beside himself. He concluded his basketball tirade by exclaiming: "Boy, he's cold-blooded, Bill. Whoo! That young man can play some basketball."[3] Ford had seen enough. Bryant's greatness had sent him into a frenzy too, albeit a religious one.

In terms of leading his team to victory, I believe Bryant's most important show of all-around skill actually took place in Game 3 of the 2010 NBA Finals versus the Boston Celtics. No need to educate the world on the history of the Celtics-Lakers rivalry. I will get straight to the juicy details. While this particular game does not get a lot of airplay in ESPN and YouTube, it serves as the most important game of the most important NBA Finals that Bryant participated in. With the series tied 1–1, the Lakers had lost home-court advantage and they had to play the next three Finals games in Boston. In this critical game, Bryant ended up with 29 points and 7 assists against a stifling Boston defense. But it was not his scoring that caught my attention. I was impressed with his dazzling display of leadership on and off the court. In addition to coaching his teammates during the timeouts about what they must do to steal back home-court advantage, Bryant was dominant offensively and defensively. He blocked many shots in the paint, stole the ball on many occasions, finished beautifully in the paint, knocked down his long-range jump shots, rebounded the ball, caught alley-oops at the rim, sacrificed his body on numerous hustle plays, and he made the clutch shots at the end of the game. Bryant played with a ferocious sense of urgency, for he knew the importance of winning the all-important Game 3. Losing Game 3 would mean the Celtics could end the series at home in five games. I am sure Bryant did not want a repeat of the 2004 NBA Finals when they were eliminated by the Detroit Pistons in five games. The historical significance of the Lakers winning Game 3 of the 2010 NBA Finals is that the win put the Lakers up 2–1. This slight advantage allowed the Lakers to

3. JL Hoops, "2000 Lakers VS Rockets," 1:31:17–1:31:28.

win the last two games of the series and gave Bryant the all-important fifth NBA title with the organization that traded Vlade Divac for his services. As always, Bryant played the game with an immeasurable amount of passion. His performance was inspiring to say the very least.

Even though he was wearing a Team USA uniform, Kobe inspired the world again when he led a group of NBA All-Stars to Olympic gold in 2008. In representing the United States in athletic competition, Kobe wore jersey number 10. While many speculated that Kobe's number 10 was a way of one-upping Michael Jordan's Olympic number 9, the truth is that Kobe wanted to honor all-time soccer great Lionel Messi. Because of Messi's European roots and his soccer genius, he was one of Kobe's greatest inspirations. It can be argued that Kobe Bryant was both the most important basketball Olympian in history and the greatest European player to ever play in the NBA. I say that because Kobe grew up in Italy. With his dad, Joe Bryant, playing for a number of professional clubs throughout Italy, Kobe lived there with family until he was fourteen years old. Growing up in Italy, Kobe learned the fundamentals of basketball in the European fashion. Kobe's unique blend of basketball skills was tailor-made for the international game. Because he was superior on the offensive and defensive ends of the court, Kobe used the aggressive nature of the international game to his advantage. Kobe's knack for making three-point shots, two-point shots, and finishing at the rim complemented his ability to put all-out pressure on the ball-handler. Kobe was Team USA's best defender and their most outstanding scorer. Kobe was also the team's hardest worker. He was the first one working out in the weight room, and he was the last one to leave the basketball gymnasium after practice.

As the team's top perimeter defensive player, Kobe was also the team's best individual scorer. His main focuses were playing great defense and leading his team to the gold medal. More important than winning gold, Kobe inspired his Olympic teammates to be better basketball players. Because his teammates witnessed firsthand Kobe working out in various places and at the earliest of hours, they increased their own workouts. Some worked out with him. Kobe's work ethic was just as great as his performances on the basketball court. Kobe was just as dominant competing in FIBA tournaments as he was competing in the NBA. Kobe played the international game of basketball.

The reason why preparation was so important to Bryant is because preparation created both a strategy to compete and the incentive to dominate the opponent. In order for domination to take place, Kobe knew that he and LeBron James had to be on the same page. Bryant believed in leading by example in both practice and in the actual game, always challenging Team USA to be the best version of themselves.

During the Blue/White intersquad scrimmage before Team USA began playing in the FIBA Qualifying event in Las Vegas 2007, Kobe showed LeBron firsthand what the Mamba Mentality looked like. Just as Magic and Jordan played opposite one another during those Dream Team scrimmages in 1992, Kobe and LeBron were on opposite sides for the tune-up scrimmage. Both superstars played well in leading their respective teams in scoring. That was to be expected. Bryant and James were the two best players in the world. Both teams went back and forth exchanging dunks and leads. As the scrimmage came down to the waning moments, Kobe showcased his infamous clutch gene. With James guarding him, Bryant scored on three consecutive possessions to give the Blue squad a one-point lead. Jason Kidd put the White squad ahead with a late bucket and then Kobe did what he had done so many times in his career. Now with the 6'9" Tayshawn Prince guarding him, Kobe sized him up with the clock running down. After he took a couple dribbles, Bryant stopped on a dime, pump-faked Prince one time and went up for his patent jump shot. The basketball swished through the white net, just as Kobe had planned. LeBron had a chance to win the game at the end with Kobe guarding him. James's shot rimmed out. The Blue team won the scrimmage. Kobe had hit the game-winning shot and the tables were set for Team USA to resume its winning ways. After Kobe hit the last jump shot over Prince, the color commentator who was calling the game live said with obvious excitement: "You knew it was coming. You just couldn't stop it. . . . They knew who the best player on the planet was."[4]

What we do not hear much about is the historical context which undergirded Kobe's matriculation to Team USA Basketball. Unlike the 1992 Dream Team and the few teams that followed them, Kobe was not walking into a situation of dominance. He was not following a certain pattern of success. Team USA was not expected to blow everybody out by 50 points en route to Olympic gold. Unlike the Dream Team, Kobe's Redeem Team was not the heavy favorite to win gold in Beijing. Team USA had not won the Olympic gold medal since 2000. In 2002, Team USA finished a disappointing sixth place out of sixteen teams. In 2006, Team USA finished in third place of out of twenty-four teams. According

---

4. LjP24, "Kobe Bryant Game Winner," 0:12–0:24.

to many commentators and pundits, Team USA had fallen off the world basketball map. Some were saying that under the guiding hands of Jerry Colangelo and Mike Krzyzewski, Team USA had developed a culture of losing. The displeasure of not winning the gold medal at the 2004 Olympics (Team USA took third place out of twelve teams while losing three games) only made things worse. Colangelo and Krzyzewski knew that if things were to change, they would need to bring the best basketball player in the world on board Team USA: Kobe Bryant.

The steady development of world basketball had begun to catch up with USA basketball. Basketball was becoming a global sport and NBA basketball had grown a bit stagnant in its passion to play the best basketball in the world. Kobe Bryant was added to Team USA for the purpose of helping to transform the basketball culture from one of losing to one of winning. After all, Kobe Bryant was a winner. He came to Team USA a three-time NBA champion and the NBA's reigning MVP. He also came to Team USA hungry to win gold as his Los Angeles Lakers had recently lost the NBA Finals to the Boston Celtics in six games.

Kobe was hungry to win. Even as he was the greatest scorer in the NBA, Kobe's primary identification with Team USA was that of a defensive stopper and a hustle guy. LeBron James, Tracy McGrady, Vince Carter, Kevin Garnett, Dirk Nowitzki, and others have said Kobe was the single-greatest player they played against. Nowitzki also stated that Kobe could have won the 2008 Olympics by himself. Kobe showcased his value as basketball's premier clutch player when he took over the 2008 Gold Medal Game. While Dwyane Wade led Team USA with 27 points, Kobe scored 13 of his 20 in the 4th quarter alone, leaving the Spanish national team with no answer for his twisting drives or three-point swishes. Late in the 4th quarter, Coach Krzyzewski told Kobe he needed to see the Mamba Mentality to help Team USA pull out the gold medal victory.

Even though he was playing alongside NBA superstars, Kobe Bryant single-handedly put Team USA back on the world basketball map. He was the 2008 Olympic Team's superstar of superstars. Bryant played in the 2012 Olympics and helped Team USA win back-to-back gold medals. Including Team USA's gold medal in the 2007 FIBA qualifying tournament, Kobe won three gold medals while going undefeated in international competition. Quiet as kept, it can be argued that Kobe's performance in the 2007 FIBA tournament in Las Vegas was his greatest display of basketball dominance. It was then that Bryant very easily could have been at the peak of his basketball powers. With the addition of Bryant, Team USA instantly went from losers to winners. Along with a peak Bryant, Jason Kidd played a major role in the team's transformation as well. By way of affirming Kobe Bryant as the greatest basketball player ever, it is important to talk about what he did for USA Basketball. To me, Kobe is the greatest Olympic basketball player to ever wear the United States uniform. Bryant and others paved the way for the 2016 team to win a third straight gold medal, in the process reestablishing Team USA as the greatest basketball power in the world.

In addition to winning an Oscar, having murals erected and painted in his honor all over the world, being a published writer many times over, leading the Body Armour initiative, challenging the Jordan-led Gatorade movement (catapulting Kobe Inc. into a worldwide brand), and developing the Mamba and Mambacita Training Facility as his base for teaching the game of basketball to all those who needed assistance, Kobe inspired me personally when he confessed to his wife that he had committed adultery. I was already a basketball fan of Bryant. As a fan of cultural liberation and truth-telling, I wanted to see how the great Bryant would respond to adversity. I wanted to observe how he would conduct himself in basketball and in life, following the Denver situation. Kobe responded to those moments of adversity in the most inspirational of ways. In doing so, he reminded us yet again of what made him such a great ballplayer and human being.

My academic research and life experiences have taught me that the greatest are those who serve others with humility and who are like children. The greatest NBA player is the one who inspires others to greatness in their own lives without being narcissistic. This theory may or may not be a part of the ever-developing culture of sport. But certainly these particular descriptions lead us straight to Kobe Bean Bryant. He checked the box in all three categories. Kobe inspired the world by playing through injuries, through his own hard work, and through his YouTube interviews, speeches, presentations, comments, tweets, books, basketball camps, other types of training sessions, and promoting girls basketball, College women's basketball, and the WNBA.

Even though Kobe wanted to destroy his opponent on both ends of the basketball court, it seemed as if he was also providing a service to those who were watching him. When I use the word "service," I am implying that Kobe left room for future generations to be inspired by his work ethic and the way he played the game. Jordan, on the other hand, was obsessed with a certain type of basketball dominance that left no room whatsoever for anyone else to approach his throne. And his contemporaries fell for it hook, line, and sinker. Like Jordan, Kobe was ruthless and dark at times. But unlike Jordan, Kobe carried a spiritual light with him that enabled him to empower other basketball players to be the best versions of themselves on and off the court. Ever the supreme intellectual, Kobe provided James, Durant, Curry, Irving, Lillard, Jayson Tatum, Kawhi Leonard, Devin Booker, and future generations of NBA players the physiological blueprint to greater greatness within and beyond the game of basketball. This is the way Kobe served humanity and God. He gave back to the game without fear of someone surpassing him. These are the true stories that defined the unfamothable mythology of Kobe Bryant.

8

The Culture of Sport and Saying Goodbye to the Inspiration of Zoom

ONE OF THE THINGS that impressed me about Kobe was his ability to create the most unique basketball shoes on the market. Kobe's basketball shoes creatively symbolize his career. As one who was schooled in aesthetics, Kobe preferred the concept of Zoom over that of Air. Nike Zoom and Lunarlons give Kobe the flexibility to create the exact look and feel of the shoe. They also gave Kobe, the designer, the wiggle-room to play around with the inner sole of the shoe. According to Kobe, the concept of Air restricts the particulars of Kobe's creative design in that it limits what Nike can do to produce a nontraditional basketball shoe. When it came to creating the designs for a new low-top basketball shoe, Kobe believed in the sharing of ideas. Even as the high-top shoe followed his Achilles injury, this particular shoe was meant to emulate Muhammad Ali's boxing shoes. Always trying to tell a story, Kobe wanted to inspire people with his shoes. Like an artist who paints a picture or a musician who plays instruments or a singer who sings songs, Kobe saw the creation of new shoes as a journey within life. Because he believed that people create in some shape, form, or fashion, Kobe did not fear taking risks in designing his signature shoes. As one who is inspired by stories, all of Kobe's signature sneakers tell a story. Each shoe was meaningful to Kobe because they symbolized him looking forward to greater innovation and greater designs.

Kobe revolutionized the basketball shoe landscape in 2008 when he decided he decided that his next signature sneaker would be a low-top. Bryant's decision was evolutionary in scope because all basketball shoes at that time were either high-top or medium-high-top shoes. This was because the high-top provided much-needed support for the basketball player's ankles.

At the end of the day, Kobe did not have to fill anyone else's basketball shoes. He played the game of basketball at an elite, all-world level while wearing Adidas, Reebok, and Nike tennis shoes. Spike Lee was wrong in his playful assertion to Jordan that it must be the shoes. It ain't the shoes. It's the skill set within the individual game that matters. No one in the history of professional basketball had game like Kobe Bryant. The same way he created his own shoes, Kobe filled his own shoes with the way he played the game and the shoes he created for himself and others. While many will attempt to place Bryant below his idol Jordan because they feel like he intentionally mimicked him, the truth is that what Kobe did on the basketball court was done with his own God-given basketball abilities. Jordan did not physically help Kobe score any of his 33,643 total points. Kobe did that on his own within his own human body of basketball talent. . Nobody did anything for him. Kobe did what he was called by God to do on the basketball court because he was determined to be the best.

Let us not forget, Kobe won multiple championships playing in both Adidas (2000–02) and Nike (2009–10). Because Kobe was successful playing in different types of basketball shoes, I think both companies (Adidas and Nike) should collaborate on creating a collaborative Kobe basketball shoe. The name of this history-making shoe should be the Kobe Forever Inspiration Shoe. The fact that more NBA players play in Kobe's basketball sneakers than anyone else's means Kobe's shoes must be comfortable to the feet of the NBA athlete. There is a reason why NBA players are shelving out astronomical amounts of money just to have Kobe's basketball shoes in bulk stock. In the words of Bryant, "More so, if you are wearing it, we must be doing something right."[1]

Like many other sneaker-heads and ex-athletes, I am disappointed that the Bryant estate discontinued their shoe-producing relationship with Nike. While I am sure this is what Bryant himself wanted, I am equally sure why the media reported that Kobe's people were not pleased

---

1. Slade, "Interview," para. 6.

The Culture of Sport and Saying Goodbye to the Inspiration of Zoom   151

with Nike's unwillingness to give Bryant the same lifetime commitment that was given to Jordan and James. Where Kobe's shoe contract with Nike is concerned, I am sure that Vanessa will make the correct business decision in regards to the decision to continue making Kobe Bryant basketball shoes. Similar to the way the media and other basketball pundits have favored Jordan and James over Bryant, I am not surprised by Nike's decision. What we do not talk enough about is the fact that more NBA players wear Kobe Bryant sneakers than any other basketball sneaker in the world—Jordans included. The myth that Kobe only succeeded on the basketball court when he was wearing Nike shoes is totally false. Similar to the myth that Shaq would have won those three championships with other superstar sidekicks. I say that for two reasons. First, there is no way to actually prove it. This particular myth is a simple opinion based upon bias. And second, there was not a more gifted, talented, committed, and clutch player in the NBA during the 2000s than Kobe. In other words, there was not another player in the NBA that could have done what Bryant did as a Laker during those three-peat years.

    Most of the myths concerning Bryant's weaknesses, basketball shoes included, were designed to stop him from becoming the greatest player of all-time. No one wanted Bryant to surpass his idol Jordan as the G.O.A.T. because people had already determined there would never be a greater player than Jordan. When Kobe began to show some signs he could be headed in this direction, and when he publicly stated that his goal was to be the G.O.A.T., the whole dynamic of the G.O.A.T. conversation began to change. With Bryant being raised in Italy, one could argue that Kobe is the greatest European player of the all-time. Not only was Bryant the greatest basketball player in the history of the NBA, but he was also the greatest and most important basketball Olympian of all-time. In this vein, Kobe transcended the political culture of national and international basketball popularity with the way he played the game. Bryant's Olympic journey is an important part of his G.O.A.T. status.

    Speaking on the sometimes biased culture of professional basketball in the United States, it must be stated that Isiah Thomas of the Detroit Pistons and Dominique Wilkins of the Atlanta Hawks should have been named to the 1992 Dream Team. Simply put, that basketball team was an American celebration of the NBA in the 1980s. That team did not need specialists like John Stockton and Chris Mullins. They did not need the services of Christian Laettner either. Talent-wise and position-wise, the Dream Team was already far superior to any of the teams that would be competing against them in Barcelona. If they were going to include the greatest active NBA players of the 1980s, then there is no way that Thomas and Wilkins should have been excluded from the original Dream Team. Outside of Magic's five rings, Bird's three rings, and Jordan's two rings (at that time), Thomas's two rings would have placed him on top of the NBA Championship hierarchy and made him no worse than the fourth-overall selection of the Olympic Team.

Outside of Jordan, Magic, Bird, and Thomas, the rest of the 1992 Dream Team were all middle-of-the-pack Hall of Famers. None of them are considered all-time greats. None of them achieved superstar status (Pippen came the closest with six rings as Bulls' #2 option). None of them led their team to an NBA title. Even though Drexler (one) and Robinson (two) went on to win an NBA title, neither led their team to the title. With the Dream Team situation we can see how the culture of professional sports includes the presence of unwise decisions. Neither Patrick Ewing, Reggie Miller, Karl Malone, John Stockton, Chris Mullins, Charles Barkley became NBA champions or are all-time greats. Of all the 1992 Dream Team members, only Drexler and Robinson (in addition to the Big Three of Jordan, Magic, and Bird) went to win an NBA Championship. Neither Drexler nor Robinson are considered as all-time greats.

One of the most important lessons I have learned in life is that perception is not always truth, and truth is not always perception. It is more like a popular myth turned into a reality show. Theology is philosophy blended with history, the Bible, culture, and intellectual revelations. Mythology is fantasy turned into the truth for the purpose of establishing strong opinions as the foundation of weak truths. Because of society's fascination with the hypothetical realm of sports in general, and professional basketball in particular, people have been convinced that 90s-era Jordan is the greatest player in NBA history, being disrespectful of Bill Russell and others who have more NBA Championship rings than Jordan. Jordan's perfect 6-0 record in the NBA Finals is not the first of its kind. One could argue that Hakeem Olajuwon was the best player in the NBA during both his team's championship runs of 1993–94 and 1994–95. However, he never opposed Jordan in the NBA Finals. Jordan's teammate, Scottie Pippen, was the second-best player of the 1990s. Pippen won six titles with Jordan, and he took a Jordan-less Bulls team to the Eastern Conference Semifinals where the Bulls lost to the New York Knicks in seven games. Even without Jordan, the 1994 Bulls were still formidable.

This shows that Jordan was surrounded by a great team. He did not win those championships by himself.

To me, Pippen's greatest moments in the NBA were his leading the Bulls in 1994 and the Portland Trail Blazers to the 2000 Western Conference Finals, where they lost a heartbreaking Game 7 to the Los Angeles Lakers. Quiet as kept, Pippen came closer to winning an NBA Championship without Jordan than Jordan did without him. The reason why Pippen came the closest to basketball immortality is because he kept playing basketball beyond his years with the Bulls. There is a good reason why Pippen publicly laments losing to Kobe and Shaq's Lakers in the 2000 Western Conference Finals: he knew if he could lead the Trail Blazers past the Lakers and win an NBA Championship over the Pacers (without Jordan), he would be mentioned among the greatest players to ever play the game. One thing is for sure: Pippen's all-around game made Jordan's undefeated NBA Finals record more feasible. Pippen's lockdown defense on the opposing team's best perimeter player helped Jordan conserve his energy so he could score more.

Perhaps Hall of Famer Scottie Maurice Pippen is the preeminent voice of reason when it comes to placing Kobe Bryant over Michael Jordan as the greatest basketball player in NBA history. If anyone in the history of the game would have sufficient knowledge of this particular comparison/debate, it would be Pippen. I would easily take Pippen's basketball analysis over the likes of television analysts Stephen A. Smith, Max Kellerman, Skip Bayless, Shannon Sharpe, and Jalen Rose. A six-time NBA Champion, Pippen is one the greatest small-forward conductors and defenders in the history of the NBA. Pippen's six rings and two Olympic gold medals could very easily establish him as the greatest small forward to ever play the game. Of course, supporters of Elgin Baylor, LeBron James, Larry Bird, Julius "Dr. J" Erving, and Dominique Wilkins could argue their analytical position, but Pippen seems to know the fundamental intricacies of the game on a higher level. The truth is that Jordan could not and did not win NBA Championships without Pippen. Says Jordan: "He helped me so much in the way I approached the game, the way I played the game. Whenever they speak Michael Jordan, they should speak Scottie Pippen. When everybody says, well, I won all these championships, but I didn't win without Scottie Pippen. That's why I consider him my best teammate of all time."[2] If Kobe Bryant was the

---

2. Garcia, "Michael Jordan Believes," para. 10.

playing bridge between Jordan and James, then Pippen is the playing bridge between Jordan and Bryant because he played against Jordan and Bryant throughout his illustrious NBA career. Both Jordan and Bryant hold Pippen in extremely high basketball regard. And rightfully so. He was blessed to see Jordan and Bryant during the various stages of their respective careers. Again, if anyone knows who the basketball G.O.A.T. is, it would be Pippen.

Even though Pippen adamantly disagreed with Mark Jackson when Jackson stated that Bryant would ultimately go down as the greatest basketball player ever,[3] he seemed to have a more concentrated and definite opinion of Bryant's career following his untimely death. Pippen begins his important analysis by admitting that Bryant idolized and mimicked Jordan down to the T. It was no secret that Bryant was determined to be the greatest basketball player ever. This particular objective of Bryant included him surpassing his idol Jordan. Pippen says Bryant took the NBA torch and carried it for twenty years. According to Pippen, Bryant's competitive fire was unmatched as he grew into one of the greatest players in the history of the game.

Pippen also admits the Jordan-Bryant debate represents a close comparison. Both were iconic in that Jordan and Bryant set the bar extremely high for two-way wing players. Both were dominant offensively and defensively. In a 2020 interview, Pippen brings the Jordan-Bryant comparison to a summarizing head: "Kobe strived so hard to be Michael Jordan. When I go back and look at the videos, I say to myself, 'Damn, he was better than Michael Jordan.'"[4] In affirming that Bryant was a far better shooter than Jordan, Pippen referenced Bryant's legendary work ethic. As one who came into the NBA right out high school, Bryant developed himself into an all-time-great NBA player. Pippen describes Bryant as a picker of exceptional basketball brains. Pippen also laments that he never told Bryant just how great of a basketball player he really was.

In addition to playing during a talent-deprived decade in terms of all-time-great NBA players (outside of Jordan, Pippen, and Olajuwon), Jordan played on a very stable Chicago Bulls team. Scottie Pippen (and Phil Jackson) was a stabilizing force of those championship teams. The Bulls were great with Jordan playing, and they were a top-5 team without him. Either way, those Bulls teams from 1990–98 had a multitude of

---

3. Dugandzic, "[2006] Mark Jackson," para. 1.
4. "Pippen," para. 4.

talented players. Jordan won NBA titles with two different starting point guards (Paxson and Harper), two different starting centers (Bill Cartwright and Luc Longley), two different starting power forwards (Horace Grant and Dennis Rodman), *one* small forward (Scottie Pippen), an all-time-great European player (Toni Kukoc), and a boatload of good role players. Kobe Bryant, on the other hand, won his titles with two different starting guards (Fisher and Ron Harper), four different starting small forwards (Glenn Rice, Rick Fox, Trevor Ariza, and Metta World Peace), four different starting power forwards (A. C. Green, Horace Grant, Samaki Walker, and Pau Gasol), two different starting centers (O'Neal and Andrew Bynum), and a group of average add ons. Jordan had far greater team stability which was highlighted by the presence of an all-time-great small forward, Scottie Pippen.

Pippen's talent and leadership accompanied Jordan on all six of his title runs. The way that Jordan dominated the ball on offense and leaned on Pippen to defend the opponent's best wing player, I do not believe he would have won NBA titles without Pippen as his teammate. Bryant, on the other hand, won multiple titles without Shaq. I prefer Kobe's body of work over that of Jordan. According to former NBA player Brandon Jennings, "Michael Jordan had more 'help' winning his rings then Kobe. MJ never won with without Pippen. Kobe won 2 rings without another great on his team. Kobe is the GOAT."[5] Premier NBA guard Kyrie Irving affirms the all-time greatness of Bryant by stating that Kobe was the standard of his generation. Irving also believes the NBA's logo should be a silhouette of Kobe Bryant.[6] While all of the media attention has been given to Jordan, the critical importance of Pippen's leadership has been left underappreciated and understudied.

In celebrating a life of great purpose and unlimited discovery, the question of the moment is: Just how great of a basketball player was Kobe Bean Bryant? Let us ask one of Kobe's greatest contemporaries—Kevin Durant. In a 2014 interview with CBS/NBA, Durant confessed that Kobe is "the greatest of all time. His skill is second to none. Him and MJ are neck and neck as far as skill. Kobe is the top two best ever in just having skill, footwork, shooting the 3, shooting the pull-up, posting up, dunking on guys and ball handling. Kobe and Jordan are 1 and 1A."[7] In 2018, Durant

5. Chen, "Brandon Jennings," para. 4.
6. Ocal, "Kyrie Irving and Vanessa Bryant," paras. 2, 4.
7. Moore, "Kevin Durant Says," para. 2.

repeated his poignant statement about Kobe and Jordan being in a league of their own: "Kobe, MJ and Kyrie,"[8] Durant says. When Durant speaks of Bryant, Jordan and Irving, he is boasting of their offensive talents and their abilities to take over games. Obviously, Durant is a fan of how Bryant and Jordan dominated the game with their physical movements:

> Just the way they move, I don't understand why people don't realize what they're seeing in these three, especially Jordan and Kobe. Kyrie is younger than me, and that's one of my best friends, so I watch his stuff. I get to play with Steph every day so I know his game inside and out. But watching Kobe and Mike, I'm like, 'How do you not realize how good these dudes are?' How do you not say they're far better than anybody who's played the game? Just by the way they move, how fluid they are.[9]

While Bryant does not get as much media attention as Jordan or LeBron in the G.O.A.T. debate among NBA fans, the players who competed against Bryant know the truth; they knew what they were up against when they competed against Bryant.

As a basketball historian, I find it very disrespectful to the game for anyone to exclusively place James in the G.O.A.T. argument with Jordan—bypassing the legacy and greatness of Kobe Bryant. Kobe did not believe in forming superteams for the sake of winning NBA titles. Nor did he believe in changing teams for the purpose of chasing NBA titles. Bryant won all five of his NBA titles in Los Angeles with the organization that traded for his draft rights in 1996. Kobe won multiple titles with Shaq, and he won multiple titles without Shaq. He always played the hand that was dealt to him. Kobe did not chase championship rings. He won them with one team and with the way he played the game of basketball. NBA Hall of Famer Allen Iverson shares the same sentiment of frustration regarding Bryant's place in the all-time debate. "What bothers me is when they do talk about]the greatest of all time] LeBron is great first of all . . . when they talk about comparing him to Mike, I don't understand how they don't have the debate with him in Kobe," Iverson said, "You forgot? They forgot? I really think they forgot. The Mamba, man . . . certified killer, man."[10] I do not believe NBA pundits forgot how great of a basketball player Kobe Bryant was; I believe they have made the concerted

8. Moore, "Kevin Durant Says," para. 2.
9. Rivas, "Kevin Durant Says," para. 4.
10. Sanfiorenzo, "Allen Iverson Doesn't Understand," para. 4.

decision not to remember just how great Kobe was. Bryant's on-the-court brilliance, along with his polarizing confidence, struck a lot of commentators the wrong way. Kobe was punished for having aspirations of greatness and then following through on them. His basketball game surpassed the media's (and a number of NBA players as well) expectations of what his ceiling would be. In watching Bryant improve his game year after year, I realized Kobe did not have a ceiling. He had a destiny.

This particular debate reminds me that having biased opinions about who is the greatest in any sport is part of what creates the culture of sport in the first place. There are both agreements and disagreements. In disagreeing with ESPN's Kendrick Perkins when he says Kevin Durant is the greatest scorer in NBA history,[11] I read a recent stat showing that Kobe had more 40-point games (122) then LeBron James and Stephen Curry combined (115), more 50-point performances (twenty-five) than LBJ, Kevin Durant, and Larry Bird combined (twenty-two), and more 60-point (six) outings than Michael Jordan and King James combined (five).[12] One of the best things I can say about Bryant was that he was easily the greatest NBA player during the decade of the 2000s.

In scoring 21,065 points over a ten-year period, Kobe averaged 28.5 points, 5.2 assists, and 5.9 rebounds per game. During the decade of the 2000s, he ended up first in total points scored (shooting 46.4 percent from the field), first in points per game, first in the number of NBA Finals played in (six), first in the number of NBA All-Star Game starts (ten), and tied for first in NBA Championships won (four, tied with Shaq) and All Star Game MVPs received (three, tied with Shaq). Kobe also finished the decade fifteenth in assists. Kobe was the only one who scored 20,000 points during the 2000s. Most important, Kobe began the 2000s in the same way he ended the 2000s—winning an NBA Championship. Decade-wise, one could argue that Kobe was better in the 2000s than the following NBA legends during their decades of dominance: Kareem Abdul-Jabbar in the 1970s (22,000 points, one championship); Magic Johnson and Larry Bird in the 1980s (Magic—13,000 points, five championships; Bird—16,000 points, three championships); Michael Jordan in the 1990s (19,000 points, six championships); and LeBron James in the 2010s (19, 000 points, three championships).

11. Tran, "Kendrick Perkins Says Kevin Durant."
12. Jajodia, "Kobe Bryant Had More 60-Point Games," para. 4.

As a basketball historian, I believe Bryant's accomplishments during the decade of the 2000s are more notable due to the level of athletic competition and basketball talent he had to overcome at all five positions. Kobe had to deal with the greatest collection of basketball talent ever during the decade of the 2000s—especially at the point-guard, two-guard, and small-forward positions. It seems like everybody's freakish athleticism enabled them to touch the top of the square. Unlike the previous decades, the 2000s were filled with high-jumping athletes, with Kobe being the greatest of them all. Question: Can anyone name an all-time-great NBA superstar, other than the great Bill Russell in 1960 and 1969, that began and ended a decade by winning an NBA Championship? Kobe Bean Bryant won an NBA title in both 2000 and 2009.

In addition to playing against an incredibly talented core of athletic perimeter players, Kobe also competed against skilled big men during the 2000s. I am sure you all have heard of Shaquille O'Neal, Yao Ming, Tim Duncan, Kevin Garnett, Dirk Nowitzki, Rasheed Wallace, Ben Wallace, Amar'e Stoudemire, Dwight Howard, Chris Bosh, and Chris Webber, just to name a few. During the 2000s, the five-position talent pool in the NBA was absolutely amazing. I laugh when I read about NBA players talking about their legacy on the offensive end of the court as basketball onlookers brag about how this particular player "changed the game." While we laud such players as LeBron James (four rings), James Harden (zero rings), Damian Lillard (zero rings), and Steph Curry (4 rings) as ones who have moved the game forward, I do not hear much about these transcendent, perimeter-oriented players playing great defense. From where I sit, James, Harden, Lillard, and Curry are all defensive liabilities. True greatness is not just about what a player does with the ball in his hands. It is also about what he or she does without it. If you do not think playing defense is important, take a look at some of the current NBA games.

Being able to amass a large number of assists does not make up for one's inability to be a great defender. I have great respect for such players as Anthony Davis, Giannis Antetokounmpo, and Kevin Durant because they make it a point to play defense. During the decade of the 2000s, Kobe was named to the NBA All-Defensive Team all ten years. Bryant was named to the First Team eight times and the Second Team twice. Ironically, the two years Bryant was not named to the first team encompassed two of the four years Bryant won NBA Championships with the Lakers.

The generational conversation of all-time basketball greatness also depends on how deep one is willing to go with his or her analysis. When

The Culture of Sport and Saying Goodbye to the Inspiration of Zoom

it comes to winning NBA Championships, I prefer Kobe's journey to that of Jordan's. As a competitor, I would much rather win five rings the way Kobe did it than win six rings the way Jordan did it. Don't get me wrong. Jordan was great in winning his six rings. But the fact that Kobe won multiple rings with and without Shaq creates a new type of conversation in terms of what it means to be dominant in a team-sport environment. For me, it is not as much about being perfect in the NBA Finals as it is about who you won with and how you won. Pippen was the best player in the NBA when Jordan decided to come back at the end of the 1994–95 season. If you wanna get specific, the Chicago Bulls' bench played a major role in them winning Game 6 of the 1992 Finals. John Paxson and Steve Kerr made big shots. Jordan ended up getting all the credit. Kobe, on the other hand, was the one main constant on all five of the Lakers championship teams in the 2000s. In my humble opinion, the quality of Kobe's championships outweigh the quantity of Jordan's championships.

Allow me to present my argument in a different way. When I need some type of motivational inspiration to do my work as a pastor, preacher, theologian, writer, and academic scholar, I tend to peruse through Kobe Bryant's YouTube collection. I believe Kobe has the greatest collection of YouTube highlights ever. Amongst other things, Kobe's otherworldly ability to score in a solo, unassisted kind of way inspires me to greater levels of achievement in my own fields of study. Even Jordan was impressed with Kobe's ability to score high volumes of points in isolation situations. Shannon Sharpe's response to NBA Champion Andre Iguodola's claim that Kobe was the most difficult player he ever guarded[13] was that Kobe is probably the second-greatest scorer in the history of the game behind Wilt Chamberlain.

Without a doubt Kobe's signature shot was his unassisted mid-range jump shot. As a one-on-one master, Kobe's ability to create and make tough shots in the face of all types of defenders made him the most unstoppable perimeter basketball player in the history of the NBA. One particular YouTube highlight[14] stated that over the course of Kobe's twenty-year career, he scored almost 2,800 points on isolated, unassisted plays that ended in two-point mid-range jump shots. This is more than Dirk Nowitzki and Allen Iverson combined (the next closest to Bryant in the history of the game). When I use the words "solo" and "unassisted,"

---

13. Martinez, "Andre Iguodala Picks Kobe."
14. ESPN, "Kobe Bryant Dominated," 7:54–8:05.

I am referring to those plays where Kobe created his own scoring play without the ball being passed to him. Here the word "isolation" (no pick and roll) comes to mind as I consider Bryant to be the greatest isolation player in the history of the NBA.

Kobe's statement about Jordan's footwork being flawless and him wanting his own footwork to be just as flawless fueled Bryant's growing fire. I say that because I believe Kobe's footwork surpassed that of Jordan. Not only was Bryant's footwork better than Jordan's, but so were his ball-handling skills. This particular analysis is part of what made Kobe an unstoppable perimeter player. Bryant's footwork and ball handling, mixed with his mid-range mastery, helped to make Bryant, in the words of LeBron James, a player with no flaws on the offensive end.[15] Kobe's unique ability to fade away on his mid-range jump shot with distance and range, and to make a good percentage of those difficult shots over taller, more athletic defenders, is yet another reason why I believe Kobe eclipsed Jordan. Whatever moves Jordan claims Kobe stole from him, Bryant utilized them for the purpose of executing them better than Jordan did. And he did. Kobe did not emulate Jordan to be like Jordan. He emulated Jordan, Jerry West, Oscar Robinson, Hakeem Olajuwon, and Dirk Nowitzki for the sole purpose of the being the greatest player in the history of the game. Whatever Kobe took from other players, offensively speaking, he put it on a whole other level. I would not be taking the time to write this important book if I was not convinced by the Spirit that Bryant was the G.O.A.T.

The inspiration behind Kobe's Mamba Mentality and the Zoom shoe inspired people from all walks of life—baseball players, painters, schoolteachers, businesspeople, skateboarders, golfers, hockey players, tennis players, soccer players, track and field athletes, artists, mural painters, singers, actors, actresses, shark experts, boaters, rich people, poor people, Mexican, Asians, Chinese, Japanese, and Italian people. Put another way, Kobe inspired multiple generations of world culture with both his basketball game and his life philosophy. The ways and means in which Kobe inspired multiple generations of people all over the world is indicative of the positive impact he had upon the culture of sport. Kobe was an old-school athlete with the new-age mindset of what it meant to battle competitively. For Bryant, the constant practiced action of play is the total embodiment of battle within a competitive format. In other words, the instinctive action of play has always been more important

---

15. Zillgitt, "LeBron James Opens Up and Reflects," para. 16.

than its impact upon the people, places, and things around those who are playing or competing. In the words of Johan Huizinga,

> Play is older than culture, for culture, however inadequately defined, always presupposes human society, and animals have not waited for man to teach them their playing. We can safely assert, even, that human civilization has added no essential feature to the general idea of play. Animals play just like men. We have only to watch young dogs to see that all the essentials of human play are present in their merry gambols. They invite one another to play by a certain ceremoniousness of attitude and gesture. They keep the rule that you should not bite, or not bite hard, your brother's ear. They pretend to get terribly angry. And—what is most important—in all these doings they plainly experience fun and enjoyment. Such rompings of young dogs are only one of the simpler forms of animal play. There are other, much more highly developed forms: regular contests and beautiful performances before an admiring public.[16]

Huizinga's reflections shed credible light on the fact that athletes who are the most competitive usually have the deepest impact on the culture of their respective sport, and it's not because they are professional athletes or the most popular sports icons, but rather because they are both competitors and human beings.

Bryant is one of the few athletes in history who reminds me that the way we play the game or sport supersedes the effect the game or sport has on the culture of the sport. Part of the reason why Bryant competed so hard against the likes of Jordan, Pippen, James, Durant, McGrady, Carter, Miller, Anthony, Wade, Ray Allen, Grant Hill, Kerry Kittles, Anfernee Hardaway, Latrell Sprewell, Iverson, Kidd, Nash, Marbury, Pierce, Allen Houston, Joe Johnson, Curry, Klay Thompson, Harden, Irving, Westbrook, Roy, and others is because he desperately wanted to match wits with these warriors in the instinctive realms of psychology and physiology. In wanting to see who the best was in those on-the-court battles, Kobe competed against the best of the best at his positions in both mind and body. Both types of competitive battle were critical to Bryant's desire to make the most of the time he had here on Earth and on the basketball court. In being described as a bully beast and a scary monster on the court, it can be said that Bryant was an animal of sorts when it came to

---

16. Huizinga, *Homo Ludens*, 1.

his maniacal pursuit of basketball immortality as defined by the winning of multiple championships. Huizinga chimes in again:

> Here we have at once an especially important point: even in its simplest forms on the animal level, play is more than a mere physiological or psychological reflex. It goes beyond the confines of purely physical or biological activity. It is a *significant* function—that is to say, there is some sense to it. In play there is something "at play" which transcends the immediate needs of life and imparts meaning to the action. All play means something. If we call the active principle that makes up the essence of play "instinct" we explain nothing; if we call it the "mind" or "will" we say too much. However we may regard it, the very fact that play has a meaning implies a non-materialistic quality in the nature of the thing itself.[17]

Huizinga goes on to add:

> Since the reality of play extends beyond the sphere of human life it cannot have its foundations in any rational nexus, because this would limit it to mankind. The incidence of play is not associated with any particular age of civilization or view of the universe. Any thinking person can see at a glance that play is a thing on its own, even if his language possesses no general concept to express it. Play cannot be denied. You can deny, if you like, nearly all abstractions: justice, beauty, truth, goodness, mind, God. You can deny seriousness, but not play.[18]

If we are knowledgeable about the chronological totality of his body of work, one could argue that the mythology of Kobe Bryant is what defined his overall greatness on the basketball court and in his life-world of humanity. While I am certain that mythology represents a contributing part of the Mamba Mentality, it must be stated that Kobe was not God or a god, nor did he have god-like powers. Kobe was a human being who strived for greatness beyond other people's expectations of him. In being a mere human being, many people have described Kobe as a spirit. This is because his life inspired people to reflect upon the presence of God in their own lives and what it means to figure out what we were created by God to do with our time here on Earth. And not for the sake of idolatry and idol worshiping, but for the sake of inspirational hope and creative imagination. Huizinga teaches:

17. Huizinga, *Homo Ludens*, 1–2 (emphasis original).
18. Huizinga, *Homo Ludens*, 4.

Or take myth. This, too, is a transformation or an "imagination" of the outer world, only here the process is more elaborate and ornate than is the case with individual words. In myth, primitive man seeks for the world of phenomena by grounding it out in the Divine. In all wild imaginings of mythology a fanciful spirit is playing on the border-line between jest and earnest. Or finally, let us take ritual. Primitive society performs its sacred rites, its sacrifices, consecrations and mysteries, all if which serve to guarantee the well-being of the world, in a spirit of pure play truly understood.[19]

Now in myth and ritual the great instinctive forces of civilized life have its origin: law and order, commerce and profit, wisdom and science. All are rooted in the primaeval soil of play. The fact that play and culture are actually interwoven with one another was neither observed nor expressed, whereas for us the whole point is to show that genuine, pure play is one of the main bases of civilisation.[20]

In the mind of Kobe Bryant, anything other than all-world greatness, while winning multiple championships, would be an unmitigated failure. Again, Bryant wanted to be the greatest basketball player ever. And he was determined to inspire people from all walks of life to a greater level of performance achievement. Especially for those who have always been consumed and influenced by the culture of sport, Kobe wanted to show them that inspiring others is greater than voicing an opinion.

As I stated in the opening chapter, the culture of sport has always been an attractive and interesting conversation for those who like competing. I say that because the culture of sport influences society in more ways than we read about. Spoken and unspoken, the culture of sport has forced people to think about their own competitive juices. Whether it be in education, business, politics, card games, board games, or even youth sports, we find ourselves competing as if we are professional athletes. We have the desire to compete and win as if we are making millions of dollars doing so. Not only do we want to win at all costs, but we also want to be the best at whatever activity we like competing in. It is not enough to win the game or the competition. We have to be the best of the best. The culture of competition has been engrained in us for a while now. People want to compete. People want to win. People want to be the best.

19. Huizinga, *Homo Ludens*, 4–5.
20. Huizinga, *Homo Ludens*, 5.

Where do they get this desire to succeed? Professional sports. If there is one sport that places historical precedence of winning and being the best, it is professional basketball. Because basketball has grown into a global sport, second only to soccer, the culture of basketball has become more influential in terms of its ability to reach mainstream consumers. Especially where the culture of Hip-Hop is concerned. The easier it becomes for professional basketball to reach the masses; the deeper society becomes consumed with its culture of winning. Also, the fact that professional basketball players make hundreds of millions of dollars just to play a forty-eight-minute game makes the culture of the game that much more intriguing.

Because professional basketball players have both power and influence on national and world stages, it sometimes encourages a culture of idolatry. Sometimes fans take their admiration of professional athletes way too far. They either worship the ground athletes walk on as gods, or they refer to them as gods. Both are idolatrous and dangerous responses. Professional athletes are not gods, nor are they the God of the universe. They are mere human beings. For fans to place them on a pedestal or attempt to deify them at the height of their athletic powers is out of bounds. This level of fanatic admiration is not placed within the boundaries of any given society. We can be fans of our favorite athletes without worshiping them and becoming idolaters. And for professional athletes to accept the worship and praise the only God deserves is even worse. To be inspired by our favorite athletes and to place them alongside God, Jesus Christ, and the Holy Spirit are two different things.

Here the culture of sport encourages a culture of idolatry amongst those who help to pay their salaries. Without the ticket-holding and ticket-buying fans, there would be no professional sports, as I am sure those who play in the NBA would not be willing to play for free. Let me put it another way. Neither Earl "The Pearl" Monroe, Kevin Durant nor Michael Jordan were Black Jesus on the basketball court or in everyday life. Only Jesus Christ is Black Jesus, or any other color Jesus for that matter. Larry Bird had it all wrong as well when he stated that Jordan was like God playing basketball.[21] God is God, and human beings are human beings. Monroe, Jordan, and Bird were all-time-great basketball players, but there is no substantive comparison between basketball players and God. Just because someone plays basketball at a high level, that does not

---

21. Walker, "Day Larry Bird Said."

merit an identifiable comparison to our Creator God. As a theologian of color, I am not in favor of athletes using religious language or God-talk to lift themselves above others. This form of idolatry causes great harm to both the culture and the sport.

In his article, "Kobe Bryant Touched Many Lives, but Celebrity Worship Is an Opiate," Dante James speaks of such revolutionary thinkers as Karl Marx (Philosophy of Economic Science), James Cone, and Jeremiah Wright (Black Liberation Theology) in his timely analysis of how people's worship of athletes is a fundamental act of their own oppression. James attempts to utilize the existential realities of human oppression as both source and norm. James's main point is that when it comes to one's reflection upon the presence of God in their lives, that particular type of reflection is reserved only for God the Father, Jesus Christ the Son, and the Holy Spirit. Celebrity worship is an opiate to the people because it takes the worship attention away from our Creator God and places it on sinful human beings. Celebrities and athletes were not created to be worshiped. Celebrities and athletes are severely flawed human beings who were created to worship the God who created them. Nothing good comes from placing imperfect human beings alongside, or in place of, God the Father. In referencing the doctrine of Black liberation theology, Jones stresses that instead of idolizing and worshiping human beings and devaluing the lives of those who may not be as prosperous as some of our heroes, people of all races and cultures of people should

> demand that corporate and black-owned media address the issues in our communities with respect and dignity through the lens of our history (of oppression) and culture unencumbered by their corporate profit motives. Let's demand that our scholars, religious and political leaders and yes the grassroots black community recognize the value of all black lives. We must embrace our humanity and understand that corporate controlled media propagandizes black celebrityhood, sports, and entertainment as an "opioid of the masses of black people" that contributes to undermining our struggle for liberation.[22]

Both Robert Ellis's *The Games People Play* and Lincoln Harvey's *A Brief Theology of Sport* warn of the danger of idolatry within the culture of professional sports. Ellis is duly cautious about the dangers of contemporary sports, but Harvey's criticism is sharper. He warns that, "Sports is

---

22. James, "Kobe Bryant Touched Many Lives," para. 10.

corrupted, not just by win-at-all costs competitive realities of cheating and doping, but also by the cults of prowess, misplaced glory and shimmering celebrity."[23] Harvey sees a temptation of idolatry lurking in the powerful attractions of professional sports. He condemns professionalized sports as a corruption,[24] and writes, "The professional sportsperson is simply an actor or a prostitute."[25] Here the culture of sport places emphasis on one's generational (decade) identification, especially when it comes to professional basketball. Because basketball is a relatively young sport, it is easy for fans and players of the game to use their generation of basketball greats to decide who is the greatest of them all. The truth is there are no right and wrong answers in naming and claiming who we believe to be the G.O.A.T. We will never know the full absolute truth of the G.O.A.T. argument because we will never see all of these great players competing against one another in their mental and physical primes. The best we can do is speculate according to our generational observations.

The culture of sport also inspires competition beyond the games that are played and between the leaders and superstars of each team. What all this means is that there are cultural influences on sports. Many societies value competition as part of their culture. They value sports at all levels, from elementary to professional level. Competition itself is more individualized at the professional level, where our favorite players become heroes. Sports players are often given, in certain societies, hero status. I have outlined eight ways in which the culture of sport impacts the larger society.

1. In addition to the individualization of our hero ballplayers, the way we place value on our favorite athlete becomes commonplace in the culture of sport. When I use the word "value," I am referring to how the influence of individuals within a society plays a role of importance for those who value competition. The sport that is valued by specific cultures depends on many variables.

2. Societal customs play a key role in the influence of sport upon culture. I say that because society and culture are powerful influences on how valuable sports are perceived to be, what sports are most important within a community, and which teams the general

---

23. Harvey, *Brief Theology of Sport*, 102.
24. Harvey, *Brief Theology of Sport*, 105.
25. Harvey, *Brief Theology of Sport*, 105.

population cheers for. Society also influences the changes in popularity across different sports and players.

3. Because sports are engrained into a country's consciousness, the culture of sport takes on many forms and shapes. The cultural influence of sport is not only limited to the field and court. Sport culture informs the fashion of the streets, and its aesthetic has become the fabric of the Millennials. Embracing this culture simply requires awareness, focus, and the desire for a competitive edge. Sports are engrained within American culture, partially due to the longevity of organized sport in the United States.

4. The role of sport in cultural socialization suggests that the "process by which an athlete begins to acquire the habits, beliefs, skills and accumulated knowledge of society" is included in his or her ability to be trained in a particular culture.[26]

5. Sports fosters identity and friendship in that sports have a positive impact on us as dreamers, participants, and spectators. Sports give our lives meaning, purpose, and direction. They allow us to switch gears, moving from mundane to the exceptional. It excites us tremendously to be able to run, swim, and jump faster than ever before. And we do these things because we love the sport we choose to participate in.

6. For centuries, the culture of sport has impacted society and people's lives on many levels, from the businesses near sporting events to even the clothes people choose to wear. Athletes are often treated as role models, and people support teams not just as fans but as employees.

7. The culture of sport helps to shape society, too. Sports can have a great impact on people and society. Watching sports inspires people with excitement. Playing sports can give people joy. Some people work as professional players, and some people work in areas which are related to sports.

8. Culturally speaking, sports have been a contributing part of humanity. From the earliest chapters in human history, this can be proved by the games that were played in Mayan and Egyptian civilization. Games such as hockey, rugby, and football have had what

---

26. Merriam-Webster, s.v. "socialization (*n.*) (medical definition)," https://www.merriam-webster.com/dictionary/socialization.

one can call a religious following while athletics are characterized by massive celebrations.

Even as the culture of sport is a mainstream conversation of great significance, there are not a lot of references to sport and competition in the Bible. The Jews generally did not participate in, or support, Greek sports because they were done totally nude, which violated Jewish practice. However, the apostle Paul appears to have been a fan of sports. Paul's writings on the subject of sports represent the bulk of what the Bible says about sports. Even as Paul applies sports to spiritual matters, he seems to understand the physical demands. These eight pieces of Scripture elucidates the Bible's take on sport and competition.

First Corinthians 9:24–27—"Do you not know that in a race all the runners run, but only one gets the prize? Run in such a way as to get the prize. Everyone who competes in the games goes into strict training. They do it to get a crown that will not last; but we do it to get a crown that will last. Therefore, I do not run like a man running aimlessly; no, I beat my body and make it my slave so that after I have preached to others, I myself will not be disqualified for the prize." *Race . . . runners.* The Corinthians were familiar with the foot races in their own Isthmian Games, which occurred every other year and were second only to the Olympic Games in importance. In ancient times the prize was a perishable wreath (1 Cor 9:25). *Not . . . running aimlessly.* Paul says in Philippians 3:14 that "I press on toward the goal to win the prize for which God has called me heavenward in Christ Jesus." *Prize.* The winner of the Greek races received a wreath of leaves and sometimes a cash award (1 Cor 9:24). The Christian receives an award of everlasting glory (2 Cor; 2 Tim 2:10). *Heavenward.* Paul's ultimate aspirations are found not in this life but in heaven, because Christ is present in heaven (Col 3:1–2).

Galatians 5:7—"You were running a good race. Who cut in on you and kept you from obeying the truth?" *Were running a good race.* Before the Judaizers hindered them, Paul was fond of depicting the Christian life as a race (Gal 2:2; 1 Cor 9:24–27; Phil 2:16; 2 Tim 4:7).

Hebrews 12:1—"Therefore, since we are surrounded by such a cloud of witnesses, let us throw off everything that hinders and the sin that so easily entangles, and let us run with perseverance the race marked out for us." *Surrounded by such a great cloud of witnesses.* The imagery suggests an athletic contest in a great amphitheater. The witnesses are the heroes of the past who have just been mentioned (Heb 11). They are not spectators but inspiring examples. The Greek word translated "witnesses" is the origin of the English word "martyr" and means "testifiers." They bear testimony to the power of faith and to God's faithfulness. *Run with perseverance* (Acts 20:24; 1 Cor 9:24–26; Gal 2:2; 5:7; Phil 2:16; 2 Tim 4:7). According to the apostle Paul and the writer of Hebrews, the Christian life is pictured as a long-distance race rather than a short sprint.

Genesis 32:25–26 reads, "When the man saw that he could not overpower him, he touched the socket of Jacob's hip so that his hip was wrenched as he wrestled with the man. Then the man said, 'Let me go, for it is daybreak.' But Jacob replied, 'I will not let you go unless you bless me.'" *Could not overpower him . . . touched the socket.* God came to Jacob, later renamed Israel, in such a form that Jacob could wrestle with him successfully, yet he showed Jacob that he could not disable him at will. *I will not let you go.* Jacob's athletic persistence was soon rewarded (Gen 32:29). *Unless you bless me.* Jacob finally acknowledged that the blessing must come from God. It should be noted that sports were played during biblical times. At the first recorded ancient Olympic Games in 760 BC, there was only one event, a footrace. Later Games included other events such as wrestling, boxing, javelin, and jumping. From around the same time, the only sport mentioned in the Bible is wrestling.

Second Timothy 2:5—"Similarly, if anyone competes as an athlete, he does not receive the victor's crown unless he competes according to the rules." One of the three examples (along with a soldier who wants to please his commander and a farmer who works hard), if not the most important example, that Paul desires Timothy to follow is that of an athlete who follows the rules of the game. Sports cannot be competitive without rules. Even with rules in place, athletes will still make it a point to cheat just to win. I am certain that part of the reason athletes cheat is because they are not disciplined in their training.

First Corinthians 9:25—"Everyone who competes goes into strict training. They do it to get crown that will not last; but we do it to get a crown that will last forever." All athletes are disciplined in their training. They do it to win a prize that will fade away, but we do it for an eternal prize. First Thessalonians 2:19 says: "What is our hope, our joy, or our crown in which we will glory in the presence of our Lord Jesus when he comes? Is it not you? Indeed, you are our glory and joy. *A crown.* Not a royal crown, but a wreath used on festive occasions or as the prize in the Greek games (2 Tim 4:8; Jas 1:12; 1 Pet 5:4; Rev 2:10). *When he comes* (1

Thess 3:13; 4:15; 5:23; 2 Thess 2:1, 8). The expression was used regarding the arrival of a great person, as a royal visit.

Revelation 20:15 (ESV)—"And if anyone's name was not found written in the book of life, he was thrown into the lake of fire." The last portion of Revelation 19:20 reads: "The two of them were thrown alive into the fiery lake of burning sulfur." In apocalyptic literature, the fiery lake of burning sulfur was equated with the "hell" of final judgment.

Aside from what the Bible says about the competitive nature of sports, sports proper has an important impact on our society. Sports is one of the few things that transcends socioeconomic status and brings people together. According to Mark Banschick, MD, of *Psychology Today*, "Sports draw us in for many reasons, the elegance, the comptetition, the history, our identification with great athleticsim (we may not be able to do it, but they sure can!), a coming together of community in a shared story, etc."[27] Most notably, sports are important to society because they help prove the importance of rules. Without rules, games such as baseball, football, and basketball are not playable. In the same vernacular, societies of human beings cannot function without having rules and laws in place. Sports also teaches you multiple lessons that can impact your life. These include discipline, sacrifice, hard work, dealing with success and failure, setting and striving for goals, overcoming adversity, and the value of practice and preparation. Sports impacts economics on local, state, and national levels, creates jobs, impacts city pride, helps young people become active, and it improves community relations. Sports also help people balance the emotions that are tied to the playing of the sport.

The two-way toughness of Kobe Bryant is the main reason why Shaq is certain that his Lakers would defeat any of the Jordan-led Bulls of the 1990s. O'Neal is sure Bryant's toughness on both ends of the court would nullify Jordan, thus giving him the space and energy needed to destroy Luc Longley in the paint. In the mind of O'Neal, the Bulls would not have had a defensive answer for him or Bryant. Sure of the fact that Jordan would send his sidekick Scottie Pippen over to guard Bryant to help conserve his energy for the offensive end, O'Neal would argue that the Lakers two number-one options on the offensive end (himself and Bryant) would be too much for the Bulls to deal with. While I am confident Bryant would guard Jordan on the defensive end, I am uncertain about who Jordan would guard during

---

27. Banschick, "Why Are Sports Important?," para. 1.

the critical moments of this mythological series. He never seemed to want to guard Bryant in their matchups in the late 1990s and early 2000s.

Ironically, Jordan's statement about Kobe "maybe" being tougher than him[28] is half right and half wrong. Jordan stated that Kobe had to be tough in the developmental years of his basketball career because people were upset with Kobe for copying Jordan's moves. The first reason Jordan is wrong about Kobe's toughness is because Kobe never cared about what people thought about him. The second reason is because Jordan had nothing to do with Kobe Bryant being a tough basketball player, mentally, physically, and spiritually. Kobe was a tough human being way before he became a professional basketball player. The way Jordan played the game had nothing to do with Bryant's toughness. Kobe developed his own toughness within himself. The third reason is because Jordan consistently failed to understand that Kobe did not copy or steal Jordan's moves for the sake of being Jordan or the next Michael Jordan. The same way Jordan mimicked Julius Erving, Elgin Baylor, David Thompson, and Walter Davis, Kobe utilized the moves of Jordan, West, Oscar Robertson, and others for the systemic benefit of Kobe's overall game. Being tough is not an evolutionary component that is borrowed from other people. It is something that is developed from within. In my opinion, Kobe was the toughest player in the history of the game because his toughness was a by-product of his own basketball greatness.

Nevertheless, Kobe made sure his last games versus Jordan and James were memorable. He performed at a high level against both of his generational contemporaries. He scored 55 points (42 in the first half) in his last game against Jordan, and he scored 26 points in his last game versus James. Many of those 26 points came when James was guarding Bryant in one-on-one situations. Kobe did not fear anybody, nor did he fear any situation. He did not flinch in super-tense, clutch moments. At one point in a game between the Lakers and the Orlando Magic he did not even move his body at all. This was when Matt Barnes acted like he was going to throw the ball in Kobe's face. Kobe remained utterly still. Kobe got into physical altercations with the likes of Reggie Miller, Chris Childs and others. He never backed down from a challenge. Kobe did not back down from individual challenges, and he did not back down from team challenges. Kobe's historic 81-point performance against the Toronto Raptors in 2006 was not his only grand effort against them.

28. Feldman, "Michael Jordan," para. 5.

In addition to hitting two game-winning jumpers against the Raptors in 2010 and 2012, Kobe also did the unthinkable in a March 2013 home game against the Raptors. With the Lakers down late in the 4th quarter, Kobe made three straight 3-pointers (two of them with multiple defenders draped on him) down the stretch to send the game into overtime. In overtime, Kobe drove around a screened double-team and made a tomahawk dunk to win the game for the Lakers. This was the second time over the course of one year that Bryant had hit a game-winning shot against the Raptors.

One of Kobe's greatest attributes was his ability to hit the pressure shot. Kobe wanted to put the burden of winning and losing on his clutch shoulders. In hitting game-winning shots against the Blazers, Spurs, Kings, Nuggets, Clippers, Warriors, Rockets, Jazz, Raptors, Cavaliers, Hornets, Bobcats, SuperSonics, Suns, Heat, Bucks, Grizzlies, Hawks, Pacers, Mavericks, Celtics, and Hornets, Kobe established himself as the greatest clutch player ever. There is no telling how many times Bryant tied games up late in the 4th quarter or sent games into overtime. In addition to having the uncanny ability to make clutch shots with the game on the line, Kobe also knew how to wiggle himself free to take the all-important last shot. He was the master of angles in terms of his ability to get open and position himself to take the shot. He jumped into slots, came off of screens, freed himself with the movement of his hips, and he knew how to move toward the goal, north or south, to cover enough ground to take the mid-range jump shot. His knowledge of time and when to take the last-second shot was unmatched in the history of the game.

In terms of creating an exquisite vision for his signature shoes, Kobe preferred Zoom over Air. He preferred the horizontal over the vertical. The word "zoom" contains four meanings in the form of an intransitive verb. They are:

> 1. to move with a loud low hum or buzz 2. to climb for a short time as an angle greater than that which can be maintained in steady flight so that the machine is carried upward at an expense of stored kinetic energy 3. to focus a camera or microscope on an object using a zoom lens so that the object's apparent distance from the observer changes—often used with in or out 4. to increase sharply.

The word zoom also possesses three definitions in the noun form. They are:

1. an act or process of zooming 2. a zooming sound 3. a means of producing an enlarged image (as in a camera).[29]

For me, the word "zoom" means being in a constant transition from one place to another. Zoom also means moving somewhere fast while not being in a hurry. In contrast, the word "air" implies a certain type of upwardness or upward mobility.

Analogously, the word "zoom" implies that Kobe always pushed the envelope in terms of creating the most innovative basketball shoe in the world. There is a reason why more players in the NBA wear Kobe's tennis shoe than anyone else's. A playful Michael Jordan referred to Kobe's game sneakers as "those Kobe [sic] Bryant's [shoes]"[30] when he expressed his displeasure with players from the University of North Carolina as they were walking to their team bus. Meanwhile, Kobe drew inspiration from the culture of Jazz, boxing shoes, music in general, and even himself as he took risks on both the macro level (with the low-top shoes) and the micro level (with the high-top shoes following his Achilles injury). Both styles of basketball shoe were smashing successes. In 2008, Kobe brought the low-top basketball shoe back into the mainstream. Many NBA players have emulated Bryant's move to the low-top shoes. LeBron, Durant, Curry, Kyrie, and Jordan have all successfully tapped into the low-top market.

Within the culture of sport, it seems pro basketball is the one sport that attempts to create and thrive within the environment of idolatry or idol worshiping. While I do believe basketball players are the greatest athletes in the world, I also believe they feel like they should be worshiped for their athletic abilities. Because some NBA players have been blessed with the gifts of working hard, running fast, jumping high, and shooting well, they feel like they are gods among mere mortals. The notion of idolatry occupying important spaces within the culture of sports is a troublesome one. I say that because it seems like there is a two-way street in place. First, the fans worship their favorite athlete. And second, the athletes are accepting of the fan worship. When we talk about the idolatry of sports, the fact of one's immoral behavior is only scratching the surface. There is a deeper problem yet. Sin is not merely doing bad things; it is making a good thing the ultimate thing. The Bible calls this idolatry.

29. Merriam-Webster, s.v. "zoom (v. [1])," https://www.merriam-webster.com/dictionary/zoom.

30. Castillo, "Throwback," para. 2.

Human beings are made to love God, be satisfied in Him, and find their identity in Him. An idol is anything that seeks to take God's place in fulfilling those very needs, whether it be a physical object or an idol of the heart. As theologian John Calvin says, "Scarcely a single person has ever been found who did not fashion for himself an idol or specter in place of God. Surely, just as the waters boil up from a vast, full spring, so does an immense crowd of gods flow forth from the human mind."[31] So how does idolatry relate to sports? As we saw from Genesis 1–2, sports are a good thing. But in a fallen world, rather than enjoying sports as a gift from God, sports are often used to replace, or even, ironically, compete with God. In other words, many look to sports for what is meant to be found in God: identity, meaning, and even salvation. Professional basketball players are not saviors of the world. They maybe decent human beings, but there is nothing redemptive about their presence in the world. They are sinful human beings just like everyone else.

Now, coming back to the realm of professional basketball, it is very difficult not to mention the player who, along with the likes of Kareem, Magic, Michael Cooper, and Kobe Bryant, also won five NBA Championships with the Los Angeles Lakers: Derek Fisher. Fisher was drafted by the Lakers into the NBA the same year Kobe was drafted—1996. All five of Fisher's championship rings were won on the same teams as Bryant. Instead of unpacking Fisher's deep connection to Kobe in the realm of family, I opted to talk about Fisher's leadership style in light of what Kobe says about Fisher's style of play. Bryant has a high and holy respect for Fisher the leader and Fisher the guy that spent more time with Kobe in the Lakers backcourt than anyone.

One of the things that stuck out to me about Fisher was that he did not always give in to the pressure of passing the ball to Bryant every time the opportunity presented itself. Obviously, he got the ball to Kobe when it was time to do so. But unlike some of Bryant's other teammates, Fisher did not force the ball to Kobe. If the Triangle offense called for the ball to be thrown to the other side of the floor away from Bryant, then Fisher would stay within the flow of the offense—even it meant not passing the ball to Bryant. Fisher did not seem like he was willing to break the flow of the offense just to feed Bryant's insatiable appetite for scoring. Fisher the basketball guy knew it was important that he take those open jump shots. Very similar to John Paxson's role with the Chicago Bulls, it was Fisher's job to take and make those open jump shots that were created by those

---

31. Calvin, *Institutes*, 1.5.12.

Shaq and Kobe double-teams. Fisher was a leader in the locker room, and he was a leader on the court. When Kobe took over on the offensive end and scored bunches of points in a small amount of time, Fisher still took those open jump shots. While Fisher was a born or natural leader, Kobe's style of leadership was more so introspective and motivational in a probing kind of way.

The next segment of Kobe's career was when his maturation as a leader took place. After the Shaq-Kobe era ended, he became the senior statesman for a team that had lost all of its other starters via retirement or trade. He was the major thrust of the team and its nominal leader, perhaps by default. Leadership is a tough thing to master, especially when you know a championship is beyond the reach of your personnel.[32] The Lakers had been a bridesmaid the past two seasons (1997–98 and 1998–99), winning a ton of games but getting swept out of successive playoffs. Shouldering the pressure that came with that history, Kobe, of course, made the plays. The Lakers got over the stigma of coming up short and went on to win three straight championships. Each of those years was dramatic and full of memorable games and moments. Kobe was the driving force, while Shaquille O'Neal, the Diesel, was the focal point of the offense—"Get the ball to the big fella," as we'd say. The group of Lakers went to four finals in five years, in essence creating a dynasty.[33]

The undeniable truth is there was real substance behind Kobe's drive to be one of the greatest basketball players ever. This is because his supreme work ethic (commitment to the game) was equally matched by both his unique skill set (overall talent) and his ability to think the game at a high level (competitive intellectualism) in pressure situations (clutch gene). These are just a few qualities that made Bryant an effective leader. Kobe believed that leadership is responsibility. Kobe also believed that leadership is about priority.

Brian Kamenetzky summarizes Kobe's leadership doctrine:

> Kobe's central premise—that in the interest of larger goals real leadership requires a willingness to say or do unpopular things perhaps damaging to the leader's popularity or public image—is undeniable, but not universally practiced. And there's absolutely no question Kobe is willing to push whatever buttons he feels necessary if it gets his team—and himself, obviously—closer to a title. That he's willing to be unpopular (Kobe uses different

---

32. Bryant, *Mamba Mentality*, 18.
33. Bryant, *Mamba Mentality*, 18.

terminology) in the process is also self-evident. If it's not, he'll frequently remind you. It's a badge he wears with pride, actually, and not without cause. Many aren't willing to sacrifice personal popularity in the interest of larger goals. As Dwight Howard can attest, the natural desire to please and be liked is a powerful one. Kobe knows exactly how he prioritizes that sort of thing relative to winning.[34]

Kamenetzky adds that,

> Over the course of now 17 seasons in L.A., the demands on Kobe as a leader have changed. Earlier in his career, Bryant's role wasn't as expansive. He didn't so much lead (not in the way we traditionally think of the word, at least) as get out front in a very competitive environment and drag guys with him through will, stubbornness, and on-floor talent. In time, though, as more has been required Bryant has adjusted. He's softened the edges, grown less insular, and learned you can't be *that guy* all the time and expect people to follow. There is greater depth to his leadership, and never does he demand levels of hard work he's himself unwilling to meet. Still, his style [of leadership] is fundamentally abrasive and incredibly demanding, emphasizing the need for contrasting personalities around him to balance things out.[35]

According to Brian Kamenetzky:

> The '09–'10 title teams had the gravitas of Derek Fisher. Lamar Odom was the emotional core of the locker room. Pau Gasol's professionalism, skill and team-first ethic afford him wide respect and are a model of how to play on a Bryant-led team. Each displayed leadership in different forms. There have been plenty of times when I and others have questioned both the necessity and efficacy of Bryant's tactics, but measuring the degree to which his personality has ultimately helped or hurt his cause over the course of his career is difficult. If Kobe were wired differently, he might be a better (or at least more appealing) leader, but not the same type of player.[36]

I recently read where Kuzma stated that Kobe was the "Greatest ever, no question."[37] This was after Kuzma had spent a few years with

---

34. Kamenetzky, "Kobe Bryant's Leadership Doctrine," paras. 5–6.
35. Kamenetzky, "Kobe Bryant's Leadership Doctrine," para. 7 (emphasis original).
36. Kamenetzky, "Kobe Bryant's Leadership Doctrine," para. 9.
37. Sengupta, "Kobe Bryant Is the GOAT," para. 6.

The Culture of Sport and Saying Goodbye to the Inspiration of Zoom 177

LeBron James and the Los Angeles Lakers. One of the best things these younger-generation players can say about Bryant is he inspired them to put in more work in the gym to improve their overall game. Kobe's inspiration also provided the need for the younger Lakers to think deeper about the nuances of the game.

Kobe's leadership was also recognized in his ability to make clutch shots in the most pressure-filled situations. Kobe not only came through in the clutch when the Lakers needed him the most, but some of the things he did at the end of games bordered on the miraculous. I recall the Lakers being down to the Golden State Warriors and one of Kobe's teammates was at the free-throw line. He made the first free throw and then intentionally missed the second one because the Lakers were still down by one point. Kobe and his teammates desperately swarmed the rim to get a put-back or a tip-in to win the game. Using his supreme athleticism, Kobe squeezed his way into the thick of things at the rim and miraculously tipped the ball back in at the last second, giving the Lakers the victory.

Kobe's determination to win the game was not always about him taking and hitting the last-second shot. His God-given will to win also included him hustling to the get the offensive rebound and making the clutch shot. Two of Kobe's most clutch shots came as the result of him crashing the boards after his teammates had taken the critical shot. At the end of Game 4 of the 2000 NBA Finals versus the Pacers, Brian Shaw took the clutch shot. Because he was not able to get the ball to Kobe, he penetrated to the right-hand side of the rim and attempted a one-footed runner. Kobe beat Reggie Miller to the rim and positioned himself for the put-back. As Shaw's runner rimmed off to the right side, Kobe got the offensive rebound and made the shot that won the game. Another time was against the San Antonio Spurs in the 2001 Western Conference Finals. The game was close at the end and Kobe wanted to take the last shot. However, because he was defended well enough to throw him out of the passing angle, Derek Fisher was forced to take the shot. Fisher's short-range jump shot missed to the left and Kobe, seemingly knowing where the ball would land, ran towards the basket, grabbed the offensive rebound, and placed the ball in the center of rim, just barely making it over the outstretched hands of Spurs' center David Robinson.

Kobe performed another basketball miracle in 2004 as the Lakers were matched up against the Portland Trail Blazers in the last game of the regular season. With the self-proclaimed "Kobe-stopper"[38] Reuben Patterson in his face, harassing him on his every move, Kobe found a way to make two of the most impossible shots I have ever seen in my life. He first made a desperation three-pointer as the clock was winding down in regulation. He then got away from Patterson at the end of overtime and made a seemingly impossible three-pointer over the outstretched hands of one of Portland's seven-footers. Kobe had a knack for the miraculous. He either knew something nobody else knew in terms of what it meant to make game-tying and game-winning shots in the clutch, or he was simply chosen by God to perform at a high level when the stakes were the highest. Kobe's performance on the basketball court made both general managers and defensive specialists question themselves about whether or not it was actually possible to stop Kobe from scoring. Being the basketball genius he was, Kobe always knew how to outstrategize the defense for his offensive gain.

In Game 2 of the 2004 Finals versus the Detroit Pistons, Kobe made a clutch three-point shot in the face of Richard Hamilton. Even as the star-studded Lakers were struggling in their underwhelming performance against the underdog Pistons, Kobe did his best to keep the Lakers from losing their first two home games. The Lakers needed someone to make a clutch three-point shot and Kobe wanted the moment as his own. Part of Bryant's offensive genius in clutch moments was found in his ability to make a decision about how to attack the defense. When Bryant speaks of the Lakers' strategy of spreading the floor in those clutch moments, he was referencing how the Lakers would make it a point to either isolate Kobe to go one-on-one or set screens to free him for the open shot. Even in taking and hitting last-second shots, Bryant credits both his ability to get great lift on his jump shot and his commitment to being in great basketball shape. For Bryant, these acknowledgments (lift and being in shape) are small things, but they were very important.

Kevin Durant believes that Kobe was the best and most clutch player he ever faced:

> Kobe Bryant was a player that wasn't afraid of the challenges. Kobe looked for them, he embraced the crunch time, the clutch moments and he didn't run away from them. Kobe faced a lot of great players in his career, leaving a great impression. Kevin Durant had great—or bad—memories from Kobe, especially

---

38. Faigen, "Did Ruben Patterson Really Call Himself 'The Kobe Stopper?'"

in the last minutes of the game, where the Los Angeles Lakers legend stepped up to finish a game.[39]

Durant echoes Silva's sentiments when he "revealed Kobe was the best 'clutch money player' he ever saw in his career."[40] According to Silva, "Kobe was a problem when it came to the clutch. He lived for those moments and even though he did not always make those shots, that didn't stop him from keeping shooting."[41] KD described Kobe's greatness this way: "Kobe. I was scared shitless of Kobe Bryant late in games."[42] Silva concludes that, "KB24 was that dude. He lived for that and Durant saw it first hand. The last time Bryant won a championship, he got past the Oklahoma City Thunder, defeating them in the first round of the playoffs. Just like Kobe didn't know how to stop KD, Durant did not know how to beat the Lakers legend in the last minutes of the game."[43] Kobe's clutch gene is one of the many reasons why I affirm him as the greatest basketball player of all time. Like former NBA players Caron Butler and Jamal Crawford, I too refuse to respect any Top 5 Greatest NBA Players list that does not include Kobe Bryant. Former Sixth Man of the Year winner Crawford, in particular, confirmed Durant's theory of fear when he stated that, "I saw [Kobe] in his prime, I saw the fear he put in not only teams but in arenas. That aura, he could be in a room full of stars and Kobe would stand out like a whole different order."[44]

As one who loved taking and making clutch shots at the end of basketball games, I became a follower of Kobe's game when he shot those four air balls against the Utah Jazz. Kobe was only 18 years old, but he possessed the confidence of an NBA veteran. The mere fact that Kobe was the only player on the Lakers team that was willing to take those late-game shots showed me he was way ahead of his time. Those four air balls showed me that Bryant was destined for greatness. It is one thing to take shots during the first three quarters of the game when there is no immediate pressure to win or lose the game. It is another thing altogether when the game is on the line and your ability to make the last-second

---

39. Silva, "Kevin Durant Says," para. 1.
40. Silva, "Kevin Durant Says," para. 2.
41. Silva, "Kevin Durant Says," para. 4.
42. Silva, "Kevin Durant Says," para. 3.
43. Silva, "Kevin Durant Says," para. 5.
44. Chaudhary, "'I Saw the Fear,'" para. 4.

shot will decide your team's fate. The consequences associated with that one shot can be far-reaching.

It can be the difference between being one of the greatest teams of all-time and being one of the greatest disappointments of all-time. It can be the difference between being inducted into the Naismith Basketball Hall of Fame and being invited to attend your teammate's induction ceremony. It can be the difference between having your jersey retired by the team you played for and being a popular commentator for the team you used to play for. Most importantly, that one shot can be the difference between being an NBA champion and being a yearly participant in the NBA playoffs. The teenage Kobe did not seem fazed by the pressure of taking that one shot. He took those critical shots as if he had been doing it his whole life.

For Bryant, this was a critical period for his basketball development. What I am most impressed with is the fact that Kobe seems to understand the plan of God in his life at a young age. In using such words as "destiny," "already written," "undeniable" and "no one, not a person or play could derail it," it seems Kobe knew the plans God had for him in the game of basketball. It seems Kobe knew he was destined by God in that his destiny (in basketball and in life) had already been written in the annals of history (basketball and life). In stating that no one could derail his destiny or kill his future, it sounded like Kobe was certain that God's plan for his life would not be derailed by the plans of Satan. It sounds like the teenage Kobe had felt the presence of God in his life. Not only did Bryant develop physically by lifting weights and shooting in the gym, but he also developed spiritually as the result of his rookie-year failures. The tutelage of the great Michael Jackson also helped Bryant to deal with his early mistakes.

As the result of Bryant learning from his rookie-year mistakes and working his tail off in the gym on a consistent basis, "He had zero flaws offensively. Zero," said LeBron James just a day before Bryant's death as he passed Bryant on the all-time scoring list. He continued,

> He could shoot the three. He could go around you. He could shoot the mid-range. He could post. He could make free throws. That's something I admired as well. Just being at a point where the defense would always be at bay, where they couldn't guard you, where you just felt you were immortal offensively because of your skill set and work ethic.[45]

45. Axelrod, "LeBron James Reflects," para. 7.

What LeBron forgot to mention was that Kobe did not have any defensive flaws either. He was a twelve-time member of the All-Defensive Team, with nine of those being First-Team honors. He could, and oftentimes would, guard the opposing team's best player from the positions of point guard to small forward. Put another way, Kobe's in-game will always found a way to bend the arc of the basketball moment towards him and the Lakers. Team USA too. The West NBA All-Stars too. Lower Merion High School too.

CONCLUSION: NO FEAR, NO REGRETS

As a way of bringing this book to a celebratory close, I will revisit the theme of Kobe Bryant fearing nothing other than bees and losing. In the article "The Last Dance: Kobe Bryant's Former Coaches on Relationship with Michael Jordan," NBA columnist Mark Medina writes that, "Kobe Bryant outlined a bold prediction involving himself and Michael Jordan."[46] As a senior at Lower Merion High School, Bryant remained humble enough to know how challenging it would be to defend Jordan. Bryant remained confident enough, however, to predict he could score on Jordan and not feel overwhelmed by the match up. "In relishing the opportunity to match up against Jordan, Lower Merion coach Greg Downer told *USA TODAY Sports*, 'He was not afraid.'"[47] The reason Kobe wanted to turn the 1998 NBA All-Star Game into a one-on-one game with whomever dared to challenge him was because Kobe was both the ultimate competitor and he was one who had the ultimate confidence in himself and his abilities. The teenage Bryant desperately wanted to compete against Jordan in those sacredly isolated one-on-one situations.

For Bryant, everything with Jordan was a personal challenge because in addition to Jordan being his idol, Jordan was also the Black Mamba's prey. Kobe loved Jordan like a big brother, but he also had plans on eclipsing the one who had been prematurely called the G.O.A.T. As early as 1993, with only three championship rings, Jordan was called the greatest basketball player ever, over and above those who played before him and won more championships. Nevertheless, the fact that Jordan presented Kobe into the NBA Hall of Fame does not mean Bryant did not surpass his idol, because the unpopular truth is he really did eclipse

46. Medina, "Last Dance," para. 1.
47. Medina, "Last Dance," para. 3.

his big brother. Kobe did so by surpassing Jordan in several numerical capacities. Most notably, Kobe surpassed Jordan when he won multiple NBA titles with multiple star sidekicks (O'Neal and Gasol). He was not cast in any *Space Jam* movies. He was not a *Looney Tunes* cartoon character who lived below the ground in a faraway land. Kobe was a fearless, modern-day warrior who simply dared to be great at playing the game of basketball. In being what Phil Jackson calls the "Chosen One," that 19-year old "Little Laker Boy" became the greatest basketball player ever. Most importantly, Kobe Bryant was a child of God. He fulfilled his calling in the Lord. Bryant's wife, Vanessa, and their trio of daughters will carry on the outstanding legacy of Kobe and Gianna.

Subsequently, one of the unique things I noticed about Bryant was he did great interviews. Some of the greatest interviews he did took place right after the Lakers had eked out a tough win and Bryant was too tired to stand up. In trying his best to answer the questions given to him by the television reporter, Kobe was always precise and strategic. In listening to his on-the-court interviews, I noticed a pattern. When he was asked about his own abilities to score massive numbers of points and consistently lead the Lakers to victory, he never talked about how great he was or about his talents. Kobe always referenced two unique aspects of the game itself. He either lifted up his teammates in complimenting them on how hard they played, or he reflected back on the countless hours he worked his tail off in the gym with intentions of improving his game on a consistent basis. Here it must be stated again that the primary objective of Kobe's system of play was not to be like Jordan; instead, it was designed to be better than Jordan. There is a reason why Bryant flat-out told his teammate Lamar Odom that "he was better than Mike [Jordan]."[48] Kobe told him that because he believed with his whole heart that he was the better of the two. His long-time friend, Tracy McGrady, says Kobe "really, truly thought he was better than Michael Jordan."[49]

Anyone who truly understands the game of basketball is aware of the fact that unlike any of Jordan's generational contemporaries, Kobe was actually better than his idol in several facets of the game. Again, little brother surpassed big brother and became a full-fledged *brother*. One critical facet of the game in which Kobe was better than Jordan was shooting the basketball. One thing Kobe did not copy or steal from Jordan was the ability

---

48. Bohlin, "Lamar Odom Opens Up," para. 4.
49. Fernandez, "Tracy McGrady Says," para. 3.

to be a great perimeter shooter. Kobe's ability to make an array of tough shots from distance and in the mid-range was something that was developed through committed repetition and hard work; not to be like Jordan but to be the best basketball player he could possibly be. I do not think Kobe got enough credit for his otherworldly ability to shoot the basketball. Because he worked so hard on his shooting, Kobe became a great shooter. His ability to shoot the basketball only enhanced his supreme ability to dominate the game on the offensive end of the court. One thing for sure: Kobe Bryant could shoot the leather off of an NBA basketball. He was the quintessential shooting guard of his generation.

I was recently watching a Game 6 documentary of the 1977 NBA Finals between the Portland Trail Blazers and the Philadelphia 76ers. In observing the overall game and different mannerisms of Dr. J, I realized how much Jordan copied much of what Erving did in the same way Bryant mimicked him, even down to the confident way Erving dressed, did interviews, walked up the court, and how he creatively hung in the air on the offensive end to draw fouls or gain a three-point opportunity. Certainly, Jordan was in great awe of Erving's athletic prowess as he played in his last NBA All-Star Game in 1987. Almost as if he was watching his basketball hero from the bench, Jordan copied the way Dr. J dunked the basketball and how he utilized the reverse layup. Both Erving and Jordan were flashy and stylish in the way they played the game. The same can be said about Kobe Bryant.

As a Black liberation theologian and an academic scholar, I take comfort in knowing that the same spirit of hate that was shown towards Kobe by those Los Angeles police officers who took pictures of Kobe's deceased body is the same spirit of hate showed toward Kobe as he was going through his sexual assault fiasco in Colorado; is the same spirit of hate showed toward him at the end of the Shaq-Kobe era with the Los Angeles Lakers; is the same hate that was shown toward Kobe throughout his 20-year playing career in Los Angeles; is the same spirit of hate that was shown towards Kobe when he was voted a 19-year old starter in the 1998 NBA All-Star Game in New York; is the same spirit of hate that was shown towards Kobe when he decided to bypass college and enter the NBA draft. In light of how some people (NBA players included) treated Bryant throughout his career, Stephon Marbury says "Kobe was a spirit."[50] To piggyback on Marbury's profound statement, I believe that as a child of God, Kobe felt the Spirit of God while he was performing on the

50. Hot 97, "Stephon Marbury Keeps It Real," 25:01.

basketball court. One could tell just by the way he played the game that Kobe was influenced by the Transcendent God. Put another way, Kobe's basketball talent made room for him in Los Angeles and the world abroad.

Marbury argues that Kobe was spiritual enough in his faith to endure the hate of others and use it as fuel to push him to higher planes and greater heights. It is not about the shoes or the size of the hands, but rather it is about how one plays the game of basketball. As the most talented basketball player the NBA has ever seen, Kobe will always be in a class by himself.

Speaking of Kobe's abiding human spirit, I recently ran across an article that talked about how Devin Booker was thinking about Kobe Bryant during his Game 6 performance against the then-defending champion Los Angeles Lakers. Playing in the house that Kobe built, the Staples Center, Booker scored 22 points in the first quarter that immediately put the game out of reach for the Lakers, and he finished with 47 overall. It was a performance reminiscent of ones Kobe Bryant had throughout his career, and the relationship between the two is well known.[51] Bryant was very high on Booker, and the young guard has a tattoo of Kobe's message to him, "Be Legendary" on his forearm. Booker reflects on his idol Bryant:

> Honestly I was thinking about Kob[e] and the conversations that we had, kinda about what we just went through. The postseason, and being legendary, and taking the steps to get there. So seeing that 8 and that 24 up there with the way that the lighting at Staples has right here. It feels like its shining down on you. And I know he was here tonight. I know he was here tonight, I know he was in the building, I know he was proud.[52]

As one of the best shooting guards in the NBA, Booker was inspired by Bryant to be the best version of himself. Similar to such generational talents as Jayson Tatum, Kyrie Irving, and Kawhi Leonard, Booker was drawn to Bryant because Kobe inspired him with the way he played the game and the way he communicated greatness. Bryant lived to silence fans on the road and that is exactly what Booker did in Game 6.[53] Bryant had a way of inspiring other players and helping them to believe that with hard work they too could become the best player in the NBA.

---

51. Hansford, "Lakers News: Suns' Devin Booker," para. 2.
52. Hansford, "Lakers News: Suns' Devin Booker," para. 4.
53. Hansford, "Lakers News,: Suns' Devin Booker" para. 6.

The Culture of Sport and Saying Goodbye to the Inspiration of Zoom

I personally believe Bryant became the best basketball player in the world at the end of Game 4 of the 2000 NBA Finals. We all know Game 4 was the pivotal game in that series. Even though he was nursing an injured ankle, he still found a way to make all of the clutch shots that gave the Lakers an insurmountable 3–1 series lead. Very similar to Game 3 of the 2001 NBA Finals, Game 7 of the 2002 Western Conference Finals, and Games 3 and 4 of the 2002 NBA Finals, Kobe always saved his best performances for those clutch moments. Kobe's clutch performances during the Lakers three-peat in the early 2000s were no different from his clutch performances during the Lakers back-to-back championships in 2009 and 2010. Let us not forget that Kobe averaged 25.4 points, 5 assists, and 5 rebounds per game for *20 years*. I will let that sink in for a minute. And he did all of these unbelievably amazing things while playing for the most decorated basketball organization in the history of the NBA—the Los Angeles Lakers. With no regrets about anything, Kobe Bryant worked himself into being the greatest Los Angeles Laker ever and the greatest basketball player ever—nationally and internationally.

In my resourceful read and observational watch of Bryant, I recently found myself stuck in the historical moment as I watched Kobe and the Lakers win the 2010 NBA Championship in Game 7 versus the Boston Celtics. While Kobe only shot 6-for-24 from the field, he found a way to lead his team to victory. To this very day, commentators and pundits take the time to critique Bryant for that sub-par shooting performance. But I hardly ever hear these same commentators and pundits talk about how Kobe made other types of basketball contributions for the purpose of leading his team to victory. When I use the word "contribution," I am referring to assists, rebounds, blocks, playing defense, and hitting free throws in clutch moments. Detail-wise, I have yet to hear a basketball historian talk about the most important play of Game 7. Yes, Kobe carried the load down the stretch just as he did throughout his legendary career. He went hard into the paint, drawing fouls and trying to dunk on the Boston Celtics. He played great individual defense against Ray Allen and Paul Pierce. He made all of his free throws in the clutch. He inspired his teammates verbally and physically. He sacrificed his body. Kobe did everything a great leader should do.

Nonetheless, Bryant's most important play came in the latter stages of Game 7. With less than five minutes left in the game and the Lakers up 66–64, Kobe took one hard dribble to the right and rose up over Ray Allen for one of his patented mid-range jump shots. Kobe's clutch jump shot gave the Lakers a four-point lead and propelled them to a historic win. This clutch jump shot, along with his 23 points, 15 rebounds, and 11 made free throws, helped to define the mythology of Kobe Bryant, that even when he was not at his best, Kobe still found a way to lead his team to victory. This particular moment (Bryant's fifth ring and second without Shaq) was an important part of Kobe's mythological (inspirational greatness) contribution to the culture of sport in the United States and throughout the world. Upon analyzing the totality of Kobe's body of work, it is my humble opinion that he achieved his goal of becoming the greatest basketball in the history of the NBA. I also believe he completed the mission for which God created him—to be an inspiration to others within and beyond the game of basketball.

One thing Jordan and Kobe had in common was they refused to join up with other superstar players in other cities for the purposes of forming superteams and winning championships. Both were committed to winning multiple championships with the organization that drafted them. Neither believed in the NBA's buddy-buddy system whereas they could banana-boat their way to winning titles. Jordan and Kobe were always busy trying to defeat the very superstars that were willing to be their teammates. As a competitor and a champion, Kobe loved the challenge of competing against the superteams that were formed in Boston and Miami. The goal was to defeat the Celtics and the Heat, not to join forces with them. The NBA made sure Kobe would not win more championships than they wanted him to when the League vetoed Chris Paul's trade to the Los Angeles Lakers in 2011. Winning multiple championships while not playing on superteams stacked with overwhelming talent (the Magic-led Lakers teams and Bird-led Celtics teams of the 1980s come to mind) was a huge part of Kobe's basketball mission.

The truth is that some of us complete our mission at an older age and live a long life. Others complete their mission at a younger age and live a shorter life. Kobe completed his mission at the age of 41. In Bryant's greatest in-game highlights, I recall the opposing team's coach walking onto the court and calling an immediate timeout as both the home crowds and road crowds roared in approval of Bryant's otherworldly basketball skills. Out of the coach's growing frustration, the stoppage in action came after Kobe had gone on one of his infamous scoring runs. It was in these blazing-hot scoring runs where Kobe single-handedly swung the momentum of the game in the favor of his team. On his way back to the bench, Kobe would spread his arms out wide as an eagle's wings and he would literally fly back to the bench in celebration of his own basketball genius and his team's momentary success. Here the recessional Black-church-celebration song, "I'll Fly Away," plays again in my spiritual ears.

In Matthew 25:23, I can hear Kobe's master saying to him, "Well done, good and faithful servant! You have been faithful with a few things; I will put you in charge of many things. Come and share your master's happiness." Rest in heaven, G.O.A.T. MAMBA. Thank you for inspiring us all to be the best version of ourselves. You found your purpose in life. You finished the race. You completed the journey. The world honors you as the superior champion that you are. Fly away to a much greater place. In the words of the late Kobe Bean Bryant, "Thank God I am not from this world."[54]

---

54. Ahmed, "Kobe Bryant 'Not from This World,'" para. 9.

Bibliography

Ahmed, Shahan. "Kobe Bryant 'Not from This World' at Lakers Practice." *NBC4 Los Angeles*, December 11, 2014. https://www.nbclosangeles.com/local/kobe-bryant-trash-talk-at-lakers-practice/59323/?amp.

Altrogge, Mark. "There Are No Accidents with God." *BibleStudyTools.com*, 2021. https://www.biblestudytools.com/blogs/mark-altrogge/there-are-no-accidents-with-god.html.

Andrew, Scottie. "Read Vanessa Bryant's Speech at the Memorial for Kobe and Gigi Bryant." *CNN*, February 24, 2020. https://amp.cnn.com/cnn/2020/02/24/us/kobe-bryant-memorial-vanessa-bryant-statement-trnd/index.html

Axelrod, Ben. "LeBron James Reflects on Relationship with Kobe Bryant One Day before Bryant's Death." *WKYC Studios*, January 26, 2020. https://www.wkyc.com/article/sports/nba/lebron-james-reflects-on-relationship-with-kobe-bryant-one-day-before-bryants-death/95-abbe43d6-4a0b-4444-898b-d6172ec5e1ca.

Baker, Kenneth L., ed. *Zondervan NIV Study Bible*. Grand Rapids: Zondervan, 2008.

Baker, William J. *Playing with God: Religion and Modern Sport*. Cambridge: Harvard University Press, 2009.

Banschick, Mark. "Why Are Sports Important?" *Psychology Today*, February 5, 2012. https://www.psychologytoday.com/us/blog/the-intelligent-divorce/201202/why-are-sports-important.

Bartholomew, Craig G., and Michael W. Goheen. *Christian Philosophy: A Systematic and Narrative Introduction*. Grand Rapids: Baker Academic, 2013.

Basketball Reference. "2002–03 Los Angeles Lakers Roster and Stats." https://www.basketball-reference.com/teams/LAL/2003.html.

Bohlin, Michael. "Lamar Odom Opens Up about Kobe Bryant's Desire to Be the Best: 'He Said He Was Better than Mike.'" *CBS | NBA*, April 19, 2021. https://www.cbssports.com/nba/news/lamar-odom-opens-up-about-kobe-bryants-desire-to-be-the-best-he-said-he-was-better-than-mike/.

Boswell, Josh "'Can You Imagine a Black Hole? It's Empty.' Kobe Bryant's Former Coach and Father's Best Friend Tells How the NBA Star's Close-Knit Family Are Struggling to Deal with the Tragedy and Will Miss Him 'More Than You Can Begin to Imagine.'" *Daily Mail*, January 27, 2020. https://www.dailymail.co.uk/news/article-7934221/Kobe-Bryants-former-coach-says-close-knit-family-struggling-deaths.html?_twitter-impression=true.

Brow, Jason. "Anthony Davis Dedicates NBA Finals Win to Kobe Bryant: He's 'Looking Down On Us'" *Hollywood Life*, October 11, 2020. https://hollywoodlife.com/2020/10/11/anthony-davis-kobe-bryant-nba-championship-tribute-lebron-james/amp/.

Bryant, Kobe. *Mamba Mentality: How I Play*. New York: Farrar, Straus and Giroux, 2018.

BSO Staff. "Kobe Bryant's Response to Michael Jordan. 'He Knows I'm a Bad Mother***er.'" *BSO*, July 13, 2012. https://blacksportsonline.com/2012/07/kobe-bryants-response-to-michael-jordan-so-what-he-knows-im-a-bad-motherfer/.

Buseck, Craig von. "Kobe Bryant: Man of Faith and Flaws." *Inspiration Ministries*, October 17, 2020. https://inspiration.org/entertainment/kobe-bryant-man-of-faith-and-flaws/.

Calvin, John. *Institutes of the Christian Religion*. Edited by John McNeil. Translated by Ford Lewis Battles. Louisville: Westminster John Knox, 2006.

Camilo, Christian. "Bill Simmons and the 'Secret of Basketball.'" *Epicbuzzer*, December 22, 2019. https://epicbuzzer.com/2019/12/22/bill-simmons-and-the-secret-of-basketball/amp/.

Carson, D. A. *Themelios 40.3*. Eugene, OR: Wipf and Stock, 2015.

Castillo, Oscar. "Throwback: Michael Jordan Tells UNC Player Not to Wear [sic] Kobe's." *Modern Notoriety*, December 16, 2014. https://www.modern-notoriety.com/throwback-michael-jordan-tells-unc-player-not-to-wear-kobes/.

Chaudhary, Aikansh. "'I Saw the Fear': Jamal Crawford Labels Kobe Bryant as This Generation's Michael Jordan." *Essentially Sports*, October 31, 2020. https://www.essentiallysports.com/nba-news-i-saw-the-fear-jamal-crawford-labels-kobe-bryant-as-this-generations-michael-jordan/.

Chen, Brian. "Brandon Jennings Calls Kobe Bryant 'The Greatest Ever,' Says MJ Had Better Cast." *Bleacher Report*, August 19, 2014. https://syndication.bleacherreport.com/amp/2168979-brandon-jennings-calls-kobe-bryant-the-greatest-ever-says-mj-had-better-cast.amp.html.

Conway, Tyler. "Gilbert Arenas: Michael Jordan Told Kobe Bryant He'd Never Fill His Shoes in '03." *Bleacher Report*, September 2, 2019. https://bleacherreport.com/articles/2852062-gilbert-arenas-michael-jordan-told-kobe-bryant-hed-never-fill-his-shoes-in-03.

——. "Kobe Bryant Comments on AAU Basketball's Impact on Sport." *Bleacher Report*, January 24, 2016. https://bleacherreport.com/articles/2610640-kobe-bryant-comments-on-aau-basketball-impact-on-sport.

Deveney, Sean ed. *Remembering Kobe Bryant: Players, Coaches, and Broadcasters Recall the Greatest Basketball Player of His Generation*. New York: Sports, 2006.

Drakos, Adam. "3 Ways St. Augustine's Confessions Describes the Fallen Modern World." *Thinking West*, May 18, 2021. https://thinkingwest.com/2021/05/18/3-ways-st-augustines-confessions-describes-the-fallen-modern-world/.

Dr. KaMilan. "Pat Riley about Kobe and MJ." *YouTube*, April 6, 2016. 1:19. https://www.youtube.com/watch?app=desktop&v=QVRBTxtlvI8.

Bibliography

Dugandzic, Matthew. "[2006] Mark Jackson: Kobe Will Go Down as the Greatest of All Time." *Basketball Network*, January 20, 2019. https://www.basketballnetwork.net/old-school/2006-mark-jackson-kobe-will-go-down-as-the-greatest-of-all-time

Ellis, Roberts. *The Games People Play: Theology, Religion and Sport*. Cambridge: Lutterworth, 2014.

ESPN. "Kobe Bryant Dominated the Midrange and Hit Unassisted Jumpers at a Historic Rate | Signature Shots." *YouTube*, 8:58. https://www.youtube.com/watch?v=zV7T2TLSz4k

———. "Kobe Bryant Praises Kyrie Irving's Shooting Prowess | MuseCage Basketball Network | ESPN." *YouTube*, January 3, 2018. 4:35. https://www.youtube.com/watch?v=cTLrMyrZNCk.

ESPNSportFirstTake. "First Take—Dr. J Lists His All-Time Top 5 NBA Players." *YouTube*, 6:19. https://www.youtube.com/watch?v=-OLmgmQ6jCs.

EssentiallySports. "I Saw Fear." 2020.

Etienne, Vanessa. "Kareem Abdul-Jabbar Remembers Kobe Bryant as Family Man and Tremendous Talent." *BET*, February 20, 2020. https://www.bet.com/article/7q60vv/kareem-abdul-jabbar-remembers-kobe-bryant-as-family-man.

Faigen, Harrison. "Did Ruben Patterson Really Call Himself 'The Kobe Stopper,' and Did Kobe Bryant Actually 'Torch' Him?" *Silver Screen and Roll*, October 27, 2018. https://www.silverscreenandroll.com/platform/amp/2018/10/27/18032606/kobe-bryant-espn-torch-ruben-patterson-calling-himself-kobe-stopper-mamba-mentality-lakers-book.

Feldman, Dan. "Michael Jordan: Kobe Bryant Was 'Maybe Even Tougher than I Was.'" *NBC Sports*, May 11, 2021. https://nba.nbcsports.com/2021/05/11/michael-jordan-kobe-bryant-was-maybe-even-tougher-than-i-was/.

Fernandez, Gabriel. "Tracy McGrady Says Kobe 'Really, Truly Thought He Was Better than Michael Jordan.'" *CBS | NBA*, May 21, 2020. https://www.cbssports.com/nba/news/tracy-mcgrady-says-kobe-bryant-really-truly-thought-he-was-better-than-michael-jordan/.

Fillingham, Hanna. "Jennifer Lopez and Alex Rodriguez Share Personal Memories of Friendship with Kobe Bryant in Heartfelt Tributes." *Hello!*, January 27, 2020. https://www.hellomagazine.com/celebrities/2020012783817/a-rod-jennifer-lopez-shares-memories-kobe-bryant-following-death/?viewas=amp.

Freeman, Eric. "Michael Jordan Thinks Only Kobe Bryant Deserves Comparisons" *Yahoo! Sports*, January 17, 2002. https://sports-yahoo.com/amphml/michael-jordan-thinks-only-kobe-bryant-deserves-comparisons-222702003.html.

Garcia, Bob. "Michael Jordan Believes You Can't Mention Him without Scottie Pippen." *Sportscasting*, April 22, 2020. https://www.sportscasting.com/michael-jordan-believes-you-cant-mention-him-without-scottie-pippen/.

Gharib, Anthony. "Lakers Video: Grant Hill Says Kobe Bryant Is Best Player He Played against." *Lakers Nation*, June 19, 2022. https://lakersnation.com/lakers-video-grant-hill-says-kobe-bryant-is-best-player-he-played-against/2022/06/19/.

Gleeson, Scott. "Kobe Bryant, 'Man of Faith,' Attended Mass with His Family Morning of Helicopter Crash." *USA Today*, February 3, 2020. https://www.usatoday.com/story/sports/nba/lakers/2020/02/03/kobe-bryant-attended-mass-family-morning-crash/4646895002/.

Goldstein, Joella. "Kobe Bryant Apologizes for Calling Out Girl on Basketball Team for Attending Recital Instead of Game." *People*, September 11, 2019. https://people.com/sports/kobe-bryant-apologizes-calling-out-girl-missing-basketball-game-for-dance-recital/.

Hansford, Corey. "Lakers News: Grant Hill Says Kobe Hit More 'Tough Shots' than Jordan." *Lakers Nation*, June 6, 2014. https://lakersnation.com/lakers-news-grant-hill-says-kobe-hit-more-tough-shots-than-jordan/2014/06/04/amp/.

———. "Lakers News: Suns' Devin Booker Was Thinking about Kobe Bryant during Game 6 Performance." *Lakers Nation*, June 5, 2021. https://lakersnation.com/lakers-news-suns-devin-booker-was-thinking-about-kobe-bryant-during-game-6-performance/2021/06/05/.

Harvey, Lincoln. *A Brief Theology of Sport*. Eugene, OR: Wipf and Stock, 2014.

———. "A Christian Perspective on Sport." *Union Publishing*, July 21 2021. https://www.unionpublishing.org/resource/a-christian-perspective-on-sport/.

Hearon, Sarah. "Vanessa Bryant Says 'Life Truly Isn't Fair' on the 4th Anniversary of Kobe Bryant's NBA Retirement." *People*, April 13, 2020. https://www.usmagazine.com/celebrity-news/news/vanessa-bryant-says-life-isnt-fair-4-years-after-kobes-last-game/.

Hoffarth, Tom, and Steve Lowery. "Why Kobe Bryant Took His Catholic Faith so Seriously." *Angelus*, February 4, 2020. https://angelusnews.com/local/la-catholics/kobe-the-catholic-a-quiet-witness-to-the-faith/.

Hot 97. "Stephon Marbury Keeps It Real on Knicks, Jay-Z, Kobe Bryant, Influence + Playing in China." *YouTube*, March 6, 2020. 35:57. https://m.youtube.com/watch?v=y2RstVha51c/.

Huizinga, Johan. *Homo Ludens: A Study of the Play-Element in Culture*. Boston: Routledge and Kegan Paul, 1944.

The Jacksons. *The Jacksons: Legacy*. With Fred Bronson. New York: Black Dog & Levanthal, 2017.

Jajodia, Advait. "Kobe Bryant Had More 60-Point Games than Michael Jordan and LeBron James Combined?!": NBA Twitter Goes Crazy after an Absurd Stat of the Lakers Legend Goes Viral." *The Sports Rush*, August 2, 2021. https://thesportsrush.com/nba-news-kobe-bryant-had-more-60-point-games-than-michael-jordan-and-lebron-james-combined-nba-twitter-goes-crazy-after-an-absurd-stat-of-the-lakers-legend-goes-viral/?amp.

James, Dante. "Kobe Bryant Touched Many Lives, But Celebrity Worship Is an Opiate." *Black Agenda Report*, February 26, 2020. https://www.blackagendareport.com/kobe-bryant-touched-many-lives-celebrity-worship-opiate.

Jha, Shreyansh. "Only Michael Jordan, Kobe Bryant, and Hakeem Have Ever Had 15 Games with 30 or More Points during a Single Playoff Run" *Clout*, August 2022. https://cloutnews.com/only-michael-jordan-kobe-bryant-and-hakeem-have-ever-had-15-games-with-30-or-more-points-during-a-single-playoff-run/amp/.

JL Hoops. "2000 Lakers VS Rockets || Kobe Bryant Scored 45 Points." *YouTube*. 1:33:26. https://www.youtube.com/watch?v=xaBsejHRbWM.

Johnson, Martenzie. "Not to Be Forgotten, Kobe Bryant Was a Black Man." *Andscape*, March 4, 2020. https://andscape.com/features/kobe-bryant-black-man/.

Kamenetzky, Brian "Kobe Bryant's Leadership Doctrine." *ESPN*, October 15, 2012. https://www.espn.com/blog/los-angeles/lakers/post/_/id/33473/kobe-bryants-leadership-doctrine.

Kimble, Lindsay. "Kobe Bryant Says Friends Joke 'It Takes a Real Man to Make a Boy': I Tell Them 'It Takes a King to Make a Princess.'" *People*, July 7, 2017. https://people.com/parents/kobe-bryant-talks-having-daughters-no-sons/.

Bibliography

Klas, Klano. "Bill Russell Thinks Michael Jordan Played in an Era Worse than the One He Played in." *OpenCourt*, May 3, 2019. https://www.opencourt-basketball.com/bill-russell-thinks-michael-jordan-played-in-an-era-worse-than-the-one-he-played-in/.

Klosterman, Chuck. "Kobe Bryant Will Always Be an All-Star of Talking." *GQ Magazine*, February 17, 2015. https://www.gq.com/story/kobe-bryant-nba-allstar.

Lauletta, Tyler. "Tracy McGrady Says Kobe Bryant Used to Tell Him Early in His Career That He Wanted to 'Die Young' and Be 'Immortalized.'" *Business Insider*, January 27, 2020. https://www.businessinsider.com/tracy-mcgrady-kobe-bryant-die-young-the-jump-2020-1.

Lazenby, Roland. *Showboat: The Life of Kobe Bryant*. New York: Little, Brown, 2016.

LjP24. "Kobe Bryant Game Winner for Team USA." *YouTube*, n.d. 0:51. https://www.youtube.com/watch?v=19eJdbOat8c.

Loumena, Dan. "Vanessa Bryant Shares Instagram Post on Kobe's Farewell Anniversary." *Los Angeles Times*, April 13, 2020. https://www.latimes.com/sports/lakers/story/2020-04-13//vanessa-bryant-shares-instagram-post-on-kobe-farewell-anniversary.

Mack, Ben. "Kobe Bryant Told Jimmy Kimmel in a Now-Heartbreaking 2018 Interview That His Daughter Gianna Would Carry on His Legacy." *Business Insider*, January 27, 2020. https://www.insider.com/kobe-bryant-daughter-gianna-death-jimmy-kimmel-interview-2020-1.

MacMullan, Jackie. "Jordan, Russell, Kareem, Even the King of Pop—The Astonishing Mentors Who Shaped Kobe Bryant." *ESPN*, April 5, 2020. https://www.espn.com/nba/story/_/id/15193525/jordan-russell-kareem-even-king-pop-astonishing-mentors-shaped-kobe-bryant.

Martinez, Nico. "Andre Iguodala Picks Kobe Bryant as Hardest Player He Has Ever Had to Guard." *Fadeaway World*, July 5, 2019. https://fadeawayworld.net/.amp/nba-media/andre-iguodala-picks-kobe-bryant-as-hardest-player-he-has-ever-had-to-guard.

Mathur, Ashish. "How Michael Jackson Inspired Kobe Bryant." *Clutch Points*, January 27, 2020. https://clutchpoints.com/lakers-news-how-michael-jackson-inspired-kobe-bryant/.

McT, Marc. "Shaq vs. Kobe: Top 10 Rivalry Moments between the L.A. Lakers Stars." *Bleacher Report*, September 15, 2010. https://syndication.bleacherreport.com/amp/462936-shaq-vs-kobe-top-10-rivalry-moments.amp.html.

Medina, Mark. "The Last Dance: Kobe Bryant's Former Coaches on Relationship with Michael Jordan." *USA Today*, May 5, 2020. https://www.usatoday.com/story/sports/nba/2020/05/05/the-last-dance-michael-jordan-kobe-bryant-relationship/3083240001/.

Mehdi, Samir. "'Michael Jordan Is a Better Scorer and Greater Player than Kobe Bryant': Gary Payton Gives His Reasoning Behind Picking the Bulls Legend Over His Former Lakers Teammate." *The Sports Rush*, October 27, 2021. https://thesportsrush.com/nba-news-michael-jordan-is-a-better-scorer-and-greater-player-than-kobe-bryant-gary-payton-gives-his-reasoning-behind-picking-the-bulls-legend-over-his-former-lakers-teammate/.

"Michael Jackson." *Wikipedia*. https://en.m.wikipedia.org/wiki/Michael_Jackson.

"Michael Jordan vs. Kobe Bryant and Some Campers." *ESPN*, July 31, 2008. https://www.espn.com/blog/truehoop/post/_/id/5158/michael-jordan-vs-kobe-bryant-and-some-campers.

Mixon, Pat. *The Kobe Code: Eight Principles for Success*. Alief, TX: Prismatic, 2010.

Moore, Matt. "Kevin Durant Says Kobe Bryant Is the GOAT (along with Jordan)." *CBS | NBA*, March 13, 2014. https://www.cbssports.com/nba/news/kevin-durant-says-kobe-bryant-is-the-goat-along-with-jordan/.

Moreira, Gabrielle. "Vanessa Bryant Recalls Kobe as a Hopeless Romantic and Loving Father: 'He Was My Everything.'" *Fox 11 Los Angeles*, February 24, 2020. https://www.foxla.com/news/vanessa-bryant-recalls-kobe-as-a-hopeless-romantic-and-loving-father-he-was-my-everything.

Ocal, Arda. "Kyrie Irving and Vanessa Bryant Support Changing the NBA's Logo to Kobe Bryant." *ESPN*, February 25, 2021. https://www.espn.com/nba/story/_/id/30962914/kyrie-irving-vanessa-bryant-support-changing-nba-logo-kobe-bryant.

Pawar, Devika. "Scottie Pippen Chooses Kobe Bryant as His NBA GOAT Over Ex-teammate Michael Jordan." *Republic World*, May 25, 2020. https://www.republicworld.com/sports-news/basketball-news/scottie-pippen-chooses-kobe-bryant-as-his-goat-over-michael-jordan.html.

Peyser, Andrea. "Kobe Bryant Was No Rapist." *New York Post*, February 10, 2020. https://nypost.com/2020/02/10/kobe-bryant-was-no-rapist/.

"Pippen: Kobe Was Better than Jordan." *Marca*, May 26, 2020. https://www.marca.com/en/more-sports/2020/05/26/5ecd6be3ca4741a51e8b4589.html.

The PostGame Staff. "Kobe Bryant: I Can't Be a Great Friend." *ThePostGame*, February 18, 2015. http://www.thepostgame.com/blog/dish/201502/kobe-bryant-i-cant-be-great-friend.

"Read Vanessa Bryant's Words about Kobe Bryant at His Memorial." *Los Angeles Times*, February 24, 2020. https://www.latimes.com/sports/story/2020-02-24/read-vanessa-bryants-words-about-kobe-bryant-at-his-memorial.

"Religion Library: Roman Catholicism—Afterlife and Salvation." *Patheos*. https://www.patheos.com/library/roman-catholicism/beliefs/afterlife-and-salvation.

"Retiring NBA Star Kobe Bryant Praises Michael Jackson's Influence on His Career." *The Sydney Morning Herald*, February 24, 2016. https://www.smh.com.au/sport/basketball/retiring-nba-star-kobe-bryant-praises-michael-jacksons-influence-on-his-career-20160224-gn1urp.html.

Richards, John C., Jr. "Kobe Bryant: Reflections on Fatherhood, Passion and Immortality." *Broward.US*, January 27, 2020. https://broward.us/2020/01/27/kobe-bryant-reflections-on-fatherhood-passion-and-immortality/.

Rivas, Christian. "Kevin Durant Says Michael Jordan, Kobe Bryant Are the Greatest Players of All Time." *Silver Screen and Roll*, December 11, 2018. https://www.silverscreenandroll.com/2018/12/11/18136460/la-lakers-kevin-durant-michael-jordan-kobe-bryant-greatest-of-all-time-goat-allen-iverson.

Sanfiorenzo, Dimas. "Allen Iverson Doesn't Understand Why Kobe Bryant Isn't in the G.O.A.T. Discussion." *Okay Player*, April 23, 2018. https://www.okayplayer.com/sports/allen-iverson-kobe-bryant-lebron-james-mj.html.

Sengupta, Tonoy. "'Kobe Bryant Is the GOAT, No Question': Kyle Kuzma Dramatically Snubs LeBron James in the GOAT Conversation after Trade from Lakers." *The Sports Rush*, February 8, 2021. https://thesportsrush.com/nba-news-kobe-bryant-is-the-goat-no-question-kyle-kuzma-dramatically-snubs-lebron-james-in-the-goat-conversation-after-trade-from-lakers/?amp.

Bibliography

Sharp, Andrew. "Kobe Bryant Learned Game from MJ—Michael Jackson, That Is." *SBNation*, November 23, 2010. https://www.sbnation.com/nba/2010/11/23/1832551/kobe-bryant-michael-jackson-profile.

Silva, Orlando. "Kevin Durant Says Kobe Bryant Is the Most Clutch Player He Ever Faced: 'Kobe. I Was Scared S---less of Kobe Late in Games.'" *Fadeaway World*, August 30, 2020. https://fadeawayworld.net/.amp/sports/nba-media/kevin-durant-says-kobe-bryant-is-the-most-clutch-player-he-ever-faced-kobe-i-was-scared-s-less-of-kobe-late-in-games.

Skilbeck, John. "Shaquille O'Neal Reflects on Kobe Bryant's Death: 'He Was so Much More than an Athlete.'" *Sporting News*, January 27, 2020. https://www.sportingnews.com/us/nba/news/shaquille-oneal-kobe-bryant-death/1rsx1s219a9l21a5i7cqfm09w3.

Slade, Jacques. "Interview: Kobe Bryant on Retros and His Favorite Nikes He's Worked On." *Complex*, May 8, 2014. https://www.complex.com/sneakers/2014/03/kobe-bryant-speaks-on-kobe-9-retros-huarache-2k4.

Smith, Greg S. *Sports Theology: Finding God's Winning Spirit*. Indianapolis: Dog Ear, 2010.

Smith, Zachary. Review of *A Brief Theology of Sport*, by Lincoln Harvey. *Themelios* 39.2. https://www.thegospelcoalition.org/themelios/review/a-brief-theology-of-sport/.

Soni, Neil. "The Mamba Mentality Key Takeaways." *Neil Soni*, July 20, 2020. https://www.neilsoni.com/the-mamba-mentality-key-takeaways/.

Sykes, Mike D., II. "Stephon Marbury Says LeBron James Is Not a 'Real Laker.'" *For the Win*, March 11, 2020. https://ftw.usatoday.com/2020/03/lebron-james-kobe-bryant-stephon-marbury-lakers.

Talwalker, Anuj. "Jalen Rose: 'I Started Calling Kobe Bryant the Remix of Michael Jordan. Because to Me, He Looked Like MJ. He Sound Like MJ. He Move Like MJ.'" *Essentially Sports*, December 16, 2021. https://www.essentiallysports.com/nba-baskeball-news-jalen-rose-i-started-calling-kobe-bryant-the-remix-of-michael-jordan-because-to-me-he-looked-like-mj-he-sound-like-mj-he-move-like-mj/.

Thompson, Patrick. *Kobe Bryant: The Inspirational Story of One of the Greatest Basketball Players of All-Time!* Oklahoma City: Draft2Digital, 2020.

Tran, Lee. "Kendrick Perkins Says Kevin Durant Is the Greatest Scorer Ever." *Fadeaway World*, August 8, 2021. https://fadeawayworld.net/.amp/nba-media/kendrick-perkins-says-kevin-durant-is-the-greatest-scorer-ever.

Treat, Jeremy R. "More than a Game: A Theology of Sport." *The Gospel Coalition* 40.3. https://www.thegospelcoalition.org/themelios/article/more-than-a-game-theology-of-sport/.

Trenaman, Calum. "Kobe Bryant Backs Women to Play in NBA 'Right Now.'" *CNN*, January 22, 2020. https://cnn.com/2020/01/22/sport/kobe-bryant-women-nba-spt-intl/index.html.

Turbow, Jason. "Kobe's Hoop Dreaming When He Says His Team Could Beat Jordan's." *WIRED*, July 29, 2012. https://www.wired.com/2012/07/kobe-hoop-dream/amp.

United Church of God. "Why Does God Allow Christians to Die in Accidents?" *Beyond Today*, January 9, 2018. https://www.ucg.org/bible-study-tools/bible-questions-and-answers/why-does-god-allow-christians-to-die-in-accidents.

"Vanessa Bryant Says Hall of Fame Election Is 'Peak' of Kobe's Career." *ESPN*, April 4, 2020. https://www.espn.com/nba/story/_/id/28994988/vanessa-bryant-says-hall-of-fame-peak-kobe-career?platform=amp.

VanHoose, Benjamin. "Derek Jeter Remembers Kobe Bryant as Family Man Who 'Just Loved Being a Dad.'" *People*, January 27, 2020. https://people.com/sports/derek-jeter-remembers-kobe-bryant-as-family-man-who-just-loved-being-a-dad/.

———. "Kobe Bryant Was a 'Very Hands-On Dad' and 'So Proud' of His 4 Daughters, Source Says." *People*, January 27, 2020. https://people.com/sports/kobe-bryant-very-hands-on-dad-so-proud-of-daughters-source/?amp=true.

"A Victory for Vanessa Bryant." *God and Sports*, February 26, 2020. https://davihundotcom.wordpress.com/2020/02/26/a-victory-for-vanessa-bryant/.

Walker, Rhiannon. "The Day Larry Bird Said, 'It's Just God Disguised as Michael Jordan.'" *The Undefeated*, April 18, 2018. https://andscape.com/features/the-day-larry-bird-said-its-just-god-disguised-as-michael-jordan/amp/.

"Welcome to Greek Mythology." https://www.greekmythology.com/.

Welk, Brian. "Gayle King Is 'Mortified' That Kobe Bryant Comments Were 'Taken Out of Context:' 'I'd Be Extremely Angry with Me, Too.'" *The Wrap*, February 6, 2020. https://www.thewrap.com/gayle-king-is-mortified-that-kobe-bryant-comments-were-taken-out-of-context-id-be-extremely-angry-with-me-too-video/.

Young, Ryan. "Phil Jackson on Kobe Bryant: 'He went beyond the veil.'" *Yahoo! Sports*, January 26, 2020. https://sports.yahoo.com/los-angeles-lakers-coach-phil-jackson-kobe-bryant-death-helicopter-crash-052915513.html

Zillgitt, Jeff. "LeBron James Opens Up and Reflects on Kobe Bryant after Passing Him on NBA Scoring List." *USA Today*, January 26, 2020. https://www.usatoday.com/story/sports/nba/lakers/2020/01/26/lebron-james-reflects-on-kobe-bryant-nba-scoring-list/4579971002/.

www.ingramcontent.com/pod-product-compliance
Lightning Source LLC
Chambersburg PA
CBHW070322230426
43663CB00011B/2191